50 Roads

TO THE MIDDLE
OF MY LIFE

THE MEMOIR OF A FREE SPIRIT

melody ross

50 Roads To The Middle Of My Life
The Memoir Of A Free Spirit
by Melody Ross

To My Dad

Someday we'll fly
together again.

For now, I'm keeping
my promise to you.

I am free.

Before We Begin

I often skip the introduction to the books I read. I get it. Please don't skip this one. There are some things I need to say before you start reading this memoir.

For starters: I've written quite a few books, but this is my first true memoir. I've owned a few companies with big teams of people to do things that are necessary and helpful, and I've worked with big publishers who've also done those kinds of things for me, but I wrote this book without any of that kind of help. I ask your forgiveness in the places you might believe an outside editor would have been helpful. I chose every word I kept and I chose every word that got cut. Every word is intentional. This first edition is also self-published and self-illustrated. And that's just how I wanted it. I am publishing it before anyone but me has read it in its entirety, as well. One of the things I've learned with great impact is that I have cut my voice box out a million times by asking for opinions. This book is all me, come what may. I even laid it out for printing all by myself without ever asking a single other person if they like it or not.

It's a huge victory to have overcome my addiction to opinions.

But I wonder if you're also wondering what this book is about . . . and what you'll get out of it. It's a big thing to ask someone to sacrifice a few days of their life simply listening to you talk about yourself. So first I want to thank you for being willing to even consider it. I wouldn't ask you to do it if I didn't think it was an epic use of your time, I promise.

And it's not so much about me and the nervous breakdown that stripped me to my core as it is about the "teachers" who showed up in my life. Heroes and villains and helpers and mirrors. I want to honor those teachers by passing on their lessons. Most of these teachers weren't actual human beings, but experiences. Most of them I wouldn't have chosen for myself.

So many of the things in life we treasure most; we never would have had the wisdom to choose for ourselves until after they've become a part of our life story.

It's a good story. It contains the elements of a good story. I do want to warn you however, that you'll probably be left with questions. I know I'm left with big questions after reading through these 50 roads. Fact is, I'm left with big questions after LIVING through them.

So know this is a story ONLY to the middle of my life, not to the end of it. The one thing I know for sure is that I'm gonna live it out til the end, while having no idea what's going to happen next. It used to scare me not to know, but now it thrills me. I think this story will help you understand why I'm thrilled now instead of scared. I hope it will cause you to consider finding the unknown a thrill too.

I'm writing this introduction after finishing the last chapter and reading the entire book in order from beginning to end. Maybe that's what people who write books always do and I just didn't know it.

But I STARTED writing this book WITH the introduction of what I thought it was going to be, it's the first thing I wrote! After finishing every word of the book and coming back to the introduction, I saw that I wrote a different book than I thought I was writing when I started. And I wrote the wrong introduction to the right book.

So here I go, rewriting the introduction.

The one I wrote first contained a whole lot of WE. I needed backup, I suppose. I showed up to this story with witnesses and allies and protectors. But I have to take the WE out of my introduction. This is MY story from my perspective and I won't speak for anyone else. I can stand on my own.

It's also an incomplete story. As all stories are.

I suspect you'll see yourself in this memoir. That's my biggest hope in writing it to be read. I wrote it to be read but I mostly wrote it to heal. I wrote it to understand myself and where I have found myself living and breathing at this time in my life. The process of writing it was like going through a closet where old purses and backpacks and coats were piled. Full pockets and compartments that had to be shaken loose of their contents.

After a fire or a flood or a looting. I went through what was left.

While simultaneously remembering the suitcases and purses and boxes that are long gone, ones that hold pieces I can't recall clearly enough to describe, but probably hold answers to some of the questions I'll always have.

The thing is, the closet where the best stuff was hidden didn't get touched by the fires or the floods or the looting. I found it while I was writing this book. So the things that matter most to me are here.

There are parts of this memoir that have clean endings. Clean endings always feel good! For the most part, though . . . there are jagged and rough edges that try to fit as close as they can to the ill-fitting pieces next to them. So much of this story is a mosaic yet to be glued-down and grouted together.

When I sat down to start writing these "roads," I thought this memoir was about my nervous breakdown, about why I disappeared from the world for a few years (and then a few more years after that.) I thought it was about how I went from rags to riches to rags again. How I conquered the world and then got conquered. About the battles that have just about killed me and who was on the other side of enemy lines. I thought it was about how I've failed. And fallen. And tried and tried and tried. How I'd been wronged over and over again. How I'd wronged others unintentionally. How unjust it's all been. And sure, it was about my victories too . . . but I thought it was mostly about how the trials have been so big that I just couldn't do it anymore. I thought it was about my husband's brain injury and how hard we've fought to make everything okay. And how we just haven't been able to get there. I thought it was about what it's been like to feel homeless, living in an RV away from everything I've ever known. But how amazing it is too. I thought it was about how the happiest and most optimistic girl I've ever met went cold and numb. I thought it was about how I made my dreams come true and then they crumbled right before my eyes. And so I broke into pieces and blew away in the wind.

I just wanted to try to explain.

That's not what this book ended up being about at all. The nervous break-down was an incomplete story too. And trying to explain something like a breakdown is really impossible anyway. Most of the time you can't even explain it to yourself. You'll always be telling an incomplete story.

I turned 50 a few months ago. The same year my oldest child turned 30. The same year my 5th grandchild turned 1. I had to order new reading glasses twice last year. I needed stronger and stronger ones. As the vision from my eyeballs has grown weaker, I've had to find a new kind of vision to make sense of things — like we all do.

You have to submit to a new kind of vision as you age.

Somewhere along the way, I had forgotten I was getting older. I've always looked young for my age and I've always had a stubborn aversion to aging. I've always had the heart of a wild chid and a stubborn aversion to grow-ing up. I thought I could defy it. When my breakdown woke me up and I saw myself clearly as a woman who is no longer young, that wake-up call came with the gift of a relentlessly clear magnifying glass.

Maybe that's what this book is about. Accepting that we are always going to have to find new ways to see things. And that the things we see will never be the same when we revisit them as they were the first time we saw them.

I want you to remember that when you look at something in a magnifying glass, all you can really see is what's inside that circle. There's a whole world in every direction you can't see.

Maybe that's just part of what this book is about.

Our stories are always going to be incomplete.

What I've learned about the human experience is that there are things a person will remember as soon as they're born. I can see it in the eyes of every baby I've ever held. We were all babies once. We all remembered something, I just know it. Then we went on to spend the rest of our lives trying to remember those things that were born into us. Along the way, we each get tricked a million times into forgetting. But we turn a million corners, too, and sometimes things will show up around those corners as blaring reminders of what we've always known. And then we'll face the biggest battle of our lives — the fight with ourselves to believe what we've always known but forgotten somehow.

It complicates your life when you remember something you've always known.

I also learned that you can get beaten to death without a hand ever touching you - without ANYTHING ever touching you physically. And you can get brought back to life in exactly the same way . . . without human or animal or anything physical having anything to do with it at all. You can be resuscitated by things no eye can see.

It's the truth, and you can love it or you can hate it. It's all your choice. While nature is indifferent about the choice you make....your life most certainly is not.

I stepped away from my entire life to try to figure this out. It's been more than a few years since I've seen or spoken to many of the people I used to see and speak to nearly every day. I broke. My voice went away. My ability to connect or communicate with others went away. I went away to find something from my earliest memory, I didn't even know what I was looking for.

But it felt like a life or death decision. And it was both. It was life and it was death.

I've always been one to step away alone. I've stepped away from life since my first memory, always looking for something. I've run away in tears as a child. I've walked away in joy, lured by something fascinating. I've wandered away, an ancient current moving my floating body while my head was somewhere else.

I'm so grateful I stepped away. But something has become clear to me this time. Every time I've done it, no matter how I ended up somewhere, there was always a moment of waking up and wondering whether I should have just stayed where I was.

That's the thought that can kill you faster than anything else . . . the wondering whether your life would be something better if you would have just stayed put. It's a mean bully of a thought — mostly because it's rooted in an illusion that staying put is even possible. We are always moving or being moved. We are always changing or being changed. We are always beginning or being begun. It's an illusion that we could EVER just stay put. It's an illusion that we could ever really finish something entirely in our lifetime. Because we won't be finished until our last breath. And even that's an illusion, because I suspect death is just another beginning. There seems to be no end to the beginnings.

Yes, I think you'll have questions about the unfinished parts. Just know that I have those questions too. Know that I come from a family I love deeply, every one of them. I deeply love my 8 siblings and their families. I love and appreciate my parents, especially after excavating these sacred shards of my existence. I even think I understand them more than I ever have. The same with Marq's parents and Marq's family. We came from incredibly wonderful people who are also just trying to figure life out. Know that Marq and I created a family of our own and I love each of them deeply, every one of them. Know that the villains I speak of in this memoir are placeholders for my own demons. And that I am sometimes the villain myself. The heroes I speak of are placeholders for my own potential. I am sometimes the hero too. People showed up in my life as mirrors and played those parts for me in the flesh, and they were exceptional teachers. I thank them all from the deepest part of my being. As you read, please try not to think you've figured out who and what I'm talking about specifically, this isn't fodder for gossip . . . it's just a tiny glimpse in a magnifying glass at a small slice of the human experience. You'll see yourself in much of it, too.

You'll find sorrow in my words. You'll find righteous indignation. You'll find my goofy enthusiasm and dorky wit. You'll find stubborn resentment and bitterness and pride. You'll find surrender. You'll find foolishness and you'll find genius. You'll find loads of self-deprecation, too. And incredible self-respect. Then we'll get to the tenderness that comes from allowing a heart to shatter in a million pieces only to find the actual truth in the center of it all.

You'll hear the voice of a happy child in my words and the voice of a child who is hurt and scared and angry and confused. You'll hear the voice of a woman who feels like a victim and the voice of a woman who knows she's a warrior.

With all of that, it's still incomplete.

You'll also hear me talk a lot about God, but I'm not trying to get you to perceive God the same way I do. I've tried so hard, so many times and in so many ways to stop believing in God. The more I looked for myself, the more I found God. And I just can't not include God in this story the way the world seems to want us to not include God in anything. My relationship with God still has jagged, ill-fitting fragments too. And I use lots of different names for God throughout this book. I was going to go back and use the same name every time to ease any confusion, but that just wouldn't be truthful. I have lots of names for this evolving relationship. Sometimes it's just plain old God. Sometimes it's Creator. Sometimes it's Jesus. Sometimes it's Truthteller. But really, it's all the same to me. It's everything to me.

This story doesn't really have one happy ending, either. I'd love it if we all stopped looking for the happy ending we think is going to save us. A happy ending comes in the new beginnings we have to choose from every morning; every minute if we can find the courage to let the last minute go.

So there are happy endings just about everywhere in this story. Even the painful endings are happy ones because I got to close my eyes and go to sleep and wake up to a brand new morning.

So, happy beginning, fellow soul.

Are you ready to go on a little journey with me?
I present to you, 50 Roads To The Middle of My Life.

I love you, Soul Sibling.
Melody Freebird Ross
January 2022

The Roads

1
The Road Away From Everything

We drove away from Idaho on a Saturday morning in Autumn of 2019. That was the last time I have ever set foot or tire on that little road that led from Main Street to our family home (that also served as our retreat center,) and the art barn, and the magical forest by the river.

Thousands of times over 8 years I'd walked that road, driven that road, ran down that road, stared out the window at the road. I waited to see my children driving up the road so I could stop worrying and go back to sleep. I watched the UPS truck come up the road and the FedEx truck, to bring me the things I thought I needed . . . things I'd later have to part with. I'd driven down that road to buy groceries for my family, to head to church (and quickly back from church.) I drove to the hospital, to the airport, to our parent's houses, to Sonic to fuel my Diet Dr. Pepper addiction. I walked down that road to the river, to the convenience store, to my in-law's house. I picked wild blackberries on that road with my grandchildren. I watched my teenage children drive away to school, to work, to parties. I watched my adult children drive up the road with my grandchildren in the car, and back down the road to their own homes. I blessed the dirt cloud behind my husband's truck as he drove up the road, back home to us. I ran down that road to meet friends who were coming to visit. I ran down that road chasing the Brave Girl Bus full of women who had been there for a week of self-inquiry at our retreats; chasing the bus was the way we said goodbye.

You might think it was terribly emotional to drive down that little road for the last time, and I fully expected it would be. I prepared myself for this day for months. One of the biggest surprises of my life was how numb I felt, and how not a single tear fell. I wanted to cry and I couldn't get myself to. I was numb. I was tired. I was confused and weary and worn. I was numbing anger and sorrow, and simultaneously numbing how perfectly right it felt. I was actually angry and ashamed at how right it felt. How could something that felt like a cruel death feel like the right thing?

It had been one death after another preceding this drive down the road from the home where so much life had birthed and happened. Death after death after death after death. In retrospect, that last drive down the road was a funeral train of sorts. Rest in Peace, beautiful Brave River Ranch.

I was in our old red truck following my husband, who was in the white truck pulling the RV his parents gave us to start rebuilding our crumbled life. It was a long, slow and painful crumble that happened over the course of a few years. We'd built a beautiful life together over 30 years, and now it was rubble. However, almost everything starts from almost nothing, and I at least knew that. If anyone could build something from crumbly rubble, it was us. Still, it sucked.

I could hear our tires crunching right over the top of that rubble as we drove away — and toward.

I could see our bikes on the back of the RV. I could see Hilarie and Carl in my rear view mirror as they sent us off and stayed behind to lock everything up for the last time — a merciful act of love. They were standing at the tur-quoise barn, waving goodbye. They'd been there for months helping us to get on the road. I did keep looking back, but if I looked forward I could see Marq's face in his driver's side mirror ahead of me, he was numb too, only looking forward. I could see the trees as we drove by, their leaves had been falling for days, and they were almost bare. We were driving slowly, but if I had been on foot, I would have been running; away, and toward.

Running away from something and running toward something can look exactly the same from the perspective of a spectator. But each of these acts creates very different chemicals in the body of the person who is running. Running away and running toward also yield very different results in the life of the runner. I can't tell you for sure which one I was doing, but I do know that when you focus on what you are running toward, you are given the added benefit of also moving away from wherever you've been. And when you are focused on running away, you could end up anywhere, maybe even somewhere worse than where you were trying to get away from.

I didn't really know where we were going to end up, I only knew that getting away had turned into a life or death decision that had to be made. If you ask Marq, he was running toward something. Like I said, I still can't say for sure whether I was running away or running toward. Both of them felt too cruel and senseless and humiliating and punitive to claim at that moment. Both of them also felt like relief, and then I felt ashamed to feel relief from something that felt cruel. Hence the numbing, I didn't want to feel any of it.

The 5 years preceding that last drive down our little ranch road, my husband Marq had been suffering what I perceived as a relapse from his traumatic brain injury (it happened back in 2004.) For the last 5 years, around the end of October, he would start to drift into dark caverns of hell, and by the time Thanksgiving came he had no will to get out of bed. He barely spoke. He didn't look at me, even when I was the only human he would see for weeks at a time. His body was there but the rest of him was gone away to war, battling the fierce monsters in his head. We would spend the holidays without him, he'd try to come out to the living room and see our little grandchildren, but would end up quickly back in bed. This would last until March when the first signs of Spring came. I knew this routine well because the first 6 years of his brain injury he spent in our bed or at the Elk's Rehab hospital, so each in our family were not strangers to his body being there without the rest of him.

But we had some really good years in between there, so it felt particularly cruel when this Winter relapse started to happen.

Over those 5 years of relapse, we tried SO MANY THINGS to help him through the Winters. And ultimately, the doctors, healers and fellow brain injury survivors helped us come to the conclusion that if we tried to winter in a sunny place, maybe that would help.

So that's reason #1 that we had to find a road to get away on, and to go to-

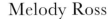

ward something else. We were racing the sun, hoping maybe the brightest light of all could chase away this darkness. It was a solid enough reason, I suppose. What I didn't know at the time (thankfully) is that there were countless other reasons to be revealed later.

So we waited until our last child was a legal adult, and we drove away from the place where we were born and raised. We drove away from 4 generations of family who had created a home in that land. We drove away from lifelong friends. We drove away from painful memories and memories that were so sparkling with love and goodness that it would blind your eyes. We drove away from the identities we had so carefully forged in an effort to belong. The young entrepreneurs. The fun ones. The ones who were sickeningly in love. The guy with the tools who would drop everything to help you. The girl who could create something beautiful. The ones who had the parties at their house. We drove away from the other identities too. The failures. The guy with the head injury. The ones who seemed to attract disasters. The woman who hardly comes out of her house anymore. The woman who hides in her bedroom so she doesn't have to talk to you. The couple who seems to have come undone.

The identities were a crushing weight. And no one gave them to us but our own selves. When you invest everything in an identity that you hope will give your life the meaning you so desperately feel you need, and then that identity gets stripped away, it feels like death. Even the crummy identities you forge for yourself are at least something. You even have to grieve the crummy identities.

So I begin this travelog of 50 Roads with this Road Away From Everything. This road is not where it all started, but it's a fine place to start this memoir because that day driving away (and toward) down our little dirt road was one of those defining experiences in life where you later catch yourself saying either "that was before we left Idaho" or "that was after we left Idaho."

I am going to share 49 more roads with you and I just want you to know that this story is not a sad one. Like all good stories, it has sad parts. It also has very good parts. It has heroes and villains and helpers and guides and tricksters. One of the biggest lessons I've learned is that ALL OF US play every single one of these roles at sometime in our life, whether we want to or not. I have been the hero and the villain and the helper and the guide and the trickster. And I have learned something from every other person who has ever come into my life, no matter what role they were playing in my life at the time. I have been molded, changed and transformed by my interactions with every hero, every villain, every helper, every guide, every trickster. I have also learned, unforgettably, that a person can be the hero and the villain in the very same story — it all depends on who you ask, where you're standing, what you're seeing and how willing you are to be truthful with yourself.

On this day, as I write this, it's been just about 2 years since we drove down that broken road of rubble that was our life. I wrote a poem sometime in the last few years that I will end Road #1 with:

WHEN WE BROKE

When we broke, we thought it was over -
we thought we were ruined.

When we broke, it was the last action we took
with our last drop of energy.

When we broke, we surrendered to the fractures
and
we surrendered to the fire that ignited
after the explosion.

When we broke, we were soaked in tears
but on the inside we were dried out
and used up .

But even so…
Things flowed from somewhere.

Because…

When we broke, we didn't know that out of every crack
would flow out of us all that wasn't good for our lives anymore.

Until
Every last drop of all of it
was gone.

Melody Ross

When we broke, we didn't know that pieces of what used to be
Would be scattered everywhere.

And that we wouldn't be able to find them all.
When we broke, some of our various pieces were sharp and flew in all directions
with so much force that they may have cut people and beautiful things that mattered to us

And
When we broke, we learned that we didn't have to find all those old pieces
and when we did find them, we got to re-choose them, piece by piece

And let some of them go entirely.

When we broke, we didn't know we were a pressure cooker
pushed to the limit, and that we were bound to break

When we broke, we got the chance to know
that we have limits and we will break if they are exceeded

When we broke, we got the chance to learn
that we are worth more than what we can do and produce

When we broke, everything got so quiet
that we could finally hear our own voices

When we broke, we surprised ourselves
with how much we needed to be alone
AND how much we needed to be together

When we broke, we didn't know we were
breaking ourselves back together.

2

The Road Of Unbecoming

I admire people who can change direction swiftly and not look back long-ingly at where they used to be. I am in awe of people who can let go of things that are long past their date of usefulness without making it into a big emotional thing.

I am not that person.

I can't stand it when something beautiful is over, and I have to work really hard to not take it personally when something that was alive and thriving one day, with so much possibility ahead — dies or moves on seemingly overnight, and that big possibility in my head is just gone.

We have all these imaginings in our head of what the future is going to be with a person or a project or a dream or even a plant. Sometimes things just die or move on when you're smack in the middle of planning a future with them. I really really really can't stand it when something beautiful is over. It feels like a knife in my heart.

A person needs to be able to count on beautiful things staying alive, right? Right? I mean, how else can we prove that we are valuable if we don't have beauty and loveliness and wonder and excitement alongside us at all times?

It was that way with everything for me, even flowers that warn you on that plastic tag stuck in the soil. They say ANNUAL. That means you get to have them for ONE GROWING SEASON and then they are done. They just die, disintegrate and turn back into soil. It's so rude. I always thought that maybe if I was nice enough, they wouldn't be so rude to just die when we had so much of a future together. So, I'd plant annual flowers and even when that growing season was over it felt like a personal insult and a complete rejection when they would die. After I'd spent so many months building a relationship with them, giving them everything I had. Every Spring I would plant thousands of flowers all over the ranch. In pots on the deck, in pots on the grass, in the dirt, in the garden. In hanging pots, in cracks in boulders, in old rusty containers. Anywhere that a visitor to the ranch might find a place to sit, I would plant some flowers. I especially loved to put them in surprising places. I would paint words and loving sentences on rocks and hide them in the pots or next to the pots. Surely that would make the flowers want to stay! I loved to make surprises for people to find later, and I would even find them years later on just the right day. There were never too many flowers. Just about every time I went to the grocery store I would throw a few more little black containers of perky colorful little blossoms, ready to be somewhere in the sunshine, in my shopping cart. I would go home and plant them wherever they would grow. And then I'd have this love affair with every single one of those flowers as spring warmed into summer, and all the way into the lingering warmth of September and October.

And then the frost would come.

And overnight, dahlias, zinnias, petunias and all their pals would literally turn black from the frost. And they'd wilt and die within hours like we hadn't just been dancing together the day before.

So rude. So devastating. It seemed so impersonal to them, like it was the most natural thing in the world for them to be a blossom one day and the material for compost the next day.

Didn't they care about me as much as I cared about them?

I often worked hard to defy nature, in just about every part of my life. Maybe if I worked hard enough, they would stick around. Maybe a miracle would happen and they just wouldn't die. Maybe my love would be enough.

So I had a whole routine of watering, deadheading and talking and sing-ing to them. I would cheer them on when they grew and I would apologize to them when I accidentally pulled off too much while trimming them. When I had to go out of town, I would obsessively send text messages to my sons or Marq asking if they remembered to water my flowers. My heart would beat fast and I'd melt into love sickness when I'd look out the window and see Marq with the big gentle rain sprayer attached to the hose, carefully watering the flowers all over the deck. It was the most romantic act of love to me.

Well, that frosty morning of death would come every year and it was dev-astating every single time. I would cry every single time. I would feel angry and insulted and betrayed. I would even cry when giant branches would break off the trees in windstorms, afraid it was going to kill them. There were more than 50 trees on the ranch and some of them were very very old. You can't just replace an old tree.

There are things you have to say goodbye to, knowing that there will never be anything there again that was exactly the same.

This same way of bargaining with nature extended into ANYTHING in my life that was beautiful. I kept every piece of clothing that was beautiful, even if it didn't fit anymore. I kept every card, every letter, every gift that was ever given to me. I kept every notebook I wrote anything in. Dish-es, blankets, sketches. Anything my kids ever made. I couldn't stand the thought of anything beautiful not being in my life.

You can imagine my dramatic devastation when my children moved away from home. We won't even go there yet. And when my dad died. Ugh. Every day, I still hate that he's not alive anymore.

So when I had to start going through 30 years of belongings, and cull the herd of my beautiful proof of life, it felt like such a personal attack, such a rejection. It felt like I was going to disintegrate right along with those dead, black flowers. It didn't seem to matter how much love or care or time I had invested in anything. It all felt so incredibly personal.

As I look back, it's embarrassing how I behaved when we had to get rid of

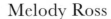

most of our belongings. I had to do it in stages. And I cried a lot. I tried to bargain and rationalize why I needed to keep things. I'd make piles of stuff that I was certain my children would want, or friends would want. I mean, I sacrificed so much of my life for all of this stuff!

In the end, nobody really wanted my old stuff, aside from a few things here and there. Turns out, it was me who had the problem.

The problem was that I couldn't let go. I couldn't let go of unfinished possibilities, good-intentions-never-fulfilled or things that had graduated to the title of "good memories." I didn't want memories. I wanted ALIVE-NESS. I wanted everything to come back to life somehow. I wanted everything that was EVER good in my life to be within arms reach so that I would be okay no matter what happened next.

In truth, I was always afraid that nothing good would happen again and so I needed to hold on to what was good before.

And the biggest truth of all was that I wanted PROOF that I did something valuable once. I wanted PROOF that I had gathered the things that make a person valuable in our culture. I wanted PROOF that I was valuable and worthy of a beautiful life.

I was a PROOF hoarder. I was a relentless coaxer of all things past their due date . . . if I just do it right, I know I can revive this.

So there were piles and boxes and bags and hangers filled with pedigreed PROOF of who I had become.

And then the frost season of my life came, and it was time to UNbecome. Just like those flowers in the pots. When this relentless season came, the old me died. And I wasn't ready.

The August before we left Idaho, my daughter Madi came over every day and asked me if I was ready to go through my clothes. I kept procrastinating. We had planned a one week stretch where neighbors, friends and strangers could come and rifle through our stuff - an estate sale of sorts. It was days before that deadline and I still had not found the strength to go through my lovely lovely lovely clothes, boots, shoes, bags, belts and jewelry. So one night, Madi showed up, set up at least 8 tables out in the driveway and came inside and started hauling my stuff out to those tables. It was getting dark, and so I told her we would do it tomorrow. She pulled her car to where the lights pointed to the driveway and shined her headlights at those 8 tables and started going through 15-20 years of beautiful costumes. Yep, I'm gonna call them costumes.

Just like with everything else, I tried to make excuses for why I needed to keep almost everything. About every 10th piece, I would say… "okay, I can let that go…" We weren't making much progress.

So Madi started doing something to make me laugh. She held up a ridiculous skirt and said "Mom, no." In a tone that helped me realize that this skirt was SO not me anymore, even though I'd worn it during a television interview years before — PROOF that I'd done something valuable. And then she put the skirt on. And then she did it with a shirt, again, held it up and made a cringey face and said "MOOOOOM, WHAT? WHY? no." Even though I remember buying it in New York City on a trip where I landed an amazing licensing deal. What other PROOF did I have that I'd done something amazing once? And another skirt. And a jacket, and a swimsuit coverup. She held them up and then put them on over the top of whatever she'd put on last. And then she found a wig, and put that on. She put on crazy tights and wild hats and just layered it all on top of the last thing and just kept layering and layering and layering clothes that I thought I just had to keep.

It was a ridiculous fashion show out there in the glow of her headlights.

And I was laughing so hard because she is just so funny, and so frank, and such a relentless let-goer. Then I started to cry because I could see that this is what I'd been doing my whole life. Hoarding proof. Hoarding future possibilities. Hoarding armor, coverings, padding — something to hide behind. Something to announce my value. Something to make me worthwhile. And I'd layer it and layer it and layer it until I was unrecognizable under it all.

I had over 120 dresses, 0ver 70 pairs of jeans ranging from size 4 to size 14. I had more than 45 pairs of boots. Countless earrings, bracelets and purses. It took most of the night to sort through it all and Madi stayed with me the whole time. I kept asking her if she wanted to keep things that I thought were particularly valuable. And she just kept saying…"Mom, no."

Well, we finished going through everything and I did keep a few boxes for myself. Coats, and a few pairs of boots and some jeans that still fit. I kept things that were practical, but I didn't keep much because you can't fit very much in an RV. I kept a few very special things to be stored for someday. But in the end, I ripped off the bandaid and let most of it go.

And over the next few days, I hid in my RV parked in the driveway and watched out the window through metal blinders as strangers stuffed my PROOF into big black garbage bags. $10 for as much as you can stuff into a bag. I'd watch them rifle through my stuff like it didn't mean much at all — discarding some of it and tightly stuffing the things they wanted into that thick black plastic. It was a reckoning. Nearly 30 years of my PROOF OF VALUE drove down that little dirt road in the cars of strangers and neighbors.

In the end, I kept t-shirts, jeans and flannel shirts. But I didn't heal this problem for a good long while - it's been 2 years and it's taken almost that long to get to the root of my need to hoard PROOF OF VALUE. After the black bag bonanza, I didn't have much to cover myself up with. So instead of covering myself with clothes, almost immediately I started to gain a lot of weight, I needed SOMETHING to cover me up if I didn't have proof of value anymore.

I was trying to disappear.

So that was when I started learning about Unbecoming. What I know now is that I was MOLTING.

molting
-to shed old feathers, hair, or skin, or an old shell, to make way for new growth.
"a caterpillar molts its skin"
-to fall out to make way for new growth.
"the last of his juvenile plumage had molted"
In biology, molting, also known as sloughing, shedding, or in many invertebrates, ecdysis, is the manner in which an animal routinely casts off a part of its body, either at specific times of the year, or at specific points in its life cycle.

Molting is an incredibly ugly process. It's the messy, raw, painful initiation into Unbecoming.

And you can get really caught up in how much it feels like a tortuous death. You can convince yourself that this is the final chapter because it feels like you are literally dying. And you are.

But you are dying because it is the **ONLY WAY** to make space for what wants to be born next.

It's a long and difficult process. It feels cruel and senseless and meaningless. It can trick us if we don't understand what is actually happening. So many things are like that.

The Road To Unbecoming was a humiliating, naked walk through dead flowers and outdated sparkly frocks.

But I was Unbecoming SO THAT I could finally BECOME. It took a long time in that chrysalis though. And I will talk about that on another road.

So, dear Fellow Molter….

What old skin are YOU carrying around that it's time to shed?

AND

What is YOUR PROOF OF VALUE you're afraid to be free of?

I dare you to slough off that old skin and see what's underneath.

And thanks for traveling The Road of Unbecoming with me.

Road #3 is The Road Where We Parted Ways.

I love you, I love who you are becoming as YOU UNbecome.

xo
melody

3

The Road Where We Parted Ways

"Goodbye always makes my throat hurt." – Charlie Brown

We sure can make up a lot of stories when we aren't together, especially if we spent a long time together before we had to part ways. I guess it's just human nature to try to make sense of things we don't understand. We fill in the gaps with "what this must mean" and then we suffer, and we make each other suffer over things that were never true to begin with.

Sometimes people who love each other have to part ways, and hope with everything in them that they will get to meet up again somewhere down the road. But still we make up stories about the "separating part" until we can't even remember the "together part." We stop remembering that love transcends time and space and even parting.

It's often like that when relationships go through the transitions that happen as a result of life's turmoils. We seem to be wired to go on a hunting expedition whenever something hurts, to look for who is the one doing the hurting. Sometimes, it's just LIFE that did the hurting, not a choice someone made to hurt someone else. It's the fallout of a bunch of people on their own path, trying to stay next to each other as much as they can — while life has all sorts of twists, turns and holes up ahead that we can't always see. Sometimes in order to stay on the path that's meant for your life, you have to go a different direction than the person next to you, who also has to stay on their own path. When you've been lucky enough to have your paths next to each other for a really long time, that's when it's hardest, that's when we start to make up painful stories about "what it must mean."

I don't know why we do it. Maybe it makes us feel better to have something solved, to accept a circumstance we never would have chosen for ourselves. We would always choose to be with the ones we love, every single day if we could! Our heart and our brain fights hard – trying to make it make sense. I get that. But goodness gracious we can make up stories that hurt.

I love the quote by Dr. Seuss that says "Don't cry because it's over, smile because it happened."

And…the one by A.A. Milne from Winnie-the-Pooh, "How lucky I am to have something that makes saying goodbye so hard."

Goodbye is the hardest word there is to say. If you and I have ever been together in person for any length of time, you know that I do not say "the G word."

I hate goodbyes. When I started writing this chapter, I sat here for longer than I'd like to admit trying to figure out why I hate goodbyes so much. I dislike them so much, in fact, that I have been known to slip out the door before something is over just so that I can avoid saying goodbye.

So I made up a phrase 10 or so years ago that has sort of become a traditional farewell for the people in my life. We just say . . . "See you at lunch!"

That way, we can pretend that it's only going to be a few more hours till we are together again, and we can high five, or fist bump or even share a little hug. But definitely not the kind of hug that means goodbye. I guess it goes back to Road #2 where I talked about how much I don't want beautiful things to come to an end.

We left Idaho without a farewell party or any kind of gathering, aside from the black bag bonanza. The friends and neighbors who so mercifully came to help us pack, or to take some of our old stuff off our hands were pretty much the only ones we said "see ya at lunch" to. We hoped to be able to see everyone we loved before we left, but it just didn't happen. The last few weeks before we left were tense and difficult. Marq's health was declining fast and the #1 focus was to just get out of there.

So there were lots of loose ends that never got tied up. There were lots of messy endings that left lots of questions. And I started to make up stories about what that must mean, that some of the people we loved most didn't even come over and say goodbye. So many didn't offer help or just show up to help. I let that hurt me a lot. When in all honesty, they may not have even known we were leaving. I made it mean that we were not important to them, that we were not loved. That we did not belong. Meanwhile, they were wondering why we would ever leave without saying goodbye. We all suffered. We all made up stories that weren't true.

What really happened is just the thing that happens. It's the thing we are hardly ever ready to have happen. Our Soul Roads curved in the opposite direction. Sometimes we have to go away to heal, or to grieve, or to lick our wounds and forgive, or to process, or to learn something critical. Sometimes we have to go away to become someone entirely new! We don't really ever know where that curve is going to take us, but it's always somewhere we need to be for some reason.

I remember the first time I watched Charlotte's Web and she sat and nurtured her baby eggs for so long and then one day they all hatched and almost immediately, they left. I cried when I watched that scene and it still makes me cry just to think about it. Why did they have to leave so suddenly? Why can't we all just be together all the time?

Why do we have to part ways?

Just a few months ago, this painful part of life finally started to make sense to me. I'd spent the better part of the month helping my soul sister and medicine-woman Kami, to build a new labyrinth on her property in the vast nowhereness of Southern Utah. Her old one had been dismantled by the horses so I had the honor of helping her move the rocks to the other side of the ranch. I always thought her labyrinth was so beautiful, but I did not understand the most paramount meaning of it until this new one was done and I was honored to walk it with her. I wish that experience for everyone alive, to walk the labyrinth with medicine-woman Kami.

If you don't know what a labyrinth is . . . it's a special path contained in a circle. Some people think it is a maze, but it's not. You don't have to try to find your way out. You just have to take one step at a time. One foot in front of the other.

From the labyrinthsociety.org :

"What is a Labyrinth? A labyrinth is a meandering path, often unicursal, with a singular path leading to a center. Labyrinths are an ancient archetype dating back 4,000 years or more, used symbolically, as a walking meditation, choreographed dance, or site of rituals and ceremony, among other things."

Kami utilizes her labyrinth as a powerful healing tool. She shares it with whomever might have the great honor of being on her ranch. I've also seen her in the labyrinth all by herself. She walks her talk and partakes of her own medicine.

The first time I walked this labyrinth was with Marq, West, Kami and 3 wonderful humans from California who came to the ranch for a week of horse and human training with West. When their week with West was over, we all walked the labyrinth together. There's a really special and meaningful way that Kami does her labyrinth meditation where you let things go on the way in, and you call things into your life on the way out. So as we started, I was ALL IN.

We started walking the labyrinth one person at a time, and as you can see in this photo (I would love it if you stopped for a moment and traced your finger around the labyrinth path til you get to the middle so you can understand this process) anyway, as you can see from this photo, it does a jiggly spiral where you end up in almost the same place lots of times before you get to your final destination in the middle. It's kind of tricky because you get SO CLOSE to the middle and then you get pulled back outward to loop around again . . . and again.

Something else that happens is that very often, when there are several people in the labyrinth together, you find yourself walking right beside each other. The first time this happened, I was walking right next to one of the women from California who I had grown to love and adore over those days together. We were walking right next to each other on the labyrinth and it felt so good. Both of us on our own paths, but next to each other. Then suddenly, our roads turned and we were walking in opposite directions. Before I knew it, we were on opposite sides of the labyrinth.

This hit me with such emotional force that I started to cry. I didn't want her to be across the labyrinth from me. I wanted to keep walking next to her. I cried as I kept walking and by the time I got to the middle of the labyrinth, I was sobbing. Then I looked up, and there she was, standing next to me in the middle. There we all were, in the middle of the labyrinth, having walked the same path that took us close to each other and then far away from each other. And then back together. And then I understood.

I believe we are all trying to get to the same place. I really do. I think there are so many things in life that we just aren't going to understand until we get to that place.

On The Roads Where We Part Ways, we have some choices to make. If there was a lot of love, it's probably always going to hurt. Heck, even if there was a lot of 'like' it's going to hurt! We ache for connection and belonging and family and togetherness, it's how we were made. So when we get those delicious spans of time where we rest in each other's presence and absorb the salve of connection and togetherness into our parched souls, it's really really really hard when it's over.

The choice we make is what we will do with the pain. There isn't always someone to blame for the pain we feel. Sometimes pain is just a byproduct of the loss we all experience as we transition to the next Soul Road we are each meant to take. It's grief more than anything.

I think we, as a human family, would do well to examine our need to find fault for the pain we feel. We hunt and hunt for the one or the ones who did something to us, the ones who left us, when the truth is that they probably didn't want it to end either.

We miss out on the crystal clarity of the love that will always remain. We cover it up with stories until it's muddied and colorless. And before long, it's a very unnecessary and unneeded fracture between us.

Because the truth is, there will almost always come a time when we are able to meet each other again on that winding path we are each on. Like the labyrinth, it's all the same route! It just tricks us into thinking it's a different one. We get to cross paths lots of times. It might last minutes, it might last years, but what happens when that collision takes place will largely be determined by how we handled the last time our paths parted ways.

I really thought at this time in my life, I would be somewhere very different from where I am right now. It takes a lot of emotional discipline to keep reminding myself that where I am is where I need to be right now. AND, where others are is exactly where they need to be right now. It doesn't mean anything about each of us, about our relationship or about the love we got to share for a while. It just means that life holds a lot of surprises and all of them will end up bringing us back together with the ones we love most if we don't submit to stories of division and false narratives. We can love each other AND be headed in the opposite direction.

Sometimes our paths just have to part ways for a while.

Let's love each other. Let's be good to each other. Let's wish each other well. Let's each stay on our own path and support others in staying on theirs. And for heaven's sake, let's dance when we get to be together and not waste a moment of time putting guilt trips on each other.

So, Dear Lifewalker,

What stories have you told yourself about the time you had to part ways with someone before you were ready?

AND

How do you want it to be when you're beside each other once again?

I love you.
See ya at lunch,
xo
melody

4

The Road With
Too Many Lights

I don't know if you've ever been somewhere so dark at night that you can actually see the Milky Way with your naked eyes, but if you haven't, I hope you find a way to experience it.

It will change your life. I used to see pictures of the Milky Way and I thought they were Photoshopped or taken with a telescope. I had no idea there were places in the world where the Milky Way became visible up there — and that what was hiding it all along was light down here.

There's such a thing as light pollution. And I love light. I love everything about light. But I learned that too much light can obscure the things we need most. Too much light can disorient us, confuse us and even blind us. Too much light obfuscates the nuances, the natural contours and the beautiful shadows where things live that need a soft and safe environment. Sometimes the best things need a semi-dark place to live, with only a candle to light what is needed moment by moment.

Sometimes when everything has a spotlight blaring on it all at once, you just have to close your eyes and put the covers over your head in order to function. We use light for the most part to be able to see things better. But sometimes it's light that hides things most treacherously.

Melody Ross

Lots of people tell me I am brave and resilient. But I need to tell you the truth about the other end of that stick. For you to understand the upcoming roads, I need to start telling you now about my complete mental and emotional unraveling that happened shortly after we left Idaho. It stepped up to the counter of my reality as if it had been waiting in line for decades to talk to me. Now that it had its turn, it wasn't going anywhere until I listened. It waited until I was on a road dark enough to see myself. And what happened next, some might call a mental or nervous breakdown, I did for a while. What I call it now is a severe allergic reaction to the blinding strobe light of self-abandonment. It showed up unapologetically as soon as things got dark enough for me to be able to see it.

I'd lost myself, or abandoned myself for a long time in the abyss of modern life's metaphorical light pollution. Too much light? It didn't make sense for a while. As a lover of truth and knowledge and love, this lesson for me was unforeseen and something I fought for a long time. How could too much light be a bad thing? Wasn't I always trying to find more light, create more light and advocate for more light?

I was actually hiding myself in the blinding lights of "too much."

What I have learned is that not all light is the same.
What I have also learned is that not all darkness is the same.

When we left Idaho to chase the sun for Marq, we first took a detour to rural Oregon, to spend some time with our dear friends, Pixie and Sky. They invited us to spend a few months there in our RV to get our bearings before we headed South to find more light.

The road between Soulodge and our ranch was about a 5 hour drive and they'd traveled it several times to see us in Idaho, to help us sort through our belongings and pack up, to visit, to spend our different holidays and rituals together. Our relationship had always been a peculiar one if you were to look from the outside, but an absolutely pure one if you could peek to the inside. Pure love. We all had different ways of devotion, different ways of prayer, different ways of belief. But it was never a problem because of the love between us all. We would take turns offering our different ways of prayer before meals. We would learn from each other about what we were devoted to and what sustained each of us. We talked openly and respectfully about what our individual Source of truth, love and creation

36

was. What God or Goddess meant to each of us. We all shared gentle light with each other over so many years. Christian and Pagan sitting in a circle, just loving and adoring and caring for each other.

I cry as I write this because I don't know a better version of love than the one that happened by candlelight or firelight every time we were all together.

Marq and I had also traveled that 5 hour road countless times over the years. We were always welcome. It always felt like home when we'd drive up the long long long gravel road to their gate. You can't believe the view once you get to the gate, an enormous rock mountain in the shape of a buffalo as the backdrop. Green fields, juniper trees, horses and cows as far as you can see. I could literally feel my heartbeat slow down as we drove up that road, every time. You had to stop your vehicle, get out and open the gate, then drive through the gate and stop your vehicle again and get out to close the gate. Then it was another drive to the house or the barn. The whole routine was like a meditation and the red volcanic gravel road would crunch underneath you like a song.

We'd been there so many times and whether or not it was printed officially on a calendar, we always made it a special occasion. We went there to recommit to each other for our 25th Anniversary, surrounded by our children and a close circle of sacred friends who threw us the best 2nd wedding we could ever imagine. We'd traveled there together and also alone. Marq had driven there alone many times during his worst bouts of depression to be on the land, to find his way in the gentle starlight. To help Sky and to be helped by Sky. They'd build fences and care for the livestock and appreciate the land the way only they could. He would go there to just be. I'd been there on my own countless times just to be with Pixie and our artist group. To sit on the couch and look out the enormous windows at the volcanic mountains and the perfect sunsets and the juniper trees and the garden. To have the best conversations with my dear soul sister. To be with her children who felt like my own. I knew the routines of gathering firewood and building the fires, opening the curtains in the morning while Pixie made us warm turmeric drinks to start the day. Lighting the candles at night.

I even got to walk that land with Pixie when she first bought it. I listened to her dreams of making a gathering place and I got to be there when it all happened.

So going there to start our journey was pretty perfect, even though it wasn't the sunny and warm place we needed to find as our ultimate destination. It was the place where we needed to start our sojourn.

I could tell you a million things about this experience but what I want to share on this road is what happened when we were away from the bright lights of our life for a sustained period of time, in a place that felt safe and restful, without a deadline to be anywhere else. And on a ranch so far out in the country that there was no light pollution.

I need you to know that Marq had his brain injury in 2004, so at this time, it had been 15 years since his accident. My inner-life had become a figurative trauma center over those years, just like you'd see on a tv hospital show, where there are surgical lights and bright bulbs everywhere, with everyone running around frantically in an over-lit hospital with loud floors and zero privacy. TV doctors yelling, people crying, dramatic relationships unfolding. Miraculous recoveries with sappy music and devastating losses with even sappier music. That's how my head felt all the time. Machines beeping, frantic messages over the loudspeaker. Waiting rooms full of people. Paramedics wheeling in new patients hectically. And then the soundtrack in the background. Dramatic music, scary music, ominous music. My head was a tv drama on full blast all the time for at least the last 15 years. Reruns playing constantly. It never ended.

I didn't know how much I was hanging by a thread until everything got really quiet and really dark at Soulodge Ranch.

I can't remember how many days we'd been there before my inner Milky Way became visible to me. I know that first Saturday afternoon, when we drove up to the house and parked the RV, something in me started to wake up. I don't know if it felt safe because of the running away or the running toward, but something in me woke up and knew I was gone from where I'd always been. I'd arrived somewhere else. Something felt both safe and very compelled to reveal itself to me. I had just turned 48 and what I've learned since this happened is that lots of people around this age are suddenly confronted with the truth of their self-betrayal and self-abandonment. And it isn't a welcome visit that was planned. This stuff shows up without an invitation. That's what happened to me.

We parked the RV right next to their house. I could look out my little kitchen window and see Pixie's kitchen. It was like having your best friend sitting next to you while you're in your hospital bed. We did a lot of things together over those few months. We all ate together every night, cooked together, played more card and board games than I can count with the kids and as adults late into the night. We watched so many movies. We went on drives and walks and to the grocery store. We made celery juice and ate ice cream and had the most wonderful Thanksgiving with a patch-work of friends, neighbors and chosen family. But a lot of the time, I was in the RV alone and Marq was out on the land with Sky. I was working, making videos, writing curriculum and doing Zoom meetings. Pixie was inside her house doing the same.

But I was finally alone. And it was finally quiet. There wasn't any light pollution at all. Inside or outside.

Within a week of being there, I started having vivid dreams. Little panic attacks. Flashbacks. I had been working with a therapist/healer over Zoom that lots of my friends had recommended to help me through the grief of the last few years. I absolutely was not expecting the locked doors of my brain to choose this time in my life to burst open and expose tightly taped boxes with secrets and anger and grief and shame and blame and rage inside, but that's what happened.

The first time I had these flashes of my inner reality, it terrified me. I was laying on the little couch/daybed in the RV, my heart was swelling and aching as I thought about what we'd left behind. Then suddenly an enormous metal playground slide opened up from the sky and a big wad of sights and sensations rolled down it into my brain. I could see it, feel it, hear it. All of it. Things I had long forgotten and stuffed away, numbed away and gaslighted away showed up like an angry mob. In an instant, I saw, felt, heard and tasted deep knowings I didn't even know I knew. Flashbacks of myself enduring soul-crushing experiences as a child, teen and young adult and then keeping it a secret. . . leading to years of so much self-betrayal as an adult. Mistakes I'd made, the way I'd put my head in the sand when I should have spoken up or taken responsibility. The people I'd hurt because of my own hurt and carelessness and numbness. The situations and people I kept attracting into my life to relive all of it, over and over again — the way this had all become a cycle.

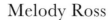

Melody Ross

Self-abandonment, self-betrayal and self-exploitation had finally broken its way out of the closet I'd stuffed it in for decades. Because it had gotten so dark and so quiet that I could see my own Milky Way.

I won't go into detail about what these sensory experiences/memories held. Some of them were heinous. But it was so real and so detailed that I can't believe I was ever able to just stuff it all away. I immediately asked God to not show me any more of it. I begged and pleaded and prayed and said . . . I get it, I don't want to see any more of this. Please.

But it didn't go away until it was time for it to go away.

I don't get angry. Well, let me rephrase that . . . I USED TO not get angry. I didn't even know how. But I suddenly got so angry that it terrified me. Memories showed up from decades back of all the times I allowed things to happen, all the times I said yes when I should have said no, all the times when I didn't have the power to say no, all the way back to the young little girl I once was. So much abuse. So many secrets.

I felt myself breaking, and I knew there was no stopping it. Some of the memories that came up were so horrific that I didn't know if I'd ever be okay again. I felt a combination of deep shame, intense rage and desperate powerlessness.

I didn't tell anyone except the therapist/healer I'd been working with. We would meet over the phone once a week and when I told her, she said she already knew there were things that I'd stuffed away. That she suspected it all along and that this was going to be one of the greatest blessings of my life. To have these things out in the open where I could heal them.

It wasn't the light that brought them out, it was the darkness.

That night the stars were so bright BECAUSE of how dark it was. I broke to pieces in that dark with the gentle light of the stars showing me why so many things happened the way they had over the course of my life. Why I was afraid of the dark, afraid of being alone, afraid of getting too close to people, afraid of quiet and stillness, afraid of success, afraid of stopping to rest, afraid of myself.

The next morning I woke up and Marq was already gone and I laid on the

40

bed and sobbed. I had no idea what to do with any of this.

Then I had one of the most sacred experiences of my life. With my eyes closed, I felt angels surrounding me. Holding me like a baby. They were over me, under me and beside me. They kept saying, you have so much to heal from…it is time….I sensed that these were beings who knew me and knew every single experience I had ever lived through — and the message that would ring in my ears for years to come was that I was even sicker than my husband was. A sports accident had broken his brain. Too many acts of self-abandonment when I needed myself most had broken my spirit. Marq would get healed by the light and I would get healed in the gentle glow in the darkness of my own Milky Way.

I'd spent most of my adult life and career passionately trying to help others to heal. I was obsessed with this mission. I have written thousands of pages of books, curriculum and Daily Truths to souls that I only knew through the connection my heart felt to them. I wrote frantically and prolifically and earnestly. Words as food. Words as oxygen. Words as medicine. Day and night I would study and write and create beautiful art in an effort to help my human family to heal. I didn't know until that day how I was really trying to heal myself. I learned that I gave those words so wholeheartedly because I needed them so desperately.

The darkness that chased away the light pollution and showed me something I needed to heal started out with that mental and emotional breakdown. That's why I disappeared from the world for a while. It lasted for months and that turned into years. I do not fool myself into believing that if I'm not careful, I will get pulled right back in for another round of unraveling. And I am not ashamed of that. I am grateful for it. Because now I know what healthy light is, and what healthy darkness is.

Not all light is the same. The Soul Road of Too Many Lights was the one that blinded my eyes and disoriented me, but it also kept me safe until it was time for me to see the stars inside of my own soul's darkness. Not all darkness is the same. Terrible and scary things happen in the dark where they can be hidden, where they can trick and deceive you, where people can do things to you that they wouldn't be allowed to do in the light. And miraculous things happen in the dark where they can be safe and protected. Babies grow in the dark of a womb. Roots grow deeper in the dark of the underground. Treasures get buried away from predators until it's safe to unearth them.

This road to middle-age is not for the faint of heart, is it? We spend the first half of our life exploring, gathering, building, proving, burying, surviving. And it seems we get to spend the second half of our life with more exploring but now dismantling, digging-up, inspecting, confronting, sorting, simplifying, appreciating and then enjoying.

We still have 46 roads to go, friends. I needed to put this one toward the beginning to give you context for some of the ones that come next. Here's what I want you to know — I have and am working through the fallout of this breakdown. When something like this gets revealed to you, it's a line of dominoes that start to fall, one by one. There's a lot of unwinding and rethinking and rewiring that has to happen. And I am doing it, I have been doing it.

If we were all at the top of a mountain in the middle of nowhere together, we would be able to see that all of us have this milky way and when we start to see it, we think we are breaking. But what's actually happening is that the thick layer of cement that we plastered ourselves with in an effort to feel safe is finally breaking off. We are not breaking, we are breaking off what can't be there anymore.

I am grateful for this breaking. It has been a long and difficult road the last few years, but the biggest gift that was under all those thick layers was something I've been searching for my whole life — self-respect.

So please just give me a fist bump. I don't want pity and I don't even need a hug about this. I feel heroic and not weak or powerless. SO MANY OF US are living with the lasting effects of trauma that bleeds into the manifestation of more trauma. It is not without consequence. At some point, we have to stop the cycle and often the first step is a complete unraveling. Thank you for witnessing me. Thank you for giving me a fist bump. I just want to dance and celebrate with you - I don't want to cry about this anymore.

Our world is sometimes far too lit. There are obnoxious lights being shined in our eyes from every direction. Let's just give each other safe places to turn off the lights so that we can see our own solar system. Let's congratulate each other, witness each other and cheer for each other as we find the courage to step away from the bright lights that have perhaps been blinding us, and face all of the pain and all of the self-abandonment that is ready to be released.

We can heal to wholeness, all of us. In the dark and in the light. But we each have the responsibility to step away from whatever spotlights are creating overwhelming competition for the beautiful little light inside of us that's always been there, ready to reveal what is most real and true.

I will tell you more about this unraveling on future roads. It's important. But for now, just know that it was a very good thing. It still is.

So, Sparkling Soul,

What are the bright lights of YOUR LIFE that are blinding you from seeing yourself?

AND

What makes you afraid of your own darkness?

Yes please, let's be a safe place for another to be in their darkness. I am so grateful for my friend and her starlit Soulodge — she's always been that safe place for me.

Road #5 is The Road I Wanted To Stay On Forever …. see you there.

xo
melody

5

The Road I Wanted
To Stay on Forever

I'm going to take a little detour now and talk about the roads I'd hoped would never end. From here on out, these 50 roads might not be in chronological order, but I promise you, they are all headed exactly where they're meant to end up.

But let's talk about life's most pleasant roads and how we wish they would never end. Something I learned from my unraveling is that when something is hurting inside and needing to be healed, we humans will often search our lives over for the one safe and magical road where everything will be okay. And every time we don't find it, we think we've done something wrong or that maybe we aren't worthy of the perfect magical road that's out there somewhere.

Never-ending magical roads sound good in theory. But let's really think through what that would actually be like.

What if we were on the same long road our whole life and we just had to wonder what was down the side roads? What if we were on a road that we could never get off of even if we wanted to someday? What if a road felt right for a while, but then it didn't…but we had to stay on it anyway just because it was perfect and magical once?

I think what would happen is that we'd have to put blinders on to survive it. We'd have to numb ourselves so that we didn't want anything different.

We are actually so lucky that we get to be on so many different roads throughout our lives. It doesn't always feel lucky though, does it?

I always loved the thought of the yellow brick road. I was a magical thinker as a kid. I have an enormous imagination and my brain feels much more comfortable playing in the non-physical than in reality. I have to pull myself down from the clouds A LOT. I dreamed up the biggest, brightest, funnest life. There's a word that floats around a lot these days — "manifest." I think I've been doing that my whole life, designing something in my head and then putting all my energy into making it a reality, and believing with all that's in me that it's possible.

I often wish life just worked in such a way that you could design it exactly how you want it to be, and nothing could stand in your way. But things do stand in our way - sometimes it's other people, sometimes it's unexpected life circumstances, and often it's our own selves.

We DO sometimes end up exactly where we dreamed and hoped we would end up, and it always feels magical at first. Sometimes it feels magical for a really long time. But then things change. We change. Other people change. Life changes.

We get signs that it's time to move on and we often ignore them, then all sorts of things start to happen because we didn't move on when our gut told us it was time. Our bodies will always tell us when something needs to change. Trusted people around us can help us know for sure that it's time to move on when we can't see it ourselves. There are times when we have lots of choices and we still don't choose. There are also times when it feels like we have hardly any choices at all.

And then there are the times where things happen that FORCE us to move, whether it feels like the right time or not. Sometimes things happen in a natural flow and sometimes things happen that are just downright crummy and unfair.

50 Roads To The Middle Of My Life

In my work, I often talk about "The 3 Hurts," which are:

1. Choices we make that leave us with painful consequences
2. Choices other people make that leave us with painful consequences
3. Things that happen that are completely out of everyone's control - leaving us with painful consequences.

Pretty much everything that hurts in life falls into one of these 3 categories.

So, sometimes you are on a road you don't want to be on as a consequence of choices you made for yourself. Sometimes you are on a road you don't want to be on because of the consequences of someone else's choices. And sometimes, you are on a road you DO want to be on, but you don't get to stay on it because of things that happen that are out of your control.

Today I am diligently reminding myself about ALL of the roads I thought I wanted to stay on forever. There's not just one. I've been on a few of those magical roads in just the last few years. I've been on perfect roads that I tried so hard to stay on forever multiple times throughout my life.

And just about every time I had to get off of that particular perfect road, I felt like my best days were over. I felt gutted. It felt unfair every time.

And then I grew. Sometimes we grow out of something while we are still in it, and sometimes we grow past something once we are out of it.

Right before we had our 5th baby, when I was 29 years old and Marq was 31 years old, we moved to a beautiful, 100 year old historic rock farm house on 7 acres. We completely remodeled it and added 2 acres of gorgeous green lawn. We planted lots of big trees to add to the ones that were already there and we started making plans immediately for how we would spend the rest of our life there. I envisioned our grandchildren coming over someday and how I'd put wreaths in every window at Christmas and luminaries lining the driveway for Halloween.

It was a magical time in our life, in our family's life. Our 4th baby had just turned 1 year old when we had our 5th. So Marq and I would sleep in separate rooms, each taking a baby and we would sometimes meet up in the kitchen in the middle of the night while we were both making a warm bottle for the baby we had in tow. Our 3 older children were 5, 8 and 11. They were old enough to be madly in love with those babies and our family was having a fairy tale life of love and laughter and growth.

Our 2 daughters shared a bedroom, and we put the two baby boys in one room and our oldest son had a room of his own. But no matter how I put those children to bed, every morning I would find them piled up in the same room, sleeping right next to each other. They're all adults now and they are still so close to each other. And now their children, as cousins, are all madly in love with each other the way their parents were when they were little.

We had so many parties at that house. We had cousins over all the time. We played in the yard, in the fields and on the wrap-around porch. There were giant trees providing shade and it was the softest grass you could ever wish for.

Our life was perfect and magical. I never wanted it to end. And I believed with my whole heart that this magical life we'd built would never end. Why would it?

And then when the babies were 3 and 4 years old, after we'd lived that perfect life for 3 magical years, Marq had his accident. A traumatic brain injury.

That's a story for another day but we had to leave that perfect magical house and drive down THAT magical dirt road for the last time too. I was able to hold up our life for 3 years after his accident, but then I just couldn't hold it up anymore and we had to leave the road that I wanted to stay on forever.

I also had a business called Chatterbox that I wanted to have forever, and we lost that after his accident too. It was a road that we paved with blood, sweat and tears — and so much joy! It was a road that we also thought we'd be on for the rest of our lives, we hoped we'd pass it on to our kids! But things happened and that road crumbled into the sea.

We have lived in 8 different houses throughout our 31 year marriage. Until we were in the last house at Brave River Ranch, I fully intended that at least 4 of those houses would be our lifetime home. I worked so hard to create a home and a perfect magical life that would last forever like it was in a safe little snow globe.

It never did last forever though.

Here's what I've learned as the result of being on COUNTLESS roads that I wanted to stay on forever — I can't know what I want forever TO-DAY. I can't know what the future will hold and what is even out there to choose from. I can't know what will be my best road next year or even tomorrow.

But I always end up on it somehow.
So do you.

Today we drove up a gorgeous dirt road to the top of a mountain in central Utah. The view was breathtaking. The sky was a clear blue with puffy white clouds. There were wildflowers pretty much everywhere that didn't have a grove of aspen or pine trees. A creek flowed through the meadow that spanned for what seemed like miles.

It was the most magical drive on the most magical road.

If you would have told me 5 years ago that I would live in Utah EVER in my life, I would not have been able to stop laughing at the ridiculous thought of it. I was a bonafide Idaho girl, through and through! Forever!

We have now lived in Utah for most of the last 2 years. We have been on hundreds of roads that blew my mind with their beauty and tranquility.

And guess what, I never want to leave here. I am currently on a road that I would love to be on forever.

BUT — I'm not doing that to myself anymore. And if you're listening, I would not recommend doing that to yourself either. It just makes you suffer when you think that if you do everything right, you'll get to stay in the magical places forever.

Here's a secret…magical places start to lose their magic after you stay past your time. Because YOUR GROWTH is what makes them magical. YOU are what brings the magic to magical places. And when you stop growing and changing, the magic fades.

But guess what? That same magic is waiting for you on the next road.

I have lived in my "dream house" a couple of times in my life. I have had my "dream furniture" and my "dream yard." I loved it.

And now I live in a medium sized RV that is 16 years old with outdated cabinets and wallpaper — and I can say with all honesty that at this exact time in my life, I am living in my "dream house." It is a magical, perfect life that we are living right now because we are learning and growing and transforming in ways that would never be possible had we stayed where we were ANY of those times that I was sure I wanted to stay forever.

It's 2021 and we are in the middle of a global shake-up on so many levels. Chances are, if it hasn't already happened, you or someone you are very close to is going to have to leave their perfect, magical life on their perfect, magical road. The one you or they were absolutely sure would last FOR-EVER.

And I promise you that you are going to be okay. There are SO MANY ROADS that you don't even know about yet, waiting for you to discover. There are roads that you will carve and pave yourself. There are roads that you'll drive down faster than you should because you'll know instantly that they are not right for you.

And no matter what road you end up on, it's going to be the perfect, magi-cal road for you at the exact right time in your life. There will be roads that you will miss forever because they were so good to you. But isn't that one of the joys of life, to have roads we can look back on fondly?

YOU ARE THE MAGIC on the most magical roads. YOU ARE THE PERFECTION when your life feels perfect. And what's totally great about that is that no matter what you have to leave behind, YOU are theone thing that will always be on whatever Soul Road you end up on.

So, Fellow Traveler . . .

What past roads did YOU think you wanted to stay on forever?

AND

What magic on your current road are you neglecting because you wish you were somewhere else?

I will leave you with one of my all time favorite quotes....

"There will come a time when you believe everything is finished; that will be the beginning."
— *Louis L'Amour*

Next up . . . I will take you to "The Road Where I Changed My Name"
See you there!

xo
melody

6

The Road Where I Changed My Name

When my dad was dying about 7 years ago, I was sitting in his hospital room alone with him and he asked me over and held my hand while he quietly and breathlessly said . . .

"Melly, you've always been my free spirit, and it has always brought me so much joy to see how free you are. Please don't ever let anyone change who you are. Keep being free, do all the things you want to do."

I have held onto those words so fiercely. I even made a piece of art that's hanging in our RV so I would never forget.

And then I changed my name to Freebird. That's the name I call myself, anyway.

Names are an interesting thing. They are so meaningful but they can also be so sticky that all sorts of other meanings adhere to them and it's hard to pull them off. I'm not so much talking about our given names. I actually love my given name. I am Melody Gae. Happy Song. I love the name my parents gave me and it is so much of who I am. I sing constantly, usually dorky songs I make up to make menial tasks entertaining. I'm not a great singer. My voice is really soft and lots of people can't even hear it very well. But I love to sing and I'm almost always singing when I'm alone. So . . . let it be documented that I love the name I was given at birth.

Melody Ross

It's the names that came after I was born that needed to be shed. The labels.

Remember the movie called "Weekend at Bernies" where the uncle dies and they just keep dressing him up and rigging up gadgets to make his arms move and make him seem alive? It's kind of gross and ridiculous, but I think we do that to ourselves sometimes. We are so hellbent on keeping things right where they are sometimes that we rig up all sorts of tomfoolery to keep things alive that are past their expiration date.

There are labels we put on ourselves and allow others to put on us. When things crumble and unravel, lots of times those old labels are revealed… along with the old packaging that suddenly feels way too small, awkward and cut for someone else's body.

Everything just feels ill-fitting and uncomfortable.

I remember this being part of the anger of my undoing. Waking up to myself and seeing that I was plastered with all sorts of labels. Nothing felt more important than doing whatever it would take to peel them off, scrape them off, chip them off. And then start working on the adhesive that was underneath them.

I just wanted to be unlabeled. I even wanted to be empty for a while. Like a clear glass bottle or an empty piece of paper.

The things that used to feel true didn't feel true anymore. Things I'd always held onto so tightly shifted and disintegrated right out from under me. I would read my own labels and think….THAT is bullshit.

Both the "good" labels and the "bad" labels. I was ready to be done with all of it. If I could have walked down the road naked, I would have. If I could have peeled my own skin off, I would have.

But in a way . . . that all started happening anyway.

I started to disintegrate.

I wrote this poem during that time . . .

Disintegrate

I am disintegrating
I'm just so tired of waiting
Can't keep in one piece anymore
Bring on the past cremating
Bring on the detonating
Bring on the tigers let them roar

Please let the pieces fly
There's just no time for goodbye
Let's let this sick thing die with grace

When you disintegrate
Think what you can create
From all the dust that's left of you

Do you know where I am
Because I don't know
I can't make out the landscape
Don't know where to go

I don't know if I exist
But this thing can't persist
So let's just let this whole thing go

I will rise from these flames
Even if all that remains
Is the inside of the inside of the inside of my soul

We can begin again
We can be whole again
But first...yes first....we have to let the sick parts end

I am disintegrating
I'm just so tired of waiting
Can't keep in one piece anymore
Bring on the past cremating
Bring on the detonating

I am a Phoenix I will soar.

Melody Ross

I have always loved birds, but I thought of myself more like a little barn swallow. I still do, actually. The barn swallow has always been my favorite bird.

But when I started to disintegrate and burn away, a different kind of bird showed up in my soul. A fierce bird.

My name has been on thousands of products and books. My name was a brand for a really long time. I think sometimes our names get hijacked and suddenly we get defined by things outside of us. We could get defined by what makes us successful, by what makes us unique, by where we were born or how we grew up. We could get defined by our mistakes, our flaws and our weaknesses.

The important thing, really, is that we decide how we will be defined on our own — because the world will define us based on the tiny fragments of us that can actually be seen at any given time.

When we don't define ourselves, other people will gladly define us.

And sometimes those definitions feel really good and so we decide to try them on and step into them. Sometimes we just want to step into a definition like a pair of pants to try on, but then we realize we actually stepped on a train and the door closed and started moving really fast. Then we realize there's no way to get off without jumping off. Jumping off of a moving train can kill a person.

Sometimes the definition of "what it means to be a good person" is already a boiler-plate checklist that someone hands us, or that we go in search of. And then we spend a great deal of our time doing ANYTHING and EVERYTHING it takes to check those boxes.

Most of us desperately want to be accepted. We want to belong, we want to fit in. We want there to be a seat for us at the table. And then we have partners and children and we want them to also belong and be accepted and fit it. So it gets really complicated. We might think the easiest thing to do is to find that magic list of things we have to do to be acceptable, to be invited, to be invited back, to be important and valuable. To belong.

We lose ourselves. Sometimes we die inside.

50 Roads To The Middle Of My Life

And then sometimes we become Uncle Bernie.

It's hard to let go of really good labels we earned by checking those boxes, it's hard to get rid of ANY really good labels. It's more PROOF that we did something amazing once. It's even harder to get rid of labels that come from crummy old beliefs about ourselves.

But think of yourself as an empty page or an empty bottle. Imagine every label you have ever had — whether you gave it to yourself or someone else gave it to you. If the next page of the story of your life was covered in a thick layer of labels, how could you write the next chapter of your life? If the beautiful container that holds your soul was covered in a thick layer of labels, how could you see what's inside of you?

Melody the wife, melody the mom, melody the artist, melody the writer, melody the entrepreneur, melody from chatterbox, melody from brave girls club, melody the brave girl, melody the failure, skinny melody, fat melody, young melody, old melody, melody the mess, tarnished melody, ruined melody, crazy melody, selfish melody, mentally ill melody, bad melody, thrown-away, forgotten, erased . . .

Some of the labels are 100% accurate, until they aren't. Some of them were never accurate but I stepped right into them and behaved as if they were. Some of them were so heavy with expectation that I never felt like I could ever quite measure up. Some of them were crutches and comfort and a perfect addition to the life-sized cardboard cutout of my perfect self I often hid behind.

I went crazy a lot of days writing down the things I'd need to do to live up to those labels and then I performed the most lifesaving surgical soul procedure I've probably ever performed on myself. I cut off all of the labels.

I just wanted to be free.

We work hard to get letters behind our name. We work hard for titles and names to put behind our name. But those are all just EXPERIENCES we get to have. They are not what make us who we are.

When our old beliefs and habits are the sticky adhesive that won't let those labels go, we have to take responsibility for how we've been believing ourselves right into old patterns...over and over and over. When we pull off the labels but the adhesive of old beliefs and patterns is still there, other stuff will just stick to the top of the old adhesive. There are a lot of broken people and organizations recruiting people with sticky habits and sticky beliefs, drooling at the thought of how easy it's going to be to stick their label right where that old label was that you thought you'd gotten rid of.

And that's the tricky part . . . that's why we run back to things after we think we've overcome destructive patterns. Because the adhesive is still there.

When the adhesive is especially sticky, you have to use some pretty strong stuff to dissolve it off.

And sometimes to get rid of the label entirely, everything under it has to disintegrate and dissolve too.

It doesn't feel good. It's not comfortable. It's both terrifying and humiliating to walk around naked without your labels. No one knows where to put you and you don't even know where to tell people to put you. You don't know what box or container you belong in.

And then suddenly . . . you get the AHA MOMENT.

I don't belong in a box or container.

I am free.

Labels get in the way of needed transformations. They keep our eyes and energy focused on what we were in the past. They trick us into thinking that what happened yesterday and last year is what needs to happen tomorrow and next year.

When I teach my courses, I often remind my students about something that I had to continuously remind myself about during this time. I still do have to remind myself of this as I'm learning to live without labels...and the lesson is this:

Our brains don't love change, so our bodies resist it. Our mind resists it.

50 Roads To The Middle Of My Life

It's hard enough to change ourselves but as humans, we also don't love when other people change. I don't know what that is. I think it's just fear, mostly. We fear losing them, or being left behind. We worry that they'll change into something that will end up hurting them, or end up hurting us. It's hard to watch someone change when you love the way things already are. It's uncomfortable to watch someone change when you've been wanting to change yourself but haven't found the strength to get started yet. One of the most uncomfortable parts of changing is that you have to give up things that still feel very very very comfortable. You have to give up where you are; places you know well. You have to give up the person you know how to be to become the person you are meant to grow into. It's uncomfortable for everyone. When we stop growing, any of us, it's time to move into a place where we can grow again. It often feels like a great big betrayal to any of the people we have grown comfortable growing with. Growth often hurts — a lot.

So we hold each other's ankles down. We hold our own ankles down.

When you make huge changes, or LIFE forces huge changes and you get stripped down to nothing more than exactly who you are.....you'll hear things like… "Wow, you've changed…"

Some people say it in a supportive tone, some people say it in a criticizing tone. I always tell my students that the best thing you could say, whether it seems like someone is trying to guilt-trip you into going back to how you were or whether someone is genuinely happy for you is….

"….well thank you for noticing, it's been a ton of work."

Rather than defending, explaining or recoiling. Rather than trying to hide your new skin or your continuing LACK of skin. Just own it. It's actually the most natural and wonderful thing that could happen.

In a culture that often teaches us to collect collect collect, attain attain attain, gather gather gather, more more more . . . it's a beautiful rebellious act to peel it all away and then dissolve what was holding it on underneath.

"To attain knowledge add things everyday. To attain wisdom, remove things everyday."
-Lao Zi

So, Beautiful soul,

What labels do you have layered on so thick that you don't even know what's underneath them anymore?

AND

What is the adhesive of your beliefs about yourself that has gotten so sticky that other labels keep sticking onto you too?

I hope you know that today you can decide to stop being whatever you're tired of being. You can start being something else as soon as you're ready….or you can just be an empty vessel or a blank page for a while. When you're ready, YOU get to decide how you're defined and what you hold.

You are a beautiful soul no matter what. You don't ever have to BE anything or PRODUCE anything or HOLD anything again if you don't want to. You just being YOU is enough.

I am melody freebird. For today.

I love you no matter what.
xo
melody ross

7

The Forbidden Road

This is the road I went down that ended up leading to what some might call a dangerous vice — because it certainly has become a habit and maybe even an addiction. Some might even say what I did was scandalous. If women did this in days of old, they might get burnt at the stake, or thrown out of the village, or shunned for life. I'm totally being dramatic but at the least, this thing I decided to do was something I had seen as a forbidden road for most of my life. It was something I would not allow myself to even think about trying out.

But I went down the forbidden road, a decision I made that was contrary to the beliefs that I'd guided my life by since the time I could start making my own decisions.

I threw tradition, convention and what I'd believed in the past as the proper way to behave - I threw it to the wind.

I rebelled.

So what was this scandalous behavior I chose to step into?

Well . . .
I started saying no.

and . . .

I also started saying yes.

and . . .

I stopped being a martyr. Ugh, I'm so embarrassed that I ever played that role in the game of life. My definition of martyr is:

Someone who says yes when they want to say no, and then feels victimized and goes on to punish just about everyone in their life because they said yes.

I looked at that forbidden road of SAYING NO for a long time. I'd drive by it and try to find the courage to go down it. It took a long time to lose the fear of rejection enough to even put one foot on that road.

But I wanted to be a warrior instead of a martyr and what I learned is that being a warrior sometimes means doing the thing you thought was forbidden before. I had to unwind so many beliefs about what it means to be a "good person." A warrior has to do the best thing and the right thing, which very often is the hardest thing.

And the hardest thing in the world was for me to say NO. Even harder than saying goodbye.

I took a small dose at first . . . yep, I micro-dosed on NO.

I loved how it felt so much that I started doing it more and more.

I started saying no to things I would have found a way to say yes to in the past, even if it killed me. I started saying yes to things I would not have allowed myself to do unless I paid dearly for it by working extra hard — most often, I would not have said yes to those things at all.

Producing was my ethic. Work was my ethic. Sacrificing was my ethic. Trying to be perfect in all ways was my ethic, though I could never even get close no matter how hard I tried.

The forbidden road was a brand new road of doing the one thing I'd never ever ever allowed myself to do — put myself on my own list. It was really difficult the first few times because there was a part of me that resisted it the way a cat would resist a bath. There was a scared little person inside of me that kept freaking out and telling me it was forbidden to just say no when there was an opportunity to be a big old martyr.

But I was in bad shape, really bad shape. It was a life or death decision that only I could make. I could choose life by starting to take care of myself, value myself and protect myself. Or I could choose to keep doing what I'd been doing for what feels like forever — do whatever it takes to be acceptable.

Forbidden or acceptable.

I chose forbidden self-nurturing, self-respect, self-care, self-healing . . . and it's my new lifestyle. I highly recommend it, especially to the ones who have the ridiculous belief that I used to have . . . that we are somehow selfish, horrible, wretched people if we ever think about ourselves at all. I had a crummy old belief that I was here on this planet to be in service of everyone all the time. And of course I STILL BELIEVE that we are here to help each other, but we have to make sure we have something to give before we head out the door to be of service, otherwise, we bleed out. We give away our own blood, our own life force. And before long, every last thing is drained out of us and we are on our last breath of will.

I started saying no to inhumane demands and expectations. I started saying no to people who bully and demean and control. I started saying no to whomever might be holding a manipulator's remote control, pushing buttons to get me to do what they want me to do. I started saying no to being a vending machine . . . lifeless but wired and plugged-in, built to give whomever whatever they need with just a push of a button, day or night without a moment's rest. I started saying no to the internal voice that would say "just a little more, just a little better, just a little sweeter . . ."

I started saying yes to rest. I started saying yes to new adventures. I started saying yes to solitude and quiet and self-respect. I started saying yes to hikes and long drives in the mountains and time to make art. I started saying yes to old Chuck Taylor sneakers, ripped jeans and old t-shirts. I started saying yes to no makeup. I started saying yes to the music I like, the places I like, the kind of art I like to make. I started saying yes to a life fueled by awe and reverence and a deep connection to the Divine. I even started saying yes to allowing myself to feel anger. I started saying yes to letting myself change whatever needed a change. I started saying yes to LIFE.

Because I'd been saying yes to whatever was asked of me by others, and saying no to what was being asked of me from my own soul.

I am the one who got myself where I was. I am not a victim, just a big dummy. I stopped being a big dummy.

Because friends, there are people who will take whatever you are willing to give. And they are not even at fault because we are the ones who are allowing it to happen. We put things out on the table to give, hoping that our offerings will be valued and will make us a productive part of the community. The problem is, there are people who have a sickness of offering and allowing WAY TOO MUCH. And there are also people with the sickness of needing to suck others dry of anything good. There are people who have the sickness of needing to actually destroy others, yep that's a real sickness, and one of the best ways they can accomplish this is to find someone who doesn't know how to say no.

....

The Journey
by Mary Oliver

*One day you finally knew
what you had to do, and began,
though the voices around you
kept shouting
their bad advice –
though the whole house
began to tremble
and you felt the old tug
at your ankles.
"Mend my life!"
each voice cried.
But you didn't stop.
You knew what you had to do,
though the wind pried*

50 Roads To The Middle Of My Life

with its stiff fingers
at the very foundations,
though their melancholy
was terrible.
It was already late
enough, and a wild night,
and the road full of fallen
branches and stones.
But little by little,
as you left their voices behind,
the stars began to burn
through the sheets of clouds,
and there was a new voice
which you slowly
recognized as your own,
that kept you company
as you strode deeper and deeper
into the world,
determined to do
the only thing you could do –
determined to save
the only life you could save.

....

When I turned the corner to step onto the forbidden road of well-being, I knew I was taking an enormous risk. I knew it was going to require the sacrifice of anything in my life that was there because of what I could produce.

There's a showdown that happens when you stop trying to over-pay for your very existence. It's like a settlement you have to reach with the part of you that wants to die a martyr. You have to give the martyr something to walk away with, so that you can be free.

It's a separation of a life partner, you and your martyr have to part ways as she wags her finger accusingly, watching you fade off in the distance down the forbidden road.

So what will you give her, that old martyr who has been passively-aggressively shaming you for most of your life?

I gave her my lists of accomplishments, my grudges, my ledger books of how I'd been wronged, my ledger books of how wrong I was. I wrapped it all nicely in a banker's box, made her a sandwich for the road and said "you head back down your road, and I'm gonna take this one….the sparkling forbidden road of self-responsibility, self-respect and humane free will."

And I slowly headed down the forbidden road of *no thank you* *nope* *not anymore* *absolutely not* and even *hell no.*

That road is where my greatest adventure began.

Because that road had the beautiful surprise of *yes please* "oh yes, I'd love to try that* *ahhhhh yes* and *absolutely, positively yes*

So, Brave Walker,

What have you said yes to that you wanted to say no to, and who did you punish for that?

AND

What forbidden NO is calling you to come and save the only life you can save?

This is holy work. You can do it too. Now let's talk about what it's like to be completely unfamiliar with your truest self on The Road Where I Was The Stranger.
See you there.
xo
melody freebird

8

The Road Where
I Was The Stranger

There are lots of ways to disappear, and being a stranger is one of them.

There's this dorky old saying that says something like — "A stranger is just a friend you haven't met yet."

I guess that depends on what your definition of a friend is. And what your definition of a stranger is. Sometimes it's okay to just remain strangers for a while, I think. Maybe even forever.

It's a bizarre experience to set off into the world and not have anyone know who you are after you've spent your whole life in the same community where almost everyone knows who you are, generations back.

Lots of people knew me that way and I knew lots of people that way. But I also "knew" lots of people across the world online and from business. On one of my Soul Roads, my social media accounts and email list were gone overnight. So over the last few years, I have had the opportunity to really experience what it's like to go from having lots of community to having almost none.

Once my social media accounts were gone, after years and years of having an online following in the hundreds of thousands, I had to really come to terms with what social media has done not just to me, but to our human

Melody Ross

family.

I had to ask myself the preposterous question of whether I had any value if no-one knew who I am, where I am and what I am doing. And this would ultimately lead to me asking MYSELF - Do I even know who I am? Do I know where I am? Do I know what I am doing?

It's like the old question....does a tree that falls in the woods make a sound?

Does a person who hardly anyone knows exists have any value?

Does that person even exist then if they are not known?

Is there any value in being the perpetual stranger?

Like I said, these are ridiculous questions, but we ask ourselves ridiculous questions a lot . . . we ask life ridiculous questions as if we are the ONE PERSON alive who doesn't matter. All of us matter.

stran·ger
/strānjər/
noun
1. a person whom one does not know or with whom one is not familiar.
"don't talk to strangers"
2. a person who does not know, or is not known in, a particular place or community.
"I'm a stranger in these parts"
3. a person entirely unaccustomed to (a feeling, experience, or situation).
"he is no stranger to controversy"

friend
/frend/
noun
1. a person who you like and enjoy being with
"I'd like you to meet my friend".
"She is such a good/close/dear friend (of mine)."
2. : one attached to another by affection or esteem
She's my best friend.
3. : a favored companion

I will never forget our first month away from Idaho. Going to the store, I

68

did not recognize or know anyone. No one recognized or knew me. Going to the laundromat . . . didn't know a soul, no one knew me. No one knew our truck when it drove by, so people only waved out of courtesy, not old familiarity. No one knew what we'd done, what we hadn't done. No one knew what boxes of acceptability had been checked on our list of life choices, accomplishments and failures. No one knew ANYTHING about us.

We were free to go about our minutes just being strangers.

It felt really good. Really peaceful. Really freeing.

When we left Idaho, I still had my online friends. I still had my online following. People still knew me if I needed to check in, and I did for a while. But then I couldn't because my social media accounts were gone. My mailing list was gone. Then I started to really experience this stranger/friend thing on a whole new level.

It was messy and internally brutal like all of this has been. I am no champion of making it through without scars. It was scarring. It was telling.

And it was lifesaving.

Seeing ourselves through the eyes of others and feeling our value through the love of others is powerful medicine. But you can overdose on it. And then what do you do when it's gone? What happens when all that's left is your own solitary self and your own self doesn't really know how to have a nurturing relationship with you?

When I became a stranger in what seemed like an overnight earthquake, I realized in a million little ways that I was actually a stranger to myself. Even Marq to a large degree was a stranger to me.

Look at the definitions up there again . . . a stranger is a person whom one does not know or with whom one is not familiar.

I was starting to learn that when I wasn't running around, wearing myself out, I was a complete stranger to myself. When I wasn't fighting for LIKES and HEARTS and validation and acceptance, when I wasn't helping people, when I wasn't loving and encouraging and lifting people out of dark places, I really didn't have a clue who I was.

When my ego started fighting with my heart, that's when I really started to break open. And breaking open requires breaking. I think I have adequately explained on the last 7 roads that I broke so we won't beat that dead horse again.

I was learning that not only was I a stranger to myself, I also wasn't a candidate to be much of a friend to myself. A friend is a person you like and enjoy being with. I didn't hate myself or anything like that, I just didn't know myself well enough to know if I liked being with her. I didn't know if she was a "favored companion" as the dictionary defines a friend.

I also had to start reckoning with the definition of enemy:

en·e·my
/en u mē/
noun
1. a person who is actively opposed or hostile to someone or something.
"the traditional enemies of his tribe"
2. a hostile nation or its armed forces or citizens, especially in time of war.
"the enemy shot down four helicopters"
3. a thing that harms or weakens something else.
"routine is the enemy of art"
4. one that is antagonistic to another especially : one seeking to injure, overthrow, or confound an opponent

Had I become an enemy to myself, even if only by putting my head in the sand during the tumbling downfall of my own well-being?

Was I hostile to myself? Was I harming or weakening myself? Was I antagonistic or seeking to injure, overthrow or confound my own life-force?

I wouldn't say I was doing this consciously, but I would say that there was a part of me that was trapped in old conditioning; when I couldn't find ways to be an enemy to myself, or destroy myself . . . it seems I was somehow trying to lure people and situations into my life who would do it for me. I attracted some of the meanest and most brutal people I have ever encountered. I let them behave in a harming, antagonistic and injurious way. I got myself in situation after situation that seemed hellbent on destroying me.

And I would turn my head as those things seized my kingdom. I sabotaged myself over and over and over again. I handed over the keys, I surrendered my golden eggs as soon as I birthed them, I passively allowed enemy attacks from just about every direction.

I did that.

That truth was a bitter pill to swallow.

I started this chapter with writing —
"There are lots of ways to disappear. Being a stranger is one of them."

I think we try to disappear when we don't feel safe, when we don't feel equipped, when we don't feel hope. It's fun for a while to be a stranger in a strange place, but after a while, you start getting lonely for human connection. You start yearning to be known, to be seen, to be heard and to be held.

When I realized the most damaging part of this stranger-ness was the way I had become my own most distant stranger, I began to realize that if I did not stop and learn to know myself, see myself, hear myself, value myself and HOLD myself . . . I was doomed.

I felt so lost when I was erased from social media. But then I learned that there is no amount of being known, heard, seen, recognized and held that can EVER make up for the act of ERASING YOURSELF from your own life.

I knew that if I was ever going to be able to move forward after so much loss, I had to stop and take the time to reclaim what I gave away, threw away, abandoned and erased about myself.

So for months that turned into years, we traveled here and there in our truck or RV and we were strangers in so many places while we took the time to get to know each other and ourselves.

Melody Ross

I'm certain there were places we stopped on our nomad adventures where we looked like we were on our first date, or on our honeymoon, or in some beginning stage of some relationship. Because after 30 years, we were.

AND the same thing was happening individually. Marq has a pretty solid sense of who he is and he's never gotten caught up in the same webs I have, but he was 50 years old when we left. And something happens when you're not young anymore. You have to decide who you are as a not-young person.

So we set off as strangers, in a land of other strangers. Learning how to be friends with ourselves, with each other and as soon as it was time, with others.

I found a quote by Mark Twain that feels especially appropriate:

"Not until you become a stranger to yourself will you be able to make acquaintance with the Friend." -Mark Twain

So, Soul Stranger, Soul Friend,

-What does it feel like when YOU are the stranger in a strange place?

AND

-In what parts of the complexity of YOU have you become a stranger to yourself?

Thank you for walking beside me on this strange road. Next we will brave our way onto "The Road to the Unwanted Truth"

I love you.
xo
melody freebird

9

The Road To The Unwanted Truth

Our world is suffering from a TRUTH crisis.

I've found you'll drive yourself mad if you need to know the absolute truth about everything. There are just too many versions of "truth" these days.

But I really thought I needed to know. I thought my life depended on it. So when I set out on my Soul Road quest, I was determined to get to the bottom of what was true. What IS true.

Here's a spoiler . . . I still don't know what's "true" about so many things - almost nothing in fact. I know that mountains are truth and birds are truth and rivers and lakes and babies and animals are truth. I know we have that God I talked about in the introduction. That's about it.

I have a great hope that lots of other things are true, but I don't know for sure.

So trying to figure out who was telling the truth about life just about did me in when everything started to unravel - it still does if I spend any amount of time trying to figure that out. My life was feeling the way the world feels right now . . . everyone screaming at once that THEY ARE TELLING THE ONE TRUTH.

That's why this road is called The Road To The Unwanted Truth — because often we want to find PROOF that everything we think/believe is ABSOLUTE. That if we search hard enough, we will find ONE VERSION that is ABSOLUTELY TRUE. And when we dig deeper and deeper we find something that maybe we didn't want — that what is true is too complicated in this incomplete human experience to be absolute.

True about WHAT, you ask? Well . . . true about just about anything, but especially the important things — the kinds of things that people use as a foundation for every decision they make in their life. When people care about you, they want you to know the truth. So usually, it's with good intention that we tell each other THE ONE TRUTH. When my disintegration started, all the different versions of everything were so deafeningly loud. I wanted to know who was telling the truth about LIFE — our world, about religion, education, medicine, politics, relationships, business, what kind of mascara to buy . . .

So much was happening in my own life and in the world at large that didn't make sense and I just wanted to KNOW FOR SURE what the truth was.

I never got there, I probably never will. And that is okay. Because the truth is complicated.

There are so many things I still don't understand, there are so many things that I will probably never understand. I felt like I was being lied to by so many people around me. I didn't know what the truth was. It was creating absolute insanity in my mind. Who is lying? Who is telling the truth? There are a million things I will never know for sure. And if you're honest with yourself, there are a million things YOU will never know for sure.

When I'm rested and fed and I haven't been binging on a zillion versions of "facts," I don't need to know for sure anymore. I hope you will get to a place where you don't sacrifice your life and your peace to KNOW FOR SURE about things that will never be entirely revealed to you. There are some things we just have to let go of, there are some things we just won't ever understand. I am at peace with not knowing and not understanding all of it, and I want to tell you how I got there.

You see . . . all I can know FOR SURE is what is true from where I am standing at this moment . . . from my viewing point. All I know is what I can see and feel and touch and taste and experience from my own unique perspective. And someone could be standing just a few feet away from me, or right across from me, and they will absolutely have a completely different point to view things from. They can see, feel, touch, taste and experience totally different things than I can from where THEY are standing, from the life they've been living in for as long as they've been alive.

Sure, I can trust what someone else tells me. I can listen closely and trust that they are telling me the truth from their perspective. But what happens when people are telling you what they know AS ABSOLUTE TRUTH and it's directly opposite of what someone else you trust just told you? And even showed you proof of?

And what happens when a person moves over a few feet and suddenly they have a totally different viewing point? And then they know something else for AS ABSOLUTE TRUTH?

It can drive you mad.

Remember on Road #1 when I said that a person can be a hero and a villain in the very same story, depending on who you are talking to and where they are standing? That's what I'm talking about.

People don't seem to remember what it's like to navigate a world full of all different beliefs, perspectives and "personal truth." I don't know when this happened to our human family, or how or why. But it's been a terrifying screenplay to watch over the years, a whole global society turning on each other in the name of TRUTH. It's happening on a large scale to our world and it's happening on a small scale in our own homes and communities. It happened in my own life. It sucks.

I truly believe the one thing that has the potential to destroy our beautiful human family and even the little families of our own homes, is the insatiable and greedy need to be RIGHT at the cost of everyone else being wrong.

Truth is tricky. Let's look at its definition:

truth
/trooTH/
noun
1. the quality or state of being true.
"he had to accept the truth of her accusation"
2. that which is true or in accordance with fact or reality.
"tell me the truth"
3. the fact of the matter
4. what actually/really happened
5. . a fact or belief that is accepted as true.
"the emergence of scientific truths"

In the same 5 minutes, through the miracle of an internet search, I can find polarized opposite "facts" for just about anything. This "crisis of truth" is truly the greatest threat right now to the vitality and survival of our precious human family.

So let me tell you about a dream I had that I'm turning into a picture book. I will give you a short synopsis and hope that you get the gist. If I could share ONE THING with the world right now…this would be it.

The dream was a story so I will tell it to you now with my rough-draft illustrations, it's called The Case of the Longest Dinosaur.

……………………………………………………………..

THE CASE OF THE LONGEST DINOSAUR
by melody ross

There was a beautiful place with an enormous mountain called Henosis. This mountain was made of stunning canyons with gargantuan boulders and rivers and streams and lakes. There were cliffs that extended high into the sky and also separated the many different terrains of the mountain.

And in between every set of cliffs and canyons, a small village of people had homesteaded.

The people of each village could not see the villages that were on either side of their own cliffs, and so thousands of people were living on He-nosis Mountain who had never sat with each other, talked to each other or even seen each other's part of the mountain.

Maybe they would have traveled to see each other if it wasn't for the Longest Dinosaur. Her name was Alethia. Lots of people on the moun-tain called her Letha for short.

Alethia the Dinosaur stretched all the way around the mountain, and made it so that every village's people could neither get off of the moun-tain or travel to each other's villages.

And she just laid there, month after month, year after year. And if you were quiet enough, all you could hear Alethia say is "I'm just doing the work I came here to do." Though it didn't look like she was doing any work at all.

Each village was very different from the next, but one thing was the same in every village — they all told stories and legends about the peo-ple of the other villages, about Alethia and about what must be beyond her large body.

The stories were scary and so almost no one dared to climb high up the mountain where the only openings to the rest of the mountain existed — at the ends of the canyons and cliffs.

One year something extraordinary happened. A flock of the most beau-tiful birds showed up and day after day, high in the sky, they would cir-cle the mountain. Every village would see them at sunrise or sunset or somewhere in between. And the children of each village were especially intrigued. After many days, there were children from every village who just HAD TO SEE these birds close up.

So children from every village, without even knowing that the other village's children were doing it, would start a climb up the mountain, and every one of those children who felt that call ended close to the top . . . and there they were, all together.

Melody Ross

At first they were afraid, because the legends and stories made them afraid of each other. But when they saw the birds, and how much every one of them loved those birds, they started stepping closer to each other.

They started telling each other their names.

And then they started talking to each other about Alethiia the Dinosaur.

A girl from one of the villages said "the pointy scales are the hardest part, they cut us when we get too close…"

and all of the other children said "Alethia doesn't have pointy scales! What are you talking about?"

another child spoke up and said, "I don't like it when Alethia's stars stay on all night and keep us awake."

and again, all of the other children said "What stars? Alethia doesn't have stars."

a boy from one of the villages said "I love it when Alethia lets us slide down her smooth skin."

and the crowd of children all started to yell at the same time, saying "Why are you lying?" "Why aren't you telling the truth?" "That is not how it is!!!"

some said "Alethia has blue dots!"

others said "Alethia has orange stripes!"

others said "Alethia has red squiggles!"

and almost all of them said "You are lying! You are a liar! Stop trying to trick us!"

and worst of all….

"this is why we aren't supposed to ever talk to people like you, we know the legends and the stories! You are all lying!"

…and then the birds came and the children stopped talking to each other or standing by each other, but they all stayed because they wanted to see the birds.

And suddenly the birds started doing beautiful flights in the air, and headed down the mountain. Their acrobatics were so exquisite that the children couldn't help but follow them. They followed them down a meadow, across a stream and then into the forest that led to one of the villages.

The children who were from that village, the ones who kept insisting that Alethia had red spots, said to the other children grudgingly,

"you can come here to watch the birds but you have to be quiet because we aren't allowed to talk to you and we don't want our parents to see us with you…."

and so the children quietly followed the birds through the forest, until they could see through the trees.

And they could see the houses that the people from that village lived in, and just beyond the houses, down Henosis Mountain, they saw Alethia.

And they all fell silent with their mouths wide open as the birds flew toward Alethia. There she was, covered in red spots for all that you could see of her — between the cliffs that separated this village from the rest.

The children of the red spotted village stood looking at the other children and one of the other children said. "He really does have red spots here, I am sorry I called you a liar."

And after Alethia spotted them she said once again, "I'm just doing the work I came here to do."

So the children headed back into the forest and sat in a circle and each one said again what Alethia looked like from where they lived.

It was getting late in the day so after they made the plan they came up with, they all headed back to their village to rest so they could meet near the top of the mountain again the next morning.

When morning came, they gathered and headed to the village of the children who said that Alethia had squiggly stripes. They walked together to a safe place where they could see the village from - and sure enough, they saw her squiggly stripes.

They headed to the next village, and the next and the next and the next.

Turns out, every child was telling the truth all along.

"We have to tell our parents!" they said.....

And they tried. And they tried and they tried and they tried. Some of the parents forbade their children from leaving the house after that. Some of them laughed and thought the children were silly. But then some of the parents could not resist their curiosity and asked the children to take them on the trails to see the other villages.

Over several seasons, the most curious parents and children of different villages would run into each other on their treks to find the truth.

And then enough parents from every village made the same plan to walk together to every village to see for themselves.

And it turns out that every parent was also telling the truth. Even though their truths were all very different.

This led to the most beautiful gathering at the VERY TOP of the mountain, where all of the children and all of the parents gathered to talk about the hard parts of living with Alethia and the parts that were good too. They were able to start sharing apples and peaches from the villages where they grew, and milk and cheese from the villages where they grew.

They laughed and danced and told each other stories from years back. They started sharing and enjoying Henosis Mountain. They started LOVING and ENJOYING each other. When they climbed to the very very very top of Henosis Mountain, all together . . . they could see every village all at once.

And they could see ALL of Alethia.
And Alethia could see all of them.

And then…

Suddenly, after decades and centuries of Alethia laying around Henosis Mountain, she suddenly stood up.

And she walked away.

And as she walked away, she turned around and said a brand new sentence to the people of Henosis Mountain….

"My work here is done….."

....

How long will we let this need to be **THE ONE RIGHT ONE** keep us from each other. How long will it be before this **NEED TO BE RIGHT** consumes us and destroys us as a human family?

There are abhorrent sicknesses of the soul and the mind that cause some sick people to LIE, CHEAT, DECEIVE, STEAL and DESTROY all that's good. But that is not the norm, folks. Most of the people in your life are telling the truth as they see it.

And it's the hidden dinosaur that is at the root of all of this, not the human family who all live on the same mountain — who all would be so much better off sharing the mountain and their lives with each other.

If you get the chance, take a nice walkabout and see for yourself what someone else is telling you is true ABOUT THEIR OWN EXPERI-ENCE. It will change your life. It will change their life. It will change the world.

I love you. I know there are parts of your truth that are different than mine. I promise you, human family, that I will keep working hard at trying to truly listen and understand, and whenever I am able, I will walk to your village with you to see it for myself.

All that I ask is that you do the same for me — and everyone else.

So, Mountain Dweller,

What is this truth you cling to so tightly that it keeps others away?

AND

What is something you've been calling a lie that's maybe been the truth all along?

I know these are tough realizations, soul sibling...but they're the ones that will heal us back together.

Thanks for walking on The Road To The Unwanted Truth, next we will take the super-fun Road To The Therapist. And the next 10 roads after that are short little roads into my psyche, letters myself about the transfor-mations I was seeking in therapy.

See you there,
xo
melody freebird

10

The Road To
The Therapist

I used to give people with depression or anxiety really bad advice.

Stuff like . . . "Just think positive!" or "Don't let that get you down, just forget about it . . . " or "Count your blessings, you're being so negative!" or "You're never going to heal until you forgive and forget, just let it go . . ."

Ugh. I wish I could go back to every person I've ever said anything like that to or thought that about. I wish I could take their face in my hands and look them in the eye and say "I am so sorry." And then just hug them so tight the way I should have when I was giving unhelpful platitudes.

I thought positive thinking could overcome anything.

Then, I became a total expert in depression and the mental illnesses that can come after a brain injury because of Marq's accident. His was a frontal lobe brain injury so the mental complications and behaviors were countless. I definitely learned that the ill-informed advice I use to give to others who were suffering with mental complications WAS NOT HELPFUL.

During Marq's worst years of recovery, his doctors would tell me that I probably needed to see a therapist. That I should probably be on some kind of antidepressant. I was taking care of my 5 small children and a big company and so I just kept saying I don't have time to go to a therapist. I went to counseling a few times but I never stuck with it. I was too afraid to go on any medication because I thought it would take my creativity away and that was how I earned a living for our family. One doctor told me that if I wasn't going to go to therapy or take medication, I, at the least needed to make sure to get a lot of exercise every day.

So that's what I did. That and LOTS of caffeine. Energy drinks to be precise. I lived on protein bars, energy drinks and SO MUCH ADREN-ALINE. And the gym. I used to get up at 4:30am and be there when the doors open at 5am. I'd work out for at least 90 minutes pretty much EV-ERY DAY and then head home to get my children ready for school and head to the office.

It took about 7 years and I pretty much burnt out my adrenals. That's a story for another day, but I ended up very sick, inside and outside. I had hives/welts all over my body and everything just shut down. I gained 50 pounds over 3-4 months and I was in bed by 3pm every day. I'd work from my bed . . . making videos and writing courses. At this time, I had a monthly subscription box that I designed beautiful products for, and a monthly subscription to my online Soul School courses. I'd do 7 lessons a month, complete with beautiful videos and curriculum to download.

I LOVED my work and it kept me going in so many ways. But my body was shutting down and I couldn't make it past midday before I crashed.

That was the big warning sign that I just pushed aside. The hives/welts showed up in 2011 and they were relentless. I'd break out horribly all over my body whenever I was dealing with a toxic relationship, whenever I felt manipulated, whenever I had to confront something I didn't want to confront.

I still didn't go to therapy. I just went to lots of doctors and healers. And SO MANY OF THEM told me this was an emotional response and my body's last line of defense to get me to take notice. Your skin is your largest organ after all, and it's one that you can actually see. My body said…"hey, if you're not going to listen to the messages on the inside, we are going to send you a big message on the outside."

So I took a million supplements and did all sorts of things to get those hives/welts to go away, and it took 4 years. But I still didn't go to therapy.

I just didn't have time.

I kept having retreats and writing curriculum and those women kept me alive. My children kept me alive. My husband kept me alive. Because every day I woke up and wanted to do everything I could for each of them. That was my motivation. And it worked. I loved the women I had the honor to serve. I loved being with and taking care of my children. Marq took exquisite care of me whenever he was well, and when he wasn't, I went to the ends of the earth to take care of him.

I was burning the candle at both ends, however. As our company grew, the pressure grew. As our family grew, the pressure grew.

On a future road, I will tell you about how I started to comfort myself at night with the thought that I could just end my life if it got to be too much. It hurts the whole center of my body to think about that now, but that was the only solution I could think of for a long time. And when everything was just too much, I would put myself to sleep at night making plans for how I could just end it all if I couldn't take it any longer. I don't indulge in those fantasies and plans anymore, but it has taken years to get to a place where I want to be alive every day. Like I said, that's a story for another road.

So then Marq's relapses started to happen, overlapping with my adrenal sickness. And that was SO MUCH PRESSURE. I again, put my whole self into fixing HIM.

And my dear friend Kolleen, who had been telling me for years that I am codependent and need to get myself to therapy, started REALLY getting on my case about it, in the most loving way . . . that I was not going to make it through all of this without help. I still didn't go to therapy.

I did start to study CODEPENDENCY though. Another bitter pill to swallow. I learned that so much of my own suffering was because of my codependent behavior. I literally could not separate my feelings from the feelings of those I loved. I would get myself all tangled up in everyone else's stuff, maybe so I didn't have to face my own. Maybe just because I couldn't stand to see someone else suffer because it triggered my own suffering. So I would go to the ends of the earth to stop ALL SUFFERING. I learned that this is just a way of being controlling. I was trying to control

Marq's suffering, my children's suffering, and anyone else I was in contact with. For someone who values personal freedom as much as I do, I sure had become a controlling person. Ugh.

The definition of codependency that most applied to me was that I could not be okay unless everyone else was okay — so I smothered people in my life with MY NEED for them to heal. Of course out of love, I wanted everyone to be happy and whole, but if I'm honest . . . I NEEDED to see their healing, I needed to feel their wholeness because I was both trying to earn their love through my determined dedication to their healing AND I was trying to heal vicariously through them. I've mastered the art of living vicariously.

This was all subconscious, but it really was happening. And it's hard to admit. But so many times when Marq was well he would tell me that he just needs me to sit next to him when he's sick, not work myself into a frenzy and wear myself out trying to control his sickness.

Another thing that happens when you are codependent is that when you don't have someone to pour yourself into, you attract people and situations that will put you into that frenzy. Man oh man did I do that. I attracted and created all sorts of unhealthy situations to play out my need to suffer vicariously. Yes, for some odd reason, I believe I also had an addiction to suffering. Again, a story for another road.

From Mental Health America:
What is a codependent behavior?
 Co-dependency is a learned behavior that can be passed down from one generation to another. ... It is also known as "relationship addiction" because people with codependency often form or maintain relationships that are one-sided, emotionally destructive and/or abusive.
-Mental Health America

Many people define codependency by their behaviors which may include :
- always being attracted to alcoholics, drug addicts or other similarly needy and emotionally unavailable people
- feeling as if they must be in a relationship with someone -- anyone -- for their lives to be worthwhile
- trying to control others behaviors, especially loved ones
- feeling as if they are incapable of ending a relationship that they know is

not good for them or that they are unhappy in
- trying to please everyone else and never taking time for themselves, or
even forgetting that they need to take care of themselves

Many people experience these situations at one time or another, but for
those who find it to be a recurring, painful theme in their lives, recovery
can be a very healing and rewarding way of letting go of the old behaviors.

When the big revealing of my inner turmoil happened that I spoke of in
Road #4, I knew it was time for intensive therapy. I resisted, I made excuses, I waited. I mean, we were living in an RV…with just enough money to
get by every month. I couldn't afford therapy and I didn't have time with
all of the life-rebuilding we were doing.

Then it just got to a point where my mind started to shut down the way my
body had. I had an extraordinary ability to continue to work. I would still
write, make videos and curriculum. It's what kept me going.

But when I wasn't working, I was falling.

Here's what Mental Health America suggests if you're wondering if therapy is what you need:

"If you experience any of the following emotions or feelings to the extent
that they interfere with life, therapy may help you reduce their effects.
It's especially important to consider getting help if you feel controlled by
symptoms or if they could cause harm to yourself or others.

Overwhelm. You might feel like you have too many things to do or too
many issues to cope with. You might feel like you can't rest or even breathe.
Stress and overwhelm can lead to serious physical health concerns.

Fatigue. This physical symptom often results from or accompanies mental
health issues. It can indicate depression. Fatigue can cause you to sleep
more than usual or have trouble getting out of bed in the morning.

Disproportionate rage, anger, or resentment. Everyone feels angry at
times. Even passing rage isn't necessarily harmful. Seeking support to deal
with these feelings may be a good idea when they don't pass, are extreme

compared to the situation, or if they lead you to take violent or potentially harmful actions.

Agoraphobia. People with agoraphobia fear being in places where they might experience panic attacks or become trapped. Some people may become unable to leave their houses.

Anxious or intrusive thoughts. It's normal to worry about things from time to time, but when worry takes up a significant part of your day or causes physical symptoms, therapy can help you deal with it.

Apathy. Losing interest in usual activities, the world around you, or life in general can indicate mental health issues like depression or anxiety.

Hopelessness. Losing hope or motivation, or feeling as if you have no future, can indicate depression or another mental health condition. Feeling hopeless from time to time, especially after a period of difficulty, isn't uncommon. But when it persists, it may lead to thoughts of suicide.

Social withdrawal. Many people feel better when they're able to spend at least some time alone. Introverted people may need even more time alone than others. But if you feel distressed around others or fear being with other people, therapy can help you understand and deal with these feelings."

I had EVERY ONE of these symptoms in multiples.

So just like I said in a previous chapter. When we set off on our nomad adventures, it was because I thought Marq was the sick one. Turns out, he just needed some sunshine, some horses and testosterone therapy.

Turns out, I was the one who needed the healing.

So I started going to therapy. I won't say much more about it yet, but the road to the therapist was a LONG ONE over many years. And I wish it would have been a short one. I wish I would have done it long ago. But here we are and here I am and I'm just thankful for the string of events that got me there.

So Beautiful Soul,

Is your inner world calling out to you, asking for some of your time?

AND

In what ways do you try to heal and serve everyone else while ignoring your own need for healing and help?

Tomorrow I will begin a series of 7 letters to my SOUL — 7 roads I had to travel to the inside of my mind and heart- the letters that were my map for what I needed most from therapy.

The first road we will travel tomorrow is The Road To Self-Honesty. I will see you there.

As always, thanks for joining me on this road trip. You're a wonderful companion.

xoxo
melody ross

11

The Road To
Self-Honesty

(Roads #11-17 are letters to myself for what I wanted to find in therapy -
they are filled with questions that I invite you to ask yourself)

....

Dear Me,
I think I am going crazy. I don't know what is true.

*So much of what I thought was true has crumbled. So much of what I
built the foundation of my life on has disappeared, as if it was only an
illusion all along.*

*I feel like I was just a rainbow. I was never anything real or solid.
And now I am gone. I don't know where I went. I was here and then I
was gone.*

What am I?
Who am I?
What is true about everything?

*I need to know. Please give me the courage and the skills to be radically
honest. First with myself and then with life. With others. In all things.*

Melody Ross

I can not carry on as only an illusion.

Please give me the strength to keep standing when I see what I see. Please give me the grit to not turn away. Give me the endurance to keep looking, to stay with it, to stay with myself. No matter what I see, no matter what I find, no matter how it feels.

Here are my fears, Self...
Will I be able to survive what I see?
Will I be okay with the whole of what is real, but more critically, will I be okay without the stories and the myths and the fantasies and the illusions that dress things up and make them bearable?
Will I be okay once I am stripped bare?
Will I even be able to stop telling my own story long enough to just see what is true?
Is it even possible to know what is true or is everything just too muddy and flowing too fast to ever be clear again?

I need my eyes healed so that I can see what is real. I need my ears healed so that I can hear the quietest voices of myself and of Truth. I need my heart healed so that I don't have other hands pumping their own stories into it to keep it going. I need to be the beat of my own heart. I need my mind healed so that nothing uninvited can seep into the cracks of its brokenness, and nothing necessary can seep out. I need my courage healed so that I can stay with this, and not shrink back to the old myths, stories and fantasies that have clouded everything.
I need the strength to turn away opinions and even perspectives from the outside. I need the courage to ask no one "what do you think?"

I need to heal my addiction to what others think.

I want to hear my own voice.
I want to feel my own heart.
I want to see my own shadows and my own light.

I want to be stripped bare because I need to know where this disease is eating away at me. I want to be stripped bare because I need to know if I am solid underneath this all.

Raw honesty is a force that not many are equipped to handle. Please give me the skills to handle it. Radical truth is a blaring light so please turn it up slowly. Give me the skills to bear this light.

Lies have destroyed me. The way I have lied to myself. The ways the lies to myself have made me lie to others. The way others have lied to me. The way we all just continue to lie. And lie. And lie. I need to step away so that I can't even hear others. So that even if they lie to me, I don't have to lie to myself.

The times I have lied to myself have been so destructive. The times others have lied to me have been so destructive. The destroying did not come from things being taken away, it came from things being added. Layers and layers and layers and layers. Too heavy to move forward. The destruction came from adding, not from taking away.

I thought I was destroyed from what got taken, but all along, it was what got added. The only way to not see a light is to cover it with something so thick that the light can't get through.

It was never about the taking away, it was always about the adding, the covering up.

So let's start taking it away. I want to be ready for this. Help me be ready for this, for the stripping away that will reveal the truth. Take away the stories, the myths, the fantasies and the outside voices. Take away anything that keeps hiding what's underneath.

Take away anything at all that's hiding the truth.
Take away anything at all that is NOT the truth.

I don't want anything more. More only makes me feel like I have to prove, pretend and protect my bejeweled coverings. I don't want less, less makes me shrink and hide in fear and shame.

I just want the truth, the whole truth and nothing but the truth.

And the strength to see it, to accept it, to heal it. Please give me that strength. Help me feel ready, help me bear this light.

So until I know . . . I will just be quiet. I will go away and find it. And I will be quiet until I know what is underneath.

And God, wherever you are. Please be with me.
Help me bear it all.
In truth,

melody freebird

Thanks for being with me on this road to my psyche, to my heart. The next 6 roads are more roads to those inner sanctums, and then I will start telling you all about what I found on each of those 7 roads to the inside of my mind, heart and soul.

My hope is that if these letters spark questions inside of YOU, that you will also find the courage and resolve to start asking them to yourself, without the need to ask a single other person. Just you and your Truth, coming straight from YOU and your Truthteller.

Next, we will go to the Road of Self-Remembering.
I will see you there.
xo
melody freebird

12

The Road To Self-Remembering

(Roads #11-17 are letters to myself for what I wanted to find in therapy - they are filled with questions that I invite you to ask yourself)

....

Dear Me,

I need to find some pieces. And I am so reluctant because I know how tricky fragments can be. I don't want to cram pieces into the puzzle I'm putting together that just "sort of" fit. I'd rather have a hole where my puzzle is incomplete than a piece that doesn't go there.

I need to remember myself back together, but once I've done all that I can do, I want to get back to living in THIS DAY. I want the parts of me that are trapped in the taped-up boxes of my past experiences to be set free.

Help me to remember the good parts when I'm fixated on the hard parts. Help me remember the difficult parts when I'm romanticizing the hard parts. Help me to be fair and merciful to everything and everyone involved when parts of me just want to self-medicate by blaming and shaming. Help me remember the broken things back together until the blame and shame are worn out enough to exit the building, and the wisdom that remains can finally be at peace. Help me to make a beautiful room for wisdom as I see the rest of it to the door.

Melody Ross

Help me remember the value of memories, and also the hazards of memories. Help me remember that I'm in search of information to help things make sense, and it's for healing and wisdom, it's to bring up things that need healing. Help me remember that value also comes from enjoying and reminiscing - but I can get caught in a world that already happened, which makes me miss the world that's happening now

As I am working to remember, keep bringing to my mind and heart the truth that there are lots of other parts to every experience and every story, not just mine. Help me remember that there are parts that I played in others' lives that were for their good and learning. And there are parts that others played in my life that were for my good and learning. And that both of these kinds of parts can easily be interpreted in ways that make us all suffer. Help me hold on to the things I learned and let go of the hurtful parts I don't understand. Help me let myself off the hook and let others off the hook.

Help me remember how hard it is to be a human being, for all of us. And that we are all seeing a different part of the dinosaur. So my memories of something might be totally different from others who were standing right next to me. And all of us can be "right" at the same time. Help me accept that sometimes I'm the good guy in someone's story, and sometimes I'm the bad guy, all depending on where we are all standing.

Help me to remember that even if I'd make different choices with what I know now, that I did make some really solid and good decisions too. It's the same with everyone. Help me to be merciful with myself and with others.

Help me to know that I had a big part in almost all the things that still bring me pain. Help me know when to correct my thinking and also help me not to gaslight myself when I want to place more blame and responsibility on myself than is needed or appropriate. Help me let things go when scrutiny is trying to take over the usefulness of a memory.

Help me remember that I'm just not ever going to be able to remember or recall everything. And that when I strain to try to remember, my brain will try to fill in the blanks and add more to the story. Help me peel things away and not add more. Help me to not indulge in add-ons to medicate myself or tip things over to my favor, or my fault. Help me not to embellish to dramatize or take a shortcut to things making sense. Help me not to take an old memory out of its context and put it into now and add what it might mean now rather than what it meant or didn't mean back then.

Help me to stay in my own experience and not try to pull others' experiences in so that I don't feel so naked and alone. Help me not to waste time attaching meaning to things that I merely observed. It muddies up everything that I was actually a part of.

Help me to remember the destructive force of witch hunts. Help me not to want to burn myself at the stake, or burn anyone else at the stake. Give me mercy mercy mercy mercy mercy. Help me to give other people and other memories the same mercy I would want if they were remembering me.

Help me remember that every part made up the whole picture, and that sometimes there's a piece of my puzzle that looks really ugly and horrific but it was actually just the corner of the larger picture, and I might have misinterpreted it before I had all the other pieces.

Help me to be an advocate and not be an accuser whenever possible - for myself and for others.

Help me to remember that some of my memories are not mine alone. Some of my feelings and fears and traumas were inherited. Help me remember the science of epigenetics, not just that it goes backwards, but that it will also go forward...that I am literally participating in what will be either the generational trauma or the generational wisdom. I am deciding right now whether cycles will continue with me, or be broken with me - according to what I cling to and what I let go of.

Help me to remember not to invest time in trying to fix something that's already in the ground decaying...let nature do what nature does, turn it back into dust. Help me remember that all the things I remember that I am not a part of anymore have moved on in their life cycle. They are either dust or different, just like I am. Help me to remember to let myself change, let people change, let situations change. Help me not to hold any of it hostage to how I remember it.

Help me remember the together more than the apart, but to be honest about what both things feel like at different times. So when it's right, help me remember that the apart is sometimes healthier than the together.

Help me remember the wisdom of timing — that just because it's not good now doesn't mean it wasn't good then and vice versa. Help me remember also that just because it's not good now, that doesn't mean it won't be good again someday.

Help me remember that there were short term gifts or lessons that came along with my relationships with others. And just because the time together was so short, it doesn't mean that those lessons and gifts weren't meant to be carried through my whole life.

Help me remember that mistakes and disasters are often the next step to a better way that couldn't be traveled on any other route.

Help me not to want things back so fiercely that I block out the memories of why they are not a part of my life anymore. Help me remember the bad chemical reactions so I don't go back to explosive situations and people just because I'm remembering only the good.

Help me remember how I feel with certain people, in certain places, and how my body is always trying to tell me the truth for THAT moment, and that even if I felt good somewhere once, that was for that moment... and even if I felt unsafe somewhere once, that was for that moment. Let wisdom guide my next step.

Help me remember what nature has taught me about how things actually are. Help me to ground myself in those ancient stories of how a rock became a rock...how a tree got as big as it is, how a river is never the same from moment to moment. Help me remember how an animal is just doing what its instinct drives it to do. How a flower becomes fruit and seeds. How the sun keeps rising and setting every day, no matter what. Let nature help things make sense and help me not fool myself into thinking that somehow I am singled-out for a life that is not connected to an interconnected plan for me from the past and a plan for me for the future. Just like every other living thing. I am part of nature.

50 Roads To The Middle Of My Life

Help me remember that when something falls apart, that doesn't mean everything else is crumbling. Help me see what's always been solid. And help me see that other things were solid for exactly as long as they were supposed to be. And just because they disintegrated, it doesn't mean they weren't solid and whole, with absolute structural integrity before. And it also doesn't mean they were supposed to stay in that state forever. Help me see that there are seasons for everything - and that a tree isn't bad just because it loses its leaves.

Help me open the boxes in the storage unit of my psyche until I'm so sick of all the old and outdated stacks and stacks and stacks of things I thought I just had to keep, that I'm ready to have the biggest bonfire ever.

Help me remember my power, and not just my weakness.

Let's do this,
melody freebird

....

As I wrote these letters, I was learning that I have to give my mind the itinerary that I WANT to travel, or my mind will just take me to the roads it knows, out of habit.

I hope as you read these letters, you'll jot down any instructions you might want to give to your own heart and your own brain, and that you'll know you have the strength and courage to go down these roads too, even if you don't feel it yet.

Thank you for coming with me on The Road of Self-Remembering, further down this journey, I will tell you where this road took me.

Next we will go down The Road to Self-Responsibility. As always, thank you for being with me.

xo
melody freebird

13

The Road To Self-Remembering

(Roads #11-17 are letters to myself for what I wanted to find in therapy - they are filled with questions that I invite you to ask yourself)

……………………………….............………………………….............

Dear Me,

It's time for me to take responsibility. It's time to set aside the damsel in distress garb and put on my true clothing, the regalia of a warrior.

It's time for me to grow up. It's hard to go from youth to elder, but it is time. I am done crying. I am done molting. I am done waiting.

I want to stop looking outside of myself and outside of my connection to the Divine. I want to take responsibility for myself and give up the oppressive need to have someone save me - that same need that quickly turns to an addictive need to save others.

I want to stop feeling like others are responsible for my future, and that I am responsible for the future of others. I want to stop feeling like others are responsible for my bain, or that I am responsible for theirs.

I want to take responsibility for the way I react when things don't feel fair, or when I feel that broken things need to be fixed whenever I see them. I am responsible for the broken things in my own life. I am responsible for how I react to my perception of unfairness. My need for fairness and fixing blinds my eyes and ties up my hands and binds my heart in plaster wrap.

I want to remember that in regard to others, at this stage in my life, I am only responsible to show up in the circle of our human family, hand in hand, and to step outward in the circle to make room for others whenever they want to be there. I am also responsible for taking the time away from everyone and everything in order to heal sometimes. I know that there will always be a place for me in the circle of humanity and family when I am ready. I am responsible for finding the right hands to hold in that circle. I am responsible for BEING loving hands for someone else to hold in that circle.

I want to live out my own responsibility knowing that there will always be difficulty and distraction. There will always be unexpected bends and curves in the road. The road will sometimes end before I get to my destination. There will always be something confronting me that gives me the opportunity to choose between creating or destroying. Stalling or moving. Life or death. Kindness or contempt. Love or fear. Almost every single moment has 2 hands outstretched with one or the other to choose from. I want to take responsibility for what I do in those moments AND what I do after I choose.

I am going to mess up, even with the best intentions. There will be times when I will wish I would have chosen differently. Those moments also hold tremendous opportunities. I want to take responsibility for choosing course correction over shame or blame. I want to extract the powerful lessons that come from "failure" and "mistakes" and I want to utilize the resulting potent energy of knowing I've missed the mark to fuel another try…and another.

I want to stop giving my own responsibility away for the results and rewards and consequences of my own life's choices. Every action has a consequence. Every choice, every thought. Every next moment, and what happens in that moment, it all has consequences. Whatever I choose, I want to take responsibility for.

50 Roads To The Middle Of My Life

When triggers come up, I don't want to point my finger at the person who just showed up at an unfortunate time and place and bumped up against an old wound that has nothing to do with them. I want to take responsibility for my triggers and see them as sacred opportunities to look at what needs to be addressed and healed. I want to take responsibility for my own healing.

I don't want to point fingers anymore, except to point my own finger back at my own heart and gently remind myself...look here, look here, listen here....don't look away from here....

I want to take responsibility for the fact that everything that is not love is a distraction from the next good move. Everything. All of it. If there is no love to choose from, I have the power to create it and it's always going to be better to start from scratch than to choose something that is not love — just because it's the least destructive thing to choose from. I want to have the strength to take responsibility for walking away from non-love distractions and creating love in the right places where there is no love.

But I also don't want to give my life-force away to places that will only suck my life-force away as I try to force my love into it or onto it. When I force the things that I think are right, it is taking away the choices of another.

I want to take responsibility for the times I try to force things.

There are things I don't get to choose but I get to choose what I do next with those things — blame and shame and self pity are such a waste of time and energy.

I want to take responsibility for what I take-in to my body, my mind and my spirit — and what reactions those things create in my body and my mind and my heart. Food, media, expectations, demands, hugs, help, mercy...taking-in any of these things has dramatic consequences, to create or to destroy.

When it's time to cut a cancer out in my life, I want to take responsibility for focusing on the life that this act of removal will save, and not on the anger and bitterness that I could succumb to once the knife is in my hand. Mercy. Life. The miracle of regeneration. Rather than blame, death and the sting of contempt.

The way I wake up in the morning and set my day is my responsibility.
The way I let myself think as I'm going to sleep is largely my responsibility.

When my mind is weary and turns on me, I need to ask for help.
When I am grieving, I need to sit with my grief.

But when I can, I need to use my life-force to move forward rather than backward.

I want to take responsibility for my habits, my old conditioning, my brain wiring, my heart fractures, my destructive behaviors, my stagnation.

But not mistake shaming myself for personal responsibility.

I want to take responsibility for finding what works best for me, for us… and I want to live into it - even if it is so different from what others are doing or from what others believe I should be doing.

I want to take responsibility for my mistakes…for my blunders, for my carelessness, for my recklessness, for my default behaviors.

I want to take responsibility for what happened because of risks I took or didn't take - for the times I listened to my gut and did the right thing by myself. For the times I didn't listen to my gut and lived out uncomfortable consequences. I want to take ownership of what both of those life experiences taught me, and how different the internal outcomes are. I want to learn from that and preserve it forever as wisdom that I can draw from until my last breath.

I want to take responsibility to stop medicating the heartbreak I feel with the slow drip of blame. It's poison, not medicine. It might make me stop feeling the heartbreak for a while, but it's a soul-eating poison that tricks me because it distracts me from the immediate pain and numbs away the alarm sound that pain is meant to bring. I want to sit with my pain and listen to it. It has so much to teach me, so much to tell me, so much to grow me. Blame just kills me slowly from the inside, without me even knowing it's happening.

I want to take responsibility to listen to what another person is saying, and

104

what they're truly trying to communicate. And then hold my tongue until I have something useful to say. Not every conversation is a duel. Sometimes it's just an opportunity to learn and understand. And it's always an opportunity to grow in some way.

I want to take responsibility for the choice to grow or shrink. The choice to grow in light or shrink in anger because of another's intimidation and destruction. I don't want to be a destroyer. I want to be a creator. I want to trust that if I put enough effort into the life of good things, and zero effort or nourishment into the life of destructive things, then the natural consequence is starvation and death of the destructive things, and a beautiful accelerated growth of the good things. Attention, focus and belief are what make things grow.

I can't save anyone and no one can save me. This is all between me and God. Everyone else's life is between them and their Truth.

I don't owe my life, my time, an explanation, or a defense to anyone and no one owes that to me.

When I don't have what I need, I have to go find it. It is no one else's responsibility to do that for me.

I want to take responsibility and stop thinking about what's wrong and start thinking about what's right. I want to stop running away and start running toward.

I want to take responsibility for finding what makes me feel like myself, what makes life feel whole. I want to stop blaming other stuff for how it doesn't feel like me, how it broke me. I just want to take steps toward what feels right and whole and then I'll be stepping away from what doesn't.

I want to take responsibility for the power of my words, the power of music, the power of action, the power of thoughts, the power of beauty, the power of imagination, the power of sitting with my emotions, the power of listening, the power of love, the power of honesty, the power of taking responsibility.

I want to pour my life into love. I want to only allow love to pour into me…and when I falter, I will take responsibility for getting myself back on track

I will stop lumping people into one group, I will stop lumping myself into one group - I get to choose, and they get to choose individually

I will stop being a victim. I will stop participating in things that feel wrong from almost the beginning. I will stop pointing my fingers outward to find fault. I will stop turning my light down to make others feel more comfortable.

I will stop silencing my voice. I will stop doing dumb things in an effort to maintain "peace." I will stop waiting for the apology, for the mess to be cleaned up, for the monsters to go away. I will stop waiting for the circumstances to be perfect. I will stop waiting.

I will stop stop saying yes when I want to say no
I will stop saying no when I want to say yes

I will stop stepping in front of fists that will be swinging whether I'm there or not. I will stop trying to love and serve and impress the cruelty out of people who have no desire to stop being cruel. I will stop hoping endlessly that situations and people who have been very consistent will somehow be something different just because I want and need them to be.

I will hold tight to the ones who feel like love.

I will stop expecting others to save me. stop expecting others to validate me. stop expecting others to understand me. stop expecting others to value me. stop expecting others to own their part. I will stop expecting others to do what I think is the right thing. I will stop expecting cruel people to be kind.

I will stop moping as soon as it's time.
I will stop hiding as soon as it's time.

I am not a child anymore. I am halfway through my life. I want to know that in very few instances do I need someone to come and rescue me or save me. I want to take responsibility for every aspect of my life. When I need help, I want to remember to look up and trust my Creator - for every other human needs to be on their path and not mine. I will never grow

50 Roads To The Middle Of My Life

I'm on someone else's path, only mine.

I take responsibility, and I am free.
xo
melody freebird.

....

This road was a painful one accompanied with lots of grief over my youth.
It's hard to realize that we are older and no one is going to come and save
us, but it's the best feeling in the world to realize not only that you get to
save yourself, but that you are capable of it. It's freedom.

I love you and I believe in you. I believe in myself too.

Next we will start the beautiful journey on The Road to Self-Nurturing.
See you there (I'm so happy you are here)
xo
melody freebird

(

14

The Road To Self-Nurturing

Roads #11-17 are letters to myself for what I wanted to find in therapy - they are filled with questions that I invite you to ask yourself)
…………………………………………………………………..

Dear Me,
I know that one of my most pervasive and destructive beliefs has been that it's selfish and unacceptable to take time to nurture and care for myself.

I want to do this deep work because my greatest joy is connecting with, learning from and sharing what I've learned with others.

And I deny myself my greatest joys when I fail to refuel my life-force because of the old belief that taking care of myself makes me a bad person.

I know that this belief has led to physical and mental health crises way too many times to count. When I go on self-betrayal binges, in the name of "service and selflessness" I almost always end up on emergency missions to save my own life. These end-of-the-line situations require me to go so far inward and for such long lengths that I become an isolated hermit and I have to relearn how to be in society.

I have limitations. I hate that I have limitations, but I do.

I am ready to accept that although my work and my ways of being with others in the world is the best part of my life, it can quickly and easily become a coping mechanism, a way to avoid my own inner world and an unhealthy addiction.

I know I try to dig-deep vicariously. I know that I try to cope with my own pain by helping others dig into their pain and ignoring my own. I know that this is the most ridiculous and inefficient and destructive pattern. It's humiliating and humbling to take a good hard look at how many times I have done this to myself, somehow believing that "this time" it will be different. Somehow believing that self-sacrifice is noble and right in all situations.

I want to stop doing it. I HAVE TO stop doing it. Only I can stop doing it.

I know that I have real and enormous fears that I will become a selfish and self-indulgent person — and therefore a completely unacceptable person. I know that there's a part of me that finds this to be so unacceptable that I am willing to risk my present and future health to avoid ever becoming that. Yet, I push myself so far that the only way to recover is to stop everything and sequester myself. And then here I am, only able to focus on myself, just to stay alive. Here I am in an emergency self-focus — and I have just created my worst fear.

This pattern is NOT OKAY WITH ME anymore. These old beliefs are NOT OKAY WITH ME anymore.

I know that if I'm not careful, I also find myself needing to over-pay if I ever have to stop and take care of myself. I am aware of how I pre-punish myself when I start needing to take care of myself. I punish myself for being weak and selfish, yet I'm willing to pay that price of punishment because I feel like I'm going to die if I don't get the care from myself I need.

This has become a pattern, an addiction, a loop. It's time for it to stop.

I can't ever love everything and everyone else enough to make-up for not loving and caring for myself - I've tried and it doesn't work. The paradox is that when I stop and take care of myself, I have so much more to care for others. I have an abundance, an overflow to work with, and to do what I love most — connect and share with others.

I know that it's not fair to others when I give them more than I have to give. It serves no one. It's not a healthy relationship. I want to offer those I love a healthy relationship. No one benefits if everyone doesn't benefit. There are ways for everyone to benefit from connection.

I know that one of the problems I face is that connecting and sharing with others is essential to my well-being. My work and my purpose is to sit in a circle with humans to learn from each other and love each other. Learning from others as well as sharing what I have learned is oxygen to me. So, I have to find a way to care for myself enough that I have sufficient energy to do what I love most — teach, share, guide, connect, learn and create creative solutions to thrive through the human experience.

I am not willing to give up this essential part of my life. So, I have to learn ways to nurture and care for myself so that I can experience the greatest joys I know of. When I am forced to step away from life just to recover, I become starved of what I most want to be doing.

This cycle cannot continue.

So I am committed to rewiring my beliefs and cultivating the discipline necessary to change my behaviors.

I will see my time and energy as my stewardship of resources. When I invest in my well-being, it compounds like a savings account. I always have exponential growth and an abundance of love and solutions to offer when I invest in my own well-being savings account.

I will stop overdoing. It is not necessary.

I will abandon my need to justify, defend and over-explain my need for rest. OR FOR ANY NEED AT ALL! I will just rest when I need to rest. No apologies, no excuses. In fact, I will give myself a gold star when I stop and rest.

I will give myself the same compassion, care and regard that I give to others.

I will stop treating myself in demoralizing and inhumane ways, because somehow this always leads to me attracting other people and situations who want to participate in treating me in demoralizing and inhumane ways. The stopping of this cycle starts with me.

I will remember that my work in the world IS IMPORTANT, and IT IS SACRED to me . . . but it is not so important that it's worth losing a life over. A person's life is the most sacred thing there is. I will hold my own life as sacred as I hold everyone else's life.

I will remember that there are nourishing things to fill my body, soul and life with. And there are also toxic things to choose from. I will personally veto toxic situations, toxic foods, toxic interactions and toxic relationships and instead welcome nourishing situations, nourishing foods, nourishing interactions and nourishing relationships. I will remember that things can change, and that it's possible that the state I am in at certain times in my life contributes to the toxicity of what I am drawing into my life. I will remember that as I am healing and growing, other things are also growing and changing — and there is a possibility that so much healing could take place that things that were once toxic are now healthy.

I will remember that I have learned a lot, and I am not the same person I used to be. So when I find myself retreating and isolating out of fear that I will get hurt again, or hurt someone else again — I will remember that I have new skills, new beliefs and new wisdom. I don't need to be afraid anymore.

I will remember that I am not on a mission to be perfect anymore, just to be whole.

I will stop berating myself for being who I am just because not everyone likes who I am. I will be acceptable to myself instead of being acceptable to others at the expense of being acceptable to myself. When I am true to who I am, I will attract the people who like who I am.

I will break the cycle of belief that my value comes from how busy I am or how much I can produce or how much endurance I have or how much I can do for others..

I will stop putting things on the table for anyone to take that I cannot afford to give away.

50 Roads To The Middle Of My Life

I will make time and room in my life EVERY DAY for the unique things that bring me joy and nourishment. I will do this without apologizing and defending and over-explaining.

I will take responsibility for my own well-being. I will treat myself the way I would treat a child I love and cherish.

I will be a good example to my own daughters and granddaughters, my own sons and grandsons. I will treat myself the way I want them to treat themselves. I cannot expect more from them than I am willing to expect from myself.

I will embrace and accept my own magnificence, my own talents and abilities and my own uniqueness, knowing this will silence my need to be acceptable to others.

I will remember that my default behavior of "fixing myself" is different from caring for myself. I don't always need to be fixed. Sometimes I just need to rest and refuel, that doesn't mean there is anything wrong with me.

I will remember when I don't respect my own needs, I cannot expect that others will. When I don't respect my own well-being, I will constantly attract other people who disrespect my well-being. So I will stop blaming others when I spiral down, and I will instead investigate where I took a self-betraying turn and see how I can avoid doing it in the future.

I want to make self-nurturing a solid value that I guide my life by, without feeling guilt and shame that I need it.

I want to heal from this.
I want to change this.
I want to rewire my beliefs about this.
I want to break this cycle.

I will sit with the discomfort and shame that comes up when old beliefs are making their way out the door, shouting shame and accusations at me. I will sit and observe those old voices and patterns. I will not allow old shaming voices to keep me from doing what I know is good.

Melody Ross

*I will shut out every voice that's not my own truest voice and the voice of
my Creator who knows me, loves me and wants the best for me.*

*I will remember that the great reward from this difficult rewiring of
thoughts and behaviors will be that I will have the energy, inspiration and
resources to do the creative and connective work I love most — to get
back in the circle with my beloved human family and be part of the flow
again.*

It will be worth it.

*Please help me to get there, highest self. Please extract my wisdom and
motivation. And God, please show me the right way to do this. I want to
change my behavior. I want to restore my soul.*

*In gratitude,
melody freebird*
....

You've just taken a look at my most difficult request to myself and what
I most needed/need from therapy. It's been so eye-opening to see that
this old belief is the root of so many of the snags I've tangled myself in
throughout life. This is some of my biggest work. Is it the same for you?

Thanks for being on this difficult and important road with me. Next we
will powerfully step on to The Road to Self-Correcting

I love you.
xo
melody freebird

15

The Road To Self-Correcting

(Roads #11-17 are letters to myself for what I wanted to find in therapy -
they are filled with questions that I invite you to ask yourself)
....

Dear Me,
I am tired of life correcting me in ways that feel like being dragged behind
a truck. I know the only way to stop this pattern is to correct myself.

I know that in moments when decisions must be made, I have had the
tendency to either weigh hundreds of options at once, or simply distract
myself, procrastinate or make no decision at all. I have had a tendency
in the past to hope for others to make decisions for me. Because I fear
making the wrong decision or because the right decision is going to bring
uncomfortable consequences.

NOT deciding for myself has caused more need for correction than mak-
ing the wrong decision ever has. I want to remember that NOT deciding
is a decision in itself. NOT moving forward is a decision. And both not de-
ciding and not moving have caused more problems in my life than taking
a wrong road could ever dream of causing.

I've taken some big risks and had some epic adventures, and I know that
the more I do and try, the more I will experience the inevitable beginning

stages that could be mistaken as failure.

I want to cultivate the consistent courage to make the truest decision I can make for myself in every moment, knowing there will be missteps, missed marks, missed signs and MIStakes. And none of this is failure.

I want to remember what every past move in my life has taught me, whether I aced a stretch in the road, or whether I "wasted" a massive amount of time walking down the wrong road. I have learned all of the most valuable things I've ever learned just from moving, and moving, and moving. Even in the stillness, when I am not physically moving - the allowing the thoughts to move forward, the dreams to move forward in my mind and heart — not stuffing them away or holding them hostage to over-analyze them . . . just observing them and letting them move through.

Stagnation, stuffing things away, hiding things and procrastinating has caused the greatest need for correction I've ever experienced. When I do nothing, there is no failure, but there is also no progression.

So the first self-correction I wish to make is my MIStaken belief that it's better to hide in a corner and play dead than to make a move that might end up needing correction.

The next self-correction I wish to make is to give up any need I might have to ask others what my next move "should" be, or to pay any mind to uninvited opinions about what I "should" do, or how I "should have" done it.

Correction is a quiet and very personal process , between me and my Truthteller. I don't want to let a mob mentality correct me, because there will be hundreds of different ideas being directed at me for how I can do better if I open up that dangerous door to opinions. We live in a voyeuristic society that has developed an insidious habit of seeing each other as a video game avatar, with a game controller — we often think we know the strategy to help each other "win." We need to get back into our own lives. I need to get back into my own life.

I want to self-correct by getting quiet and healing everything inside of me to the point of being able to hear my kindest, strongest, clearest and most determined voice telling me how to get back on track. It's holy and sacred work to correct yourself - it's not a group project meant for the masses.

50 Roads To The Middle Of My Life

Lots of times we all make MIStakes in public. Publicly missing the mark is humiliating and humbling, but not many are willing to try things publicly so I want to remember that those who step up and try things in front of others are brave, a rare group who have the courage to fail in front of a crowd if that's what it takes. I want to be that kind of person.

I want to remember that coming to terms with mistakes, missed marks and disastrous choices takes tremendous courage and yields lasting respect for self and others. It makes me respect all of life. I respect those heroic enough to try and succeed, to try and fail, and to try and have to come to terms with missed marks. I want to be that kind of person.

The times when I have caused the most trouble in my life and respected myself least are the times when I placed no value in course correction. The people who have caused the most trouble in my life and who I have the least respect for are the ones who place no value in their own course correction.

I don't want to get self-correction and self-criticism confused. Correction is a loving coach who wants the best outcome. Criticism is harsh and demoralizing and makes a person feel like they're never going to make it. Correction is a cheering voice saying, "you're getting there, why don't you try this next?" I want to remember that encouragement helps massively when combined with correction and is certainly more effective than criticism.

I want to remember that what often has felt like the worst and most devastating experience or situation in my life has turned out to be an accelerated course correction - a shortcut. But it often feels like a giant soul cut.

I want to remember that without correction, it will be a long road to improvement, and that with the right kind of correction and coaching, I can make long strides quickly.

I also want to remember that sometimes things take a long time to correct and you have to go a centimeter at a time, you have to have patience. Some improvement is a really long game. I want to be patient and stay with it.

117

Melody Ross

I want to remember that recklessness almost always ends in disaster. There are a lot of ways to be reckless and a lot of them look like productivity and progress. I want to pay attention to the pace. I want to stop being reckless.

I want to make a daily habit of encouraging, merciful self-correction in my life, while taking ownership for every decision.

As I make decisions and correct my course as needed I want to remember to:

Stand in the chaos without believing the lies inside of it.

Stand in the discomfort without believing the lies inside of it.

Stand in the difficulty without believing the lies about it.

Stand in deceitful situations without believing the lies inside of them.

Stand in my own life without believing the lies inside of it.

Stand in my place in our human family without becoming bitter, cynical, afraid or addicted to using other's lives as my guide or my obstacle.

And NOT STAND in one place too long . . . just long enough to learn and then it's time to be brave and make the next move. To correct the moves as needed, and then move forward again.

Even in the stillness, allow my Truthteller to move, allow my heart to move, allow my thoughts to move. More forward movement is happening in the stillness than I know, if I simply trust the quiet stillness of my own intuition to move me. Sometimes the most holy movement comes in the quietest moments of rest.

I don't want to make self-correction an addiction. I only want to partake of its potency as needed. Self-correction can become its own loop of procrastination. Keep moving, listen closely, move in the next right direction. Repeat.

Mistakes are lessons.
Falling down when you're learning to walk is inevitable.

Things are almost always hard at first, and then they get easy.

It doesn't matter how many times I fall, what matters is that the amount of times I get back up matches my falling down number for number.

I am done seeking out corrections from the world. Only I can correct myself in ways that are lasting and whole — and my Truthteller is beside me as a compass. It is my job, it is my choice, and I am up to the task. I am ready.

Radical mercy always,
melody freebird

…………………………………………………...

This Road to Self-Correcting is another one that required a bit of grieving of my youth, a threshold to growing up. I had gotten addicted to opinions and addicted to being corrected by others. This created a loop that had me running in circles of confusion, resentment and cringe worthy self-pity. I had to realize I was welcoming the opinions and then feeling self-pity over what they brought to the party. What a mess. I am so done with all of that.

Next, we step onto the power-filled Road to Self-Governing. Because no one is the boss of me! And no one is the boss of you! Isn't that wonderful? (and a little bit scary)

See you there,
xo
melody freebird

16

The Road To Self-Correcting

(Roads #11-17 are letters to myself for what I wanted to find in therapy - they are filled with questions that I invite you to ask yourself)
....

Dear Me,

I have done something destructive a bunch of times and I want to stop. I know this is going to be a hard one. I have so much shame about this that I'm ready to release and heal. But I have to change, and I need help.

I want to be free more than anything else, even more than being loved, I want to be free. I don't like being bossed around. I detest being manipulated. I don't like when other people or organizations or institutions are in charge of my time or my decisions. I don't like feeling like someone else is controlling me. I don't like mean people.

Yet I have chosen a sick scenario over and over and over that would lead one to believe that I don't value my own freedom at all. I have played out this scenario over and over. Maybe the costumes were different each time, but it was always the same dance.

And I chose it. I know this. This was no one's responsibility but my own, once I was an adult.

Melody Ross

I know that sometimes my need to be loved and liked often overrides my need for self-sovereignty . . . and I have too often engaged in the dance of a weak damsel with a relentless bully. When one dance ends, I seem to go in search of a new bullying dance partner immediately.

I've danced this dance so many times that I can make perfect steps with my eyes closed.

I am addicted to a dance that I hate.

I know that every time I choose not to govern myself, I end up being governed. I don't know why it works like this, but I get it. I have to have authority over my own life if I don't want others to have authority over me.

I have to do the difficult and tedious things that come along with governing your own life. I have to stop believing that it's worth it to hand over my sovereignty for the cheap reward of having someone else do difficult and tedious things for me.

There are many who would gladly pay that price for their wanted reward of having someone to control.

I know life has been difficult and my plate has been over-full with things needing emergency attention. But I have too often handed my plate of most precious things to someone who was waiting for someone like me to play out their sickness.

I know that in the past, I have carelessly handed over my personal authority and almost always, I have been dominated, pushed-around, browbeat and bullied. I have been demeaned, talked down to and disrespected. I have handed over my own remote-control and become a machine at the mercy of someone else's whims. I have had my own life ripped from my fingers and held over my own head. I have had the things I birthed taken and hidden and used as ransom. And I didn't use any of this as fuel to rise up and fight. I just got smaller and more victim-y. This insidious pattern (that I chose) has tried to teach me over and over and over to stand up and take control of my own life.

But the dancing damsel in distress always seemed to win out.

I know I am the one who danced this dance. I know I am the one who sought out dance partners to replay this scene over and over again in a million ways. I know that I am the one who kept it going on the dance floor.

I know this is sick.

I know that someone playing out the role of a bully is really no worse than someone playing out the role of a victim. All of it is sick. We both showed up to the dance and I chose the role for myself. And then I cried about it.

I cringe as I look at this honestly. I want to change.

I know that I have been exhausted and weary beyond description so many times and I really needed help, and it was easiest to go into these default patterns of behavior.

But I didn't learn the first time, or the second, or the third.

I know I hid things from my husband that I knew he would put a stop to. Like I was hiding harmful drugs, I only engaged in this behavior in dark corners where he couldn't see. I hid it from almost anyone who would have put a stop to it, and it was easy because my dance partners always wanted to dance in the dark. They didn't want anyone to put a stop to it either.

I know I could say that I did this subconsciously but I also know that my body tried to tell me it wasn't okay. My soul tried to tell me it wasn't okay. And I kept dancing.

Because at times I thought maybe this time would be different and at other times I just felt too comfortable, I knew the dance too well. I knew my steps and I knew their steps and sometimes knowing is easier than changing. Sometimes dancing with someone is better than dancing with no one.

I could say I was hoping that love would be enough to break the cycle. I can say that I thought if I could become someone different during the dance, maybe they would too. I can say that I hoped I could do a different dance with the same dance partner. I can say I was unaware. But I danced this dance so many times that I have to take responsibility for how many times in my sick need to dance this dance, I empowered another with their sick need to be my dance partner.

None of it is healthy for any of us.

I am ready for this cycle to end.

I know my tendency to allow others to make my decisions and to get small when others get big has resulted in bruising acts of self-betrayal with consequences so far and wide that I will probably never be able to see them all. I know that those consequences spread to the people in my life I love most. I know that I chose this by not choosing to stop it. I participated in it and as an adult, I could have stopped it. I know that I didn't.

I know that others tried to step in and tell me it wasn't healthy. I know others tried to warn me. I know I closed my ears and kept dancing. I know I closed my eyes and kept dancing. Bleeding and dancing. Bleeding and dancing. Bleeding and dancing.

I know all of this, and it's another bitter pill to swallow. I have no one to blame for the destructive results of these dances that kept going until the end goal was reached — one person dominating another at all costs. One big foot crushing another's soul. One person needing to crush, another needing to be crushed. Over and over and over. So sick.

Today this changes. I know that somewhere inside of me, I have the power to change this TODAY.

I want to stop attracting controlling, demeaning and bullying people/situations. I want to stop attracting people and situations that love to tell me what I am not capable of doing on my own. I want to stop attracting people and situations who test me to see if I will allow them to publicly exploit my weaknesses and covertly exploit my strengths. I want to stop being passive and acting small. I want to stop encouraging the next sick move of a bully so that I can shine at my next sick move as a victim. I want to stop playing the part of the victim after I'm the one who took off my armor, surrendered my sword and said "have your way with me and all that is mine" to people who have a history of treating others exactly the way I abhor others being treated.

I want to recognize that my unhealthy need to have others love me, combined with others' unhealthy need to dominate, control and bully has created an exponentially disgusting cycle of destruction.

Over and over and over again.

I want to learn what true leadership is. What true guidance is. I want to lead myself and guide myself in the ways that every soul needs. I don't need someone else to do this for me.

I know that a bully's strategy is to intimidate, coerce and connive with force and threats. I know that a bully's strategy is to first seduce a person into their dark and hidden lair with faux kindness and friendship. As I learn to govern and lead myself, I DO NOT wish to use these tactics on myself. I know that bullies deal in retribution and hostile action. I know that bullies don't take responsibility for their actions, but deal in shaming, blaming and remaining spotless in front of others. I know that bullies deal their most heinous acts in the dark — with a kind smile on their face in the light.

As I choose to govern myself, I want to remember that bullying myself is no better than allowing others to bully me. I do not want to shower myself with faux kindness and friendship only to lead myself back into a dark and hidden lair where I can bully myself.

As I choose to govern myself, I want everything out in the light, no secrets in the dark where destructive things can grow unchecked. I want to be transparent. I choose to stop hiding ANY bullying behavior from my husband and from those I love.

I choose to stay away from new situations and old situations that cause me to want to go back to my old dance. I choose to stay away until I have practiced the dance of self-governance long enough that I will not revert back to old dance steps that I have ingrained into muscle memory. I want to override my old dance steps with the beautiful dance of sovereignty, self-respecting boundaries and self-governance. If I'm dancing with others, I now want it to be in a line-dance...with others who are also doing their own dance of sovereignty, self-respecting boundaries and self-governance.

Melody Ross

No more secret, crushing bully dance partners.

I know this is going to be hard. I know I will have to forgive myself over and over again for how long I've done this. I want to get to the root of why I do this thing I am so ashamed of doing. I know I have a lot to clean up because of it. I know it's going to take a lot of practice and discipline every day to learn new ways of being. I know I will mess up. I choose to get up and try again every day. I choose to take responsibility. I am ready.

This cannot happen again. It has destroyed too many beautiful things and kept too many beautiful things from happening. It has been destructive on just about every level. This cannot happen again.

Please help me, self, please help me God. Help me repair what has been broken by these reckless dances and help me learn a new dance. Help me dance courageously, authentically, unapologetically, unashamed and epically.

I want to be free. I want everyone to be free.

In deep gratitude,
melody freebird

....

I cannot begin to tell you how difficult this particular road has been. Both because of the awareness and because of the need for change. This road led down several other roads before I started to get to the root of it. We will go down those roads later.

Thank you for sticking with the journey on this very uncomfortable, cringey road. It was an absolutely necessary one that, like I said, I will be talking about more on other roads. But next, we visit the last road of letters to my psyche on the beautiful Road To Self-Renewal.

See you there,
xo
melody freebird

17

The Road To Self-Renewal

(Roads #11-17 are letters to myself for what I wanted to find in therapy - they are filled with questions that I invite you to ask yourself)
……………………………………………………………………........................

Dear Me,

I know that at this stage in my life, when something needs renewal, it is usually because something has died or is living with the threat of death. I guess I fall into both of those categories.

I know that there are only a few choices left at this point. To die all the way to death, or to see all of this death and loss as an opportunity to grow a fresh new stalk of ME from what has been chopped down.

I want to live, and I know that in order to live, I'm going to have to let something new grow. I am going to have to choose a new life sprouting from the remains of my old life and from the miracle of life itself.

I want to become someone new. I want to become who I need to be, to be able to thrive at this time in my life. I want to become someone I enjoy being.

I know that as I watch every living thing and focus on what is true about renewal, I can trust that I will renew . . . that I am already renewing. I

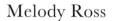

know that when things are inbetween where they were and where they are headed, it can look like a hopeless mess. I know a caterpillar turns to green slime in the weeks between being a caterpillar and becoming a butterfly.

I know what it feels like to be green slime.

I want to tell myself the truths that I know from experience — that everything alive, including me, is always on a progressive path of becoming the next version of itself. I know this is true for me at this time.

I want to trust the wisdom that is contained in my DNA about how to renew. I want to trust my body, my spirit and my Creator that this is something already programmed into me and the timing is perfect for right now, even if it just feels like so much suffering and so much death and so much failure.

I want to remember that no matter how the death and destruction happened, my focus MUST remain on the becoming rather than the unbecoming. The unbecoming will happen as a by-product of the becoming. I am becoming and renewing, and my life-force is building up again during this process. I am not just becoming, I am becoming more than I have ever been.

I know that because the cycles of renewal have their own timeline, I cannot rush my becoming. Just like it would kill a butterfly to cut it out of its chrysalis prematurely, I must allow the timing of my own renewal and becoming and not kill it by rushing it.

I know that the root of the word suffer is actually ALLOW. And I want to have the courage and strength to sit with and suffer the parts of the renewal and becoming that I wish I could stop or run away from.

I don't want to be tempted to write a sad story about this that is incomplete. Incomplete stories told as truth are actually lies. I know this story is not over yet, so I want to trust this part in the middle and not call it the end. I want to be hopeful and excited about the incomplete parts, trusting that they're headed somewhere good for me.

I know I don't have to overthink this. I don't have to try to figure out how it will happen. I know this is more a continuation of who I have always been than a new creation of who I will be. It's a becoming of continuation. It's happening and it will continue to happen. I just have to trust the process.

I want to keep this quiet, sacred and opinion-free.

I know sometimes renewal requires a forest fire, and sometimes renewal requires vigorous sanding down or stripping down. I know that renewal sometimes requires aggressive pruning, or a really hard scrub that bleeds . . . and that all of it feels like suffering and death at times.

I also know that sometimes a living thing is simply starving or thirsty. And that a wilted plant sometimes just needs to be watered and a screaming baby sometimes just needs to be fed — and suddenly they are renewed.

Sometimes I am starved of things that sustain my life. Sometimes I am so thirsty for who I am that I think I am going to die. And sometimes those things just take a remembrance of what is needed and an action to deliver what is needed, and then I'm renewed.

But this feels different. So much of me has already died. It is gone. So much of what I thought would sustain me forever is gone now. This might be a long process of being green slime and trusting that it is going somewhere good.

I don't want to be angry or bitter about this time in my life that has felt at times like such a cruel death. I want to trust it, welcome it and be grateful for it. I want to allow it. I want to let it take as longas it takes. I want it to be as complete and whole as possible.

I want to be new without crying about what is gone that felt so much like an essential part of me. I want to be new without constantly apologizing and explaining that I no longer have parts of me that others used to enjoy. I want to trust that who I become will attract the ones who like what grew from the ashes of the old me.

I want to love what I was— without clinging so tight to it that it becomes shackles that keep me from moving forward. I want to appreciate and enjoy the memories of what once was — without feeling like what should have lasted forever got stolen from me. It was just time, that's all.

Melody Ross

I want to let myself grow older without feeling like I was more valuable when I was younger. I want to appreciate my youth but welcome my wisdom years with youthful enthusiasm.

Because I have been out of commission for a while, I don't want to waste any more time feeling shame for this necessary period of being green slime. I want to be back in commission, but better than ever.

But also with better boundaries than ever. Because I have this opportunity to become new, I want to take better care of my life, my body and my spirit. I don't ever want to participate in my own unnecessary destruction again. But I do want to allow my own natural decomposition when it's time for a new part of me to be born.

I want to remember that at my age, when a new part of me is ready to be born, it's usually because it's time for an old part of me to die.

And I want to sacredly, honorably and patiently allow that death so that I can sacredly, honorable and patiently rejoice in the birth that is to come.

Because so much of me died, I am also being born.
I get to be new.

I am here for it.

With deep awe,
melody freebird

....

This wraps up the letters to myself for what I wanted/want to gain in therapy. In all honesty, it's difficult and uncomfortable to read these letters, but also very empowering.

On this Road to Self-Renewal, I started to reframe the losses and deaths in my life. I even started to reframe the betrayals and the bullies. I started to see that even though I don't believe that everything is meant to be, I do have irrefutable proof that everything that happens in life can be raw material to build something new.

50 Roads To The Middle Of My Life

Thank you for being with me on these roads.

You'd think that after putting all of this time into defining what I wanted, it would be straight and simple road to get there. But no.
You'll learn on the next road, The Road Around The Block, that I was certain there would be a shortcut. But trying to find a shortcut only made me go in circles.

So, I will see you on the road that loops right back to where it started.

I love you and I hope that as parts of my road bring things to light for you, you'll recognize the courage you have inside to find the roads your soul is ready to travel. I know you'll always end up right where you need to be.

With great love,
melody freebird

18

The Road Around
The Messy Block

So I committed to therapy, and I had a plan for how it would go. It was going to go quickly and aggressively. We were gonna get this done and move on with life!

You see, if there is one thing that's been consistently true about me, no matter what twisting turning roads I've been down, it is that I am prolific.

I get things done, and I get things done fast. And most of the time, I get things done beautifully. This is both an incredible blessing and a messy problem. Historically, another thing that's also been true is that the bigger the thing I'm creating, the bigger the mess I make. Whether it's in the kitchen, the laboratory, the library, the closet, the studio . . . every dish and tool and book and outfit gets used in these flurries. I leave no stone unturned. I make beautiful things and I make enormous messes.

I have always been able to make something out of anything. It started when I was very young and I would see possibilities in sticks and rocks and garbage on the street. I would weave grass and plants, stack rocks with mud for cement. I would make tiny worlds for fairies that I really believed in. I have been trying to create something else from my first memory.

I'm also a chronic optimist. An impossible dreamer. A girl with my head in the clouds, orchestrating sparkles of light that can only be found up there where dreams are made into reality. I can lose myself in some place a million miles from the grounded earth with the snap of a finger, and sometimes it's hard to bring me back. I am a mad scientist and a tortured artist and a perpetual seeker. It never ends, it never rests, it always finds a way to break through any way I try to stop the flow. This flow is stronger than I am most of the time.

So I have learned to be incredibly prolific. It has been paramount in the creation of so much loveliness and also so much complication. When I'm in the flow of creation it sometimes looks like a river of light and it sometimes looks like the tornado in Wizard of Oz, complete with a swirling live cow.

I get stuff done, but sometimes it's way too much. Sometimes it's way too soon. Sometimes it's way too fast. Sometimes it starts to take on an energy all its own, like a flash flood that forces its way through whatever place it can rush and flow.

I deal constantly with flash floods of thoughts, ideas, dreams and visions. My brain did not seem to have an "off" switch and even if it looks from the outside like I'm not doing much, my whole inner world is constantly having planning meetings, my brain is constantly looking at everything in the world as raw material to create something else. Give me a bag of random things and I will return having created something completely new from it.

And I don't want things to take a long time. I don't want anyone ever telling me that something is impossible. I will quietly rebel every time someone tells me a limitation of any kind, and my mind will immediately go to work figuring out how to defy impossibility — how to not only return with something useful, but also something magical and impossible. It's my favorite thing, and I couldn't have stopped doing it if I wanted to. It is who I am.

The people in my life are well versed in my cycles of creation and the messes I make while making magic. I have a suspicion that it's the hardest part about being in my life. The way I make enormous messes and then feel completely overwhelmed by what it's going to take to clean them up. The way I get "lost" in my creating and become impossible to reach. And the way I get tangled up in the chaos and mess that gets made between what was and what is now.

So many times I've emerged from these periods of deep creativity and I bring what I've created out to the open, all bundled up like a brand new baby to present to my beloveds. And then I completely fall apart when I see the mess I didn't even know I made, and it's got to be cleaned up. I mean this both literally and figuratively. The people I've worked with either embrace this and help me, or try to change me and passive-aggressively berate me. And believe me, I've tried to change. I've gotten better with age. I've learned to slow down. I've learned to plan things out and harness the energy of a flash flood rather than get swept away in it. I've learned that the flash flood is going to come no matter what I do, and that if I just plan for it and create safety around it, I can mitigate a lot of damage and a lot of mess and actually utilize it in positive ways.

I have also read hundreds of books about hundreds of things. I research incessantly. I catalog both the experiences I've had alone and with others, every book I've read, every comment I've read on every message board about every subject. I have a deep desire to know how everyone feels about everything. I want to understand every facet of every human experience. I remember the stories I hear from every human and those get cataloged too. I watch the way people move through their lives, the way they progress, what makes them happy and what puts the light in their eyes, and what takes it out of their eyes. I study how world events affect us as a human family, how we are similar and how we are different. I ask questions constantly and I have to make myself stop asking questions because sometimes a conversation with me feels more like an interrogation. But truthfully, I am just absolutely fascinated, interested and in love with almost every human I' ever meet. The entire world and the entire human family has been a beautiful 8 billion piece puzzle that I've been trying to figure out my whole life. So I am constantly seeking to find new facets, patterns in old facets, and especially what puts the light in the eyes of every precious person, and what takes the light out of their eyes.

And then I try to create solutions for suffering out of all of the things I've gathered. It's what I've always done.

It's what I love. It's who I am. It's messy and beautiful.
And then the world stopped and suddenly I was the thing that sat on my

creating table, in my sketchbook, in my pressure cooker. I was the thing that was shifting and ready to blow.

I was the mess that was about to be made.

When I came to terms with the fact that I was going to be my biggest research project, my biggest puzzle to be solved, my biggest mess to clean up and my biggest creation to put together, I knew I could do it fast and efficiently. I had created millions of things quickly and beautifully, I could do the same for myself! And then I could get back to work. I knew I could be prolific in my own creation of myself.

Boy, was I wrong.

It's like someone told me that I've got to go on a journey, and it's all about the journey. Don't we get told that a lot? It's not about the destination, it's about the journey, right?

Well, I figured I could be very prolific on my journey all the way around the block. I knew what I was capable of. So I made a plan to "fix myself" as quickly as possible. And I figured that a little bit of therapy and a new location would do the trick.

It would just be a little trip around the block and then everything could get back to normal.

I took quite a few roads around the block before I figured out that I was just going in circles, down old familiar roads that brought me right back to the place I had grown out of. And that in my need to get finished quickly and efficiently, I was just wasting time and wearing myself out. It looked like momentum, and it was, but it was really more traveling procrastination than anything.

After a few frustrating and exhausting and prolific trips around that same familiar track, I finally surrendered to what was happening, and how big of a mess it was going to make.

This wasn't going to be me doing the creating in the way I was used to, this was me being created by the energy that had been building up for eons, like a volcano. There was no stopping it.

50 Roads To The Middle Of My Life

On an upcoming road, I will tell you about how after we left in the RV, I started getting up close to mountains rather than viewing them in the distance . . . all kinds of mountains. After one particularly spectacular and steep climb to the top of a really cool place, I decided I wanted to climb 100 mountains that year. And I did it. That was quite a road that I will tell you about soon, but there's something that I learned about the mountains and the canyons and the cliffs and the ravines and the river washes that I grew to love so much on those 100 climbs . . . they all came to be from a tremendous mess of chaos.

I climbed a few mountains that were formed from volcanoes sometime way back in history. I climbed mountains that swelled up from the earth after massive earthquakes sometime back in history. I hiked canyons that got formed from the erosion of swift running water, flash floods and regular consistent flowing rivers. Destroying to create. Destroying to create. Destroying to create.

I experienced and enjoyed the result of nature's "chaos," and learned what massive amounts of energy can do to create something new. I learned when energy explodes and looks like so much destruction, it is creating something new and different at the same time. And when that pent up energy finally expels, what once was becomes something entirely new.

The heat and explosions and shifting of our earth taught me so much about myself. About my creative explosions and the messes that are an inevitable part of putting all of my own energy into something. I was at times a volcano, a flash flood, an earthquake. And the messes were the "shadow side" of how prolific I am.

I started my first big creative venture when I was 25 years old. It was a multimillion dollar, worldwide company within a few years. I had a team to help me create and to clean up. We had to let that company go after Marq's accident and then I started another, again with a team. We created and cleaned up together.

This time, it was just me and my RV. And I had a long journey ahead. And no team to help me clean up the aftermath of creative explosions. And I was the thing exploding this time, I was the thing being created. I was the mess. I was the chaos.

Melody Ross

After those few desperate trips around the block, I realized this was going to be a long game, a long process, to allow my own inner earthquakes, my own inner volcanos, my own inner floods, my own erosion, my own forest fires, my own droughts, my own fractures . . . and all of the mess that goes along with it.

And the unpredictable, uncontrollable nature of what was happening had to be trusted. I had to trust the process of my own destruction — because I knew there was the possibility of a new creation once the terrifying tremors of change calmed down.

I also had to look back at what a nightmare I must have been to work with for people who didn't love the magic of the mess. When I was stuck alone in my little RV with my own prolific nature and my own messes, I really started to understand how to some people, this chaos is exciting and magical, and to others, it is annoying and appears to be counterproductive.

I thought about all of the times in my creative career when others tried to be helpful and change my process. They wanted to stop the volcanos and stop the flash floods and stop the earthquakes. Or they wanted to be able to start a volcano or flash flood on command, and stop it on command. They wanted to harness all of this energy and bottle it up and make it more efficient. If I was going to have creative explosions, they needed it to be planned and controlled. They wanted to plan them out and calm them down and make them consistent and predictable. They wanted to control the outcome of the experiment. They didn't want any kind of mess, only beauty. They didn't want any kind of chaos or experiments, only beautiful outcomes. They wanted me to make mountains, but without earthquakes or volcanoes. They wanted me to create deep canyons, but without flash floods and fast running rivers. They wanted me to stop being messy and only be prolific. They wanted me to be able to duplicate the processes that ended up in particularly spectacular results. Most of the time they were just trying to be helpful. It must have been such a nightmare for them. I know it was for me.

Because I wanted that too, but every attempt at defying the nature of raw creation failed. And so I thought I was the failure.

50 Roads To The Middle Of My Life

I am so angry about this now. I think about the way I tried so hard to be someone different than I am, and how much I betrayed myself. I think about how I went along with plans and ideas that I knew were incomplete and would never work. I think about the way I participated in dumbing myself down, shaming myself and trying so hard to be acceptable and mainstream.

And I think about how there's a really great place for everyone to be awesome at what they are awesome at . . . but we aren't all awesome at everything, everywhere. Sometimes people and situations, even when they are both awesome, are not a good match. I am not a good match for people who need predictive structure, because you never know what kind of mountain is going to form from a volcano, you just have to trust that it's going to be just right, and totally unique and amazing. I AM a good match for people who love to be in the laboratory and love the magic of new discoveries so much that they don't mind at all that a mess comes along with trying new things and expanding on old things. I love the people who don't complain about sweeping up the confetti after a party, because the party was SO SPECTACULAR and part of enjoying the party is cleaning up the mess.

Creation is messy. It just is.

So when I started seeing that I was the thing being created, I started to understand why I was also the thing being destroyed — it was chaotic and messy. And I didn't want to shame myself about the mess. I didn't want to try to plan the outcome. I didn't want to follow some old guidebook that would just yield outdated results.

I wanted to let myself be created by the energy of a shifting environment. I wanted to trust that because all of us on this planet ARE part of nature. We are just like everything else, always becoming something new. And sometimes we become someone new in gentle and beautiful ways . . . like a rose going from a tight bud to an open flower. It's so beautiful, gentle and lovely.

But then sometimes, we get to become something new from what we might call natural disasters. Sometimes it's the storms and the earthquakes and the active volcanos that end up taking what we once were, and shifting it into something different entirely. Sometimes parts of us get washed away, blown away and burnt away. And what remains sometimes looks like an awful mess.

So I packed my bags after those first few trips around the block and I braced myself for a trip around the world, a trip around the universe — the universe I would find right inside of myself.

And I set out on a road that I didn't know at all.

So, Beautiful Mess-Maker,

What chaos do you avoid that could actually bring new creations if you embraced it?

AND

What has blown up or shaken up in your life, leaving you in a pile of rubble, and what beautiful new landscape was created because of it?

We just can't fight change, my friends. It's an awesome adventure we are all on. It's messy.

You might think when I packed my bags to travel around the universe, that I had it all figured out. But I didn't. So next, I will tell you about The Road Where I Had No Idea.

See you there.
With great love,
melody freebird

19

The Road Where I Had No Idea

I'm going to start this road by telling you that "I don't know" has become one of my favorite phrases recently, and it's almost always true when I say it. Sometimes I think I don't know but I actually do, and sometimes I know that I know but I'm too afraid of saying it out loud. But most of the time when I say "I don't know," it is positively true.

It wasn't always this way though. Somewhere along the way, I adopted the belief that if you didn't know something, you were inferior. I have been one who asks every question that crosses my mind from the time I could form a sentence. Because I really wanted to know about everything! I quickly learned in elementary school, as well as middle school and high school that kids laugh at you when you ask a lot of questions, and scoff at what you ask.

So, I always thought everyone knew but me. But the laughing didn't deter me from asking questions, it just made me think that I was the dumbest one in the class.

Then when I became an adult and I would attend meetings with other adults, I would always raise my hand and ask question after question, making sure I truly understood. It was then that other adults would pull me aside after the meeting and say, "thank you for asking those questions, we were all wondering the same thing."

What? Then why didn't you ask?

What if the kids in school didn't know either . . . and they just didn't want anyone to think they didn't know? What if I wasn't dumb after all . . . just curious?

I have since learned that almost no one wants to admit when they don't know something, especially when they think they SHOULD know it.

The Road Where I Had No Idea is the road where my prolific ideas left me, and my knowing left me. My questions even left me. I was lost in every way on that road, or I thought I was.

As a person who usually has more ideas than I could ever dream of making into reality, it was a terrifying phase in my life when suddenly I had no idea what to do next. Not a single idea . . . nothing. And I certainly didn't KNOW anything for sure.

That happened shortly after we left Idaho and all hell started breaking loose internally. And the weight of all the burdens were so heavy that all I could do was try to hold them up, I could not think of one other thing to do.

I had no idea. I knew nothing for sure.

Just this morning as I started to write about this road, I felt such similar feelings. It is now September, and I am up in the mountains with no internet, no cell service and no electricity. There are familiar feelings both because it's just about the time of year we left Idaho, and because the last few days have been a bit of a struggle in my current life, making it easy to remember the "I have no idea" feeling.

Yep, I'm back on a little stretch of a very familiar road right now. But I've been down this road before and I just have to remember that it's not an eternal road even if I can't see where it ends or where the turn-offs are.

At this exact moment, we are up in the mountains camping after spending the summer at Wild West Mustang Ranch with our friends, West and Kami. I am sitting in my RV, using my laptop powered with a solar battery that takes a large part of the day to charge. I will write until it goes dead and then I will take it back out to the solar setup in our red truck and let it charge again. When I tried to start writing this morning, I had a million notes ready to elaborate about this road. Well, as luck would have it, when I woke up at 4am I was so cold that I could hardly move my fingers and toes. The heater was off for some reason. I got up to switch it on and it wouldn't work.

It was about 35 degrees outside.

I figured we were out of propane so I decided I would wait until 6am to wake Marq up and tell him, because he needs lots of sleep to recover from the accident he had a few days ago (that's the kind of week we've had.) So I sat here in the cold and I wrote on the battery power left from yesterday until my computer went dead. To get to the solar plug-ins, it's a walk outside and across the gravel, so I put my shoes on and headed out into the cold darkness to plug it in. And I committed to learning how to change the propane tank so I don't ever have to need someone to do it for me again, I was SO COLD.

We've been here for 5 days. We came high high high up into these mountains last week because all of us who live at the ranch together were very sick.

It's something very contagious because all 4 of us . . . Kami, West, Marq and me . . . we all contracted the same sickness. And it's a doozy, it has knocked 4 go-getters straight down on our tushies.

We left because West and Kami were expecting some beloved guests at the ranch, about 20 of them, and we didn't want to pass this sickness on to them. So we all packed up our RVs and enough food for 5-7 days, and the horses and our computers and work equipment and we all had BIG PLANS that we would get so much done while we were here. Things haven't gone according to that plan. What we HAVE done is a lot of breathing treatments, a lot of eating of soup, a lot of fire building and a lot of coughing, sneezing and blowing our noses.

And a lot of readjustments to our plans, because just last week we all told each other about the big things we are ready to do and build as we go into Fall and Winter. We all had big and exciting things to work on.

And then we got sick.

But we still thought we could all get so much done up here while we recover and quarantine.

So West and Marq had some horses to train, they were super excited to get started even though they were both sick. They'd been working with them a few hours a day when Marq got kicked by the biggest horse and knocked down with a whole lot of force. And turns out, he broke his right shoulder. He is right-handed. We took a trip into town to the doctor and got X-rays. Tomorrow we have to drive somewhere with cell service and talk to an orthopedic surgeon.

I had big plans to finish an online course while I was here, but my voice is still gone. I started feeling a little bit better yesterday, then it rained all day. I have to kick things into gear because Marq is not going to be able to work for a while, and it's going to be up to me.

So here I am again, I have no idea what to do next. I have no idea how to make up for this time we are losing and I have no idea how to make up for the financial resources we are going to lose during his recovery. So many obstacles. So much discouragement. So many unknowns. I have no idea.

I cried a lot. I got really angry. I pulled out old journals and read them and I kept seeing this pattern of not knowing what to do next. And then I realized that the next part of the pattern needs changing. That instead of freaking out and spiraling down into despair, I need to embrace the I HAVE NO IDEA ROAD.

I've been down it SO MANY TIMES and it hasn't killed me yet. In fact, it has often been the catalyst for innovative and resourceful solutions that never would have materialized otherwise. Sometimes the only reason we do something fresh and brave is because we have no other choice.

I don't know how this is all going to work out. My husband does SO MANY ESSENTIAL THINGS in our life that he's not going to be able to do for a while. I have no idea what we will do now.

50 Roads To The Middle Of My Life

Sometimes I feel like I know. Sometimes I feel like I don't know. I pretend to know. I pretend not to know.

What is KNOWING, anyway? This is a question that has shown up on so many of the roads I've traveled, and I still don't have a solid answer. That's right, I don't know if I know and I don't even know what KNOW really means.

When we left Idaho 2 years ago, we had no idea where we were going. We had ideas about where we'd like to go, but had no idea how we were going to end up there. We had no idea what was going to happen next. We had no idea who we were going to become or not become.

And here we are 24 months later, living this very unorthodox and unpredictable life, and most days we absolutely love it. But we have no idea where we will be a year from now.

We live in a time in history where none of us know if we will be going to work next week, or if the kids will be going to school. We don't know if the stores will be open or closed, or if countries across the world will be open or closed. We have all learned together to embrace I DON'T KNOW, or atleast survive it.

But there are still things that are sure. TODAY. And that's what you gotta do in times like these, find the things that are sure TODAY, or even just IN THIS MOMENT . . . and let that be enough, not try to make things certain and sure for next week or next month or next year (or even the next minute.)

Does anything feel sure anymore? I think when we can't find things that feel sure, we suffer a lot . . . we suffer to the point of complete paralyzation.

So sometimes on roads like these, I just make a list of what I know for sure is SURE. Just in this moment. It makes me feel a little bit better AND it reminds me that tomorrow there will be more sure things, and the day after that. And that sure things will show up that I never could have expected, really good sure things that act as little stepping stones to get just a little bit further.

Melody Ross

There are times that all we can hope for is just a place to take one step forward, and as for the rest of the steps . . . we have no idea. Just because we don't know, it doesn't mean they don't exist. The next step forward will always exist, lots of them will. Sometimes they just don't show up until our foot is in the air ready to land on them.

Shortly after we set off as nomads, the 2020 Pandemic started. That's when I started writing down things that were sure IN THIS MOMENT. I found my journal and here's what I wrote . . .

What are the sure things TODAY?

Today I am breathing in and out
Today I am alive
Today it is March 2020
Today I am 48 years old
Today I have been married for 30 years
Today I have 5 children and 3 bonus children and 4 grandchildren (5 soon!)
Today my husband and our children and grandchildren are alive and well and in loving and supportive relationships - they all have everything they need
Today the sun came up right on time
Today the sky is blue with white puffy clouds, it is cool and sunny
Today the leaves are starting to show up on trees and lots of flowers are starting to bloom on trees and from the ground
Today I am practicing social-distancing right along with the rest of the country and much of the world
Today I have the internet to stay connected
Today I have just about any kind of music I could ever want at my disposal
Today I could learn just about anything I could ever dream of learning with the click of a few links
Today I could connect to just about anyone in my life on video, text, email
Today I have enough to eat and drink
Today I have art supplies
Today I have a warm place to sleep and work and rest and relax
Today I am of sound mind and heart and I can choose to spend my time focusing on things that bring peace instead of anxiety

It's interesting that most of these answers are still true, though there's no way I could have known they would be. Life went on, things worked out somehow. They always have, somehow. That's something I can know for sure, that life is going to go on.

50 Roads To The Middle Of My Life

After that road, I started to ask myself these questions every time I find myself on I HAVE NO IDEA roads in other places . . . the fact is, there are lots of roads called I HAVE NO IDEA all over the world. . . so these are good questions for those roads, and they have become a way of life for me.

1. What if I really don't need to know what's going to happen tomorrow and next week and next month RIGHT NOW?
2. What if I really don't need to know if there's a purpose to all of this RIGHT NOW?
3. What if I really don't have to know how I WANT things to turn out RIGHT NOW?
4. What if I really don't have to know who I will become because of all of this RIGHT NOW?
5. I wonder if I could relax into not knowing and just EXPERIENCE my life for a while? Could I? What would that feel like?

I started learning on The Road Where I Had No Idea to be gentle and kind and merciful and HUMANE to myself. I started learning that I don't want to require more of myself than I have to give, or that life has to give! I decided not to bully myself into figuring out how I was going to get through this year and next year and the next decade of my life. Just TODAY. Just THIS MOMENT.

So, Dear Fellow-Wanderer,

How have you been handling the times in life when you HAVE NO IDEA?

AND

How could you show mercy to yourself by looking at the things that are sure RIGHT NOW and let that be enough?

Tomorrow, we will go on another journey, this time to THE ROAD MADE OF MIRRORS. It's a big one.

I love you.
melody freebird

20

The Road Made Of Mirrors

One morning in 2012 I woke up with horrific hives. I had just turned 40 years old. They quickly grew and turned to welts that swelled about 1/4 inch from where my skin was supposed to be. They would start out the size of a dime or quarter and end up growing and growing, then growing into each other until they were covering different parts of my body completely. They were hot to the touch and they itched, burned and ached. The ones on the palms of my hands and the bottoms of my feet were excruciating. The ones on my face were humiliating. The ones on my scalp were horrifically itchy and anywhere my clothing touched, the hives/welts would rub raw. It was not a fun time.

The first time it happened I went to the hospital because they started on my scalp, went down to my ears and then to my throat and mouth. My throat started swelling up and I was afraid I was going to lose my air passage.

The doctor at the hospital gave me an IV of Benadryl and told me I was probably just having some kind of allergic reaction, but that he's also seen these kinds of hives/welts show up on women about my age. There is no explanation and no cure. It's just called Chronic Urticaria - which simply means hives that won't go away.

I figured they'd be gone by morning, but they weren't. They were even

149

worse.

And this was just the beginning of a 3-4 year mystery illness that turned out to be one of the biggest mirrors of my life.

If you know me, you know that I hang mirrors all over the place, many times in places so high that a person would not be able to see their own reflection in them. I do this because I love how they reflect light, how they expand a room, how they dance with whatever is moving and create all sorts of aliveness wherever they are.

Those aren't the kinds of mirrors this road is about, but similar. The kind of mirrors this road is made of are the things in life that reflect you back to yourself, that make you take a good hard look at yourself and only yourself.

The hives/welts were a mirror because they were a manifestation of my fears, anxieties and past trauma — secrets. I would have horrible breakouts that I could not hide from when I was trying to stuff something away, avoid something or when I didn't feel safe. I had a dream the first week of those hives that told me every single hive was a secret I was keeping that wanted to be released. There was no way to hide from any of it, it stared me right in the face. For all those years, those hives disfigured me and woke me up. They didn't go away until I learned about boundaries and until I started telling the truth about some things I was keeping secret. They would show up when I said yes to things that weren't good for me and no to things that were. They would show up when I had to have conversations with people who weren't a good match for me. They were the ultimate truth serum. They were relentless until I started making some agreements with myself about what and who was allowed to have influence over my life and how close people and situations could get to the core of who I am. Of course, that was only the beginning of my boundaries journey, but I don't know that I ever would have started on that journey without those hives/welts that forced me to face things that needed facing without looking away.

Mirrors are fun to look at when you have a new outfit or you've spent a lot of time doing your makeup or you just got your hair done. They're fun to look at when you're dressed up in a costume or you're making a funny face, or when you're holding a baby.

50 Roads To The Middle Of My Life

Mirrors are not very fun to look at when you're not feeling fabulous about your life or your self or what you're surrounded by. Mirrors are incredibly difficult to look at when you're only pointing your finger outward and not taking responsibility for your life and your circumstances. But nothing can pull you back to your truest truth like having to take a good hard look at yourself.

It used to take a whole lot to get me angry, and that's not something I'm particularly proud of. It's just that I used to be so afraid of anger and I even thought that if I was angry, it would make me a bad person. What I've learned is that anger is our friend, a nice little package delivery guy bringing an urgent message that needs to be dealt with ASAP. These days, I welcome anger when it comes and I open the package at the time of delivery. Anger is not so scary after all.

But when I first stepped foot on the Road Made of Mirrors, I was one big ball of anger. And resentment. And bitterness. I felt betrayed, abandoned and discarded. I felt indignant. My anger certainly felt justified, and it was — but anger kept too long turns toxic. It's really just supposed to be there to deliver the message that something needs to be dealt with, it's not supposed to move in and change its address to yours.

At this time I had a big journal where I would write letters to Heaven. And then I'd listen and write down what I heard Heaven saying back to me. It was my way of dealing with things I didn't want to talk to any other human beings about.

So I was writing about my anger, and then an answer came back about mirrors. This message felt right on target. I was writing asking questions about what to do about the betrayal I felt. What to do about how I was wronged, hurt and left to die bleeding in the street. It was all very dramatic. And I loved the answer I got back in my writing prayers.

The message came as "visualize that you have surrounded your RV in mirrors so that when these people come toward you, all they can see is their own faces and what they have done."

And, of course I was thrilled to have gotten this answer. I felt so validated, vindicated and RIGHT.

But then more of the message came . . . "and now visualize that you have surrounded the inside of your RV with mirrors, so that wherever you go, you can see your own face and what you have done."

WHAT? ARE YOU KIDDING?

This road was like the hives, there was no getting away from what it was trying to teach me. It only escalated my anger at first but then I started to soften as I imagined others seeing themselves in this situation between us, and as I found the courage to look at myself in this situation between us.

I kept writing about this for days in that journal and I would see more and more of the roles I've played in circumstances and consequences that I really really really dislike. When there's a mirror right in your face as you're screaming accusations, it's a wake up call , and you don't always like what you see.

It's a 2-sided mirror on The Road Made of Mirrors. And you're not allowed to see each other until you take a good look at yourself. The mirrors don't become clear until you can both see yourself first. Usually by the time you're done looking at yourself, you've sheepishly put down your pointer finger and gotten to work on your own nonsense.

I don't know what the other person can see when they look on their side of the mirror. Of course when I'm in my righteous indignation, I want them to see how selfish, cruel and hurtful they've been . . . but on The Road Made of Mirrors, I first have to look at how maybe I've been selfish, cruel or hurtful - or any other variety of hive-inducing behaviors I've participated in.

This road taught me to investigate the accusing feelings I feel toward another and see if maybe there's some of those unsavory things also inside of me. I often find at least glimpses of the things I'm most fired up about right inside of me and it's a perfect opportunity for me to start healing and changing that part of ME rather than spending my energy wanting the other person to see that in themselves so that they will change and apologize.

And when there has been blatant abuse, true betrayal and gross manipulation, looking in a "mirror" can help us to see just how hurt we actually are, and instead of focusing all attention on the other person who did the hurting, we can suddenly see our own self and how much attention we need, how much healing we need, how much comfort and mercy and nurturing we need. After you see yourself in that way, suddenly proving the guilt of the other person becomes much less important than it was a few minutes ago — when you're looking in the mirror and you can see the fragments of your own crushed heart right in your own eyeballs, you know that the most important task is now to tend to your own hemorrhaging wounds.

The Road Made of Mirrors taught me that there is always so much more than we can see, and the only thing we can truly influence is what we see in our own mirror. But that we have to have the courage to look, and we have to preserve and protect our time by not spending it looking at the thing or person that we believe wronged us.

There will be hurts in life that will never be made right through apology. There will be things that happen with others that we may never understand. There are tragic things people do to each other, but what makes it even more tragic is when we either let it steal our life from us or we don't take the opportunity to look in the mirror and first see the role we played. We feel free when we take ownership of our part, we feel validated and seen and powerful. We feel whole because we aren't hiding from or leaving out parts of the story.

Don't deny yourself the whole of the story. Don't gaslight away the parts of the story that can feel unbelievable. Don't pretend not to see what you see. Being a human is hard and messy so sometimes we are going to see things in ourselves that are hard to see — we are going to see things in others that are hard to see, and messy to clean up. But man it feels good when you take your own power back and stop feeling like everyone else has all of the power.

And here's the beautiful surprise . . . when you cultivate the courage to really look at yourself, it's not all bad. In fact, it's not bad at all. It's lessons, it's learning, it's another chance to do better the next time. But mostly it's magnificence and resilience and beauty and bravery and loveliness — that's mostly what we're made of!

I hope we can see these life mirrors as enormous blessings that give us tremendous opportunities to see things as they are rather than how we thought they were. It doesn't matter what things look like, it matters how things ARE. And we are all so much more than what we look like and so much more than what we think we are. We shouldn't be afraid to look at the raw truth . . . because the truth is always what sets us free.

So, Authentic Soul,

What are you afraid to see when you look in a mirror?

AND

How can you look even deeper to see the truest and rawest beauty?

Thank you for traveling this very reflective road with me. Next, we will take an easy stroll down The Road of Unfathomable Relief.

See you there,
xo
melody freebird

21

The Road Of Unfathomable Relief

We all have our default behaviors to bring some kind of instant relief in times of severe stress. These are often behaviors that are not great for our lives in the long term, but we do them to make uncomfortable or painful feelings stop. People look for relief in overworking, or by drinking a few cocktails, or over-shopping. Mine used to be binge eating, and it still is if I'm not careful. I can find instant relief in chocolate, Cheetos and carbonated drinks. If things are really bad, I can find myself at the gas station, numbing my feelings with a hot dog that's been rolling on the warmer all day. I've learned better, so I can do better now. These days, I find that the most effective relief comes from standing right in the middle of what is scaring me or stressing me, looking it straight in the eye and not backing down.

But it took a long time to get here. And a wild horse was my teacher.

I don't know when I started doing it, but since I was younger than I can remember, I lived my life as if there were a gun to my head, making sure I did everything "right" so that I didn't get kicked out of wherever I'd found myself. Getting kicked out and rejected felt like it would kill me. If I felt like I was going to get kicked out, or that I didn't belong, I just left before someone could kick me out. I was always in a constant cycle of fear that something was going to come and take away whatever was good in my life, and something was going to come and hurt me, and something was going to come and expose the deep flaws of who I was deep down inside. I couldn't bear the thought of just relaxing and trusting life, because then not just everything would get taken away, but everyone would leave me.

It stings to write this and admit this. But until the last year or so, fear and adrenaline were my greatest reserves of motivation.

It was my core way of being, it was my energy source, it was what drove me almost every minute of the day. I was living with the goal of simply not getting hurt anymore. Or to find vicarious relief in making sure no one in my sphere of influence felt hurt or got hurt anymore.

And I pushed myself to every limit to feel safe in the world . . . but I never got there. The more I pushed the limits of what I thought would bring safety into my life, the more afraid I became, because the more I exhausted every new idea to push into being, the more I realized it didn't work. And the more it didn't work to do and be and create everything I thought would make me feel safe, the more I realized I didn't EVER feel safe, and I didn't know how I was ever going to feel safe. It was a terrifying realization.

And I didn't realize how I've lived most of my life trying to cope with this deep, clenching fear I felt until I saw myself in the mirror of a wild horse.

For the last few years, I've spent most mornings waking up within a few hundred feet of wild mustangs. And with the opportunity to witness true miracles as I watch West Taylor utilize neuroscience, the science of trauma and the vagus nerve, and what can happen when two sentient beings, horse and human, decide to grow together through presence and attention.

I tell you this because I have never had a better teacher of what brings true relief in life than that of these beautiful wild equine creatures.

What is relief anyway?

The dictionary says relief is:
 the alleviation, ease, or deliverance through the removal of pain, distress, oppression, etc. a means or thing that relieves pain, distress, anxiety, etc.

Here at the ranch, our home base the last few summers, there are several wild horses that were adopted and rescued. And many more come through to work withWest. My husband has been apprenticing with West for nearly 3 years now, and I have watched these horses tame the wild brokenness in his brain that came from his brain injury. I have watched the sacred magic that happens when both horse and human surrender to the only thing that really works. I used to think it was about building trust with each other, now I know it's about learning to trust yourself, no matter what happens next.

The horse has to find their safety inside. The human has to find their safety inside. They both have to learn this by experiencing their fears and staying still as they learn what will and will not kill them. And the only way you can truly learn that is by standing still **AS YOU EXPERIENCE** the thing you fear most. And the trick is to not believe the fear as you're standing right in the middle of it.

The old way was to "break" a horse. Tears fall as I type this sentence. Because we used to be so primitive as a society to truly believe that the way to get people or creatures to do what we want them to do is to emotionally **BREAK THEM.** And I think we have all seen the results of this. I think as a society, we are all **LIVING** the results of this.

The horses taught me that from the time I was a child, I believed that I could finally **BREAK MYSELF** into doing what other people wanted me to do, by allowing others to break me. By breaking myself. By thinking that I could use fear, punishment and intimidation on myself. And attracting other people who liked to do the same. From my perspective, a horse who has been "broken" is really just submitting to their lot in life, and tolerating their fears until they are too exhausted and defeated to fight them anymore. People are the same. When a person has been broken, their calm demeanor isn't so much about inner peace, it's about giving up and giving in to the thing that is trying to control them, the thing they fear the most . . . to the "gun against their head." They're just focusing on not getting hurt, not getting killed. That is how you break a horse. Or a person.

I think at some point in life, we all have to learn that it was never the scary thing we thought was going to kill us that was the threat. It's always been the stories we tell ourselves about what will kill us that actually kill our life. We stay stuck with the false belief that that is what will keep us safe — to play small, to avoid, to play dead — to let the more dominant ones bully us into submission and make the decisions. We don't really live, we just tolerate life.

People don't need to be broken. They need to be built. Horses don't need to be broken, they need to be built. And the building for a horse or a human has to come from the inside of their own choice, their own sovereignty, their own respect for the truth of what surrounds them.

From my observation over the last 10+ years of sitting for a week with lots of traumatized humans at my retreats, and the last 3+ years of witnessing lots of traumatized horses here at the ranch . . . building a horse or a human requires that horse or human look their fears in the face and see them for what they are. It comes from feeling SAFETY inside of themselves. It doesn't come from being taught that someone else can protect them, but that they can protect themselves. And especially that the threats they perceive are almost always not threats at all. The fear and the stories they tell themselves are the biggest threat to them. The fear and stories that others try to control and manipulate them with are the biggest threat to them.

I've watched this over and over in the "round pen" where West and Marq train the horses. These horses are afraid of sounds, people, paper, airplanes, ANYTHING. Until they learn for themselves that they are okay whether a person is standing next to them, or 100 people are. Whether there's a tractor going, a dog barking, a river to walk over, a saddle and a person sitting on their back. They learn to feel safe by facing the thing they think they are most afraid of, and finding safety inside as they stand calm right in the middle of it.

And they have to learn this by facing their fears for little moments of time, then releasing and relaxing and seeing that the thing they feared didn't kill them or hurt them after all. There is a period of pressure whether horse or human must get in that arena and stand with what they fear for as long as they can take it. And then the pressure is released and they realize what they are capable of. And then after a period of rest and relief, back to another level of facing the stories of what they think will kill them.

And after a while, they find their safety inside. They are built, not broken.

I don't like to call West a horse trainer, or even a horse whisperer. Instead, he is a horse listener. And he has taught us the supreme power in this magical form of listening. It comes from 100% presence and attention to the horse. To their every move, their every twitch, their every breath. And the only way it can work is to also give 100% presence and attention to YOURSELF and your safety, the way you are showing up, thinking and being. To have good results with the horses, you have to learn to regulate your own nervous system, you have to feel the safety inside of yourself.

You have to trust yourself, and you have to learn to be worthy of your own trust.

When these horses are first rescued, they seem to truly believe that EVERY SINGLE THING in their environment is a threat that is going to kill them. And they behave as such. They are twitchy, avoidant and clever. They all seem to have their own personalities and their own way of dealing with their feelings of insecurity. But it's clear that they're all very afraid, very on-guard and very ready to fight, flee or freeze. They're especially terrified of the 2-legged creatures called humans, no matter how much love and respect and affection a human wants to share with them.

So from my observation, a human first shows up to the horse feeling safe in themselves. Only then can they lead the horse to their own safety.

It's a relationship. It's what West calls Social Engagement. And he knows the science of all of it as it pertains to the autonomic nervous system and the vagus nerve and all of that science-y stuff. I'm a respecter of science and all, but I just call this whole process LOVE.

It's actually rooted in safety, though. Can we ever truly feel love for ourselves or others if we don't feel safe?

The horses have taught me that true RELIEF, unfathomable relief comes from feeling safe. And then the natural state of being can be love, because I truly believe that LOVE is our natural state. But no amount of outside protection can override the internal feelings of safety or non-safety we deal with inside. No one can convince us that a situation is not going to kill us if we truly believe it will.

And very often, the only way we can overcome the stories that keep that gun to our head is to step right into the story and look it straight in the eyes for as long as we can take it. And then rest for a bit, and then head right back out to that round pen of life and face it again. After a while, it doesn't scare us anymore at all. But other things do . . . so we have to keep getting back out there in the round pen and facing the next thing that scares us.

When you're in a constant state of fear and spending most of your time and resources trying to just tolerate it, your body is filled with adrenaline. Everything makes you jumpy and on-edge. You're exhausted and wired at the same time.

When you feel safe inside, you can start to experience AWE. And you can rest and relax and enjoy. And your body is filled with the right hormones and chemicals to make you feel calm and peaceful. And you make WAY BETTER DECISIONS. You can actually be present with others, because you're ENJOYING them rather than trying to strategize ways to survive once they decide to try to kill you or hurt you. Because you trust yourself, you finally feel safe to truly trust others. Because no matter what happens next in life, you know you can stand calm inside of it.

So The Road to Unfathomable Relief was a surprise. I didn't find true and lasting relief in the hiding places. I didn't find true and lasting relief in the numbing power of food or overwork or endless scrolling on the internet.

I learned that true and lasting relief comes more from showing up and doing what must be done rather than hiding under the blankets or looking for the next hero to come and save the day.

Relief comes after the uncomfortable process of lancing an infected wound so the poison can drain. It doesn't come from hiding the wound under your sleeve.

Relief comes after the painful process of putting a dislocated body back where it belongs. It doesn't come from keeping the arm in a sling and keeping it from moving.

Relief came from the bloody and painful process of pulling out a thorn that impaled you, not from putting a bandaid over the top of it and leaving it in.

Relief for me came from pairing things down to so few dishes that I have to wash them if I want to eat again, not from going to Target and buying more dishes.

Relief came from making the phone call to deal with the things that kept me up at night, not from avoiding and procrastinating the confrontation.

Relief came from telling the truth, and listening for the truth, and finding the truth. Even when the truth hurt devastatingly at first.

TRUE AND LASTING RELIEF only came for me when I stepped into the things I feared most. And not only did relief come, but suddenly I felt my old skin peeling off and the woman I truly am began to wake up, stretch and get herself ready to emerge.

She wasn't going to show up until I was ready to stop being motivated by the gun to my head. Her first order of business was to take the gun from my hand and tell me….
"there is a better way…."

And I believed her. Unfathomable relief.

So, Dear Soul,

What are your mechanisms to break yourself into submission, rather than build yourself into sovereignty and self-trust?

 AND

What fears do you need to step into in order to find your own unfathomable relief, after realizing what you're capable of staying calm through?

Thank you for going down this road with me. Tomorrow, I will take you on The Road Where I Didn't Want To Be Found.

I love you. Please love yourself. Please find it inside of yourself.
xo
melody freebird

22

The Road Where I Didn't Want To Be Found

*trigger warning - this chapter contains a sensitive account of one of the darkest times of my life, mentally and emotionally

When I set out to write these roads, I committed to being as honest, raw and vulnerable as possible. It's not an easy thing to do, and some of these roads I have written, I wanted to delete as soon as I typed them. This is one of those.

But I have to tell the truth about the roads that have led to now, and leaving this one out would not portray an accurate story. So I guess I will just cut to the chase and tell you that I started trying to disappear long before I actually disappeared from the world a few years ago on my quest to figure things out in my RV.

You see, secrets are poisonous and this is one of my secrets - I wish our whole human family could understand that we've all got to drain our secrets of their poison so we can heal together. We've got to stop causing others to feel shame about the things that have poisoned them.

So many parts of modern life drive people into the ground, people who were once healthy and vital and enthusiastic and whole. So many people end up living a very inhumane existence, pushed to their limit. And then get labeled crazy. It's messed up.

I share this road because I am certain there are some of our human family out there right now who are hiding the same dangerous secret I was hiding. And I want to do my part to bring this out in the open. The stigma around this kind of unwellness is so pervasive and destructive that I want to do all that I can to eradicate the judgment and whatever compels a person to feel so much shame about it that they keep it a secret. The only way to ease its effects is to STOP KEEPING IT A SECRET. So here I am.

And before I begin, I want you to know that I love being alive now, and I want to be alive. And this was just a temporary struggle along the way, one that called me to make some major transformations in my life. I want you also to know that working through this time was a huge turning point for lots of reasons. It actually gave me a whole new perspective on life, and a whole new way of being alive. My yearning to be done with life is actually what ended up saving my life. If you struggle with this too, I want you to know that it can and will get better. Please tell a trusted someone how you're feeling, don't carry it alone.

And if someone finds the courage to tell YOU this secret, please take it seriously. You cannot imagine the courage they had to muster-up to tell you.

I remember when one of my favorite humans of all time, our beloved Robin Williams, shocked the world when he just couldn't take the pain anymore and ended his own life. I still think about it all the time. The way most of the people in his life had no idea what kinds of battles he dealt with internally. Yet there exists a long list of Robin Williams quotes that were clues to what he was thinking and feeling. He did such a great job of smiling, laughing and caring for others that hardly anyone knew just how hard he had to work to stay around. When he lost that battle, I was devastated. I think the whole human family was.

More than 2 years before we left our home state for roads unknown, I was having a constant internal battle over whether I could find the strength and the will to continue on with life. I will never forget the day that I called my friend Lisa in California and told her about the 2 different plans I had orchestrated to end my own life and make it look like an accident. And I told her that I wanted to tell her exactly how I was going to do it because then I knew I wouldn't go through with it. Because if someone knew about my plans, it wouldn't look like an accident. And that's the only way I would ever be able to go through with it, so that it wouldn't hurt my children and my husband and anyone else I love or who loves me.

But Lisa and I talked for a while, and she was just so calm. And she thanked me for telling her. And she made me promise that I'd call her first if I ever seriously considered that option. And she told me that it was time for me to do whatever it took to want to be alive. And that she would help me.

She did the most important thing, she believed me. She is still helping me to this day.

Around this time, one of my children caught on to some of my behaviors and asked me point blank one day . . . "Mom, are you going to die? Are you planning to die? I'm just going to tell you right now how devastated your grandchildren would be to not have you in their life. I hope that is enough motivation for you."

This question seemed to come with both concern and anger. And it shocked me and jolted me awake. I knew something was very wrong inside, but I didn't have any idea how to fix it, my life was just too complicated.

After that, I decided I would not even entertain the idea anymore. But then the despair and overwhelm and hopelessness came back. And the shame. I was drowning in all of it, treading those waters with all the energy I had left.

So I started just asking God to take me away. I would ask in the car for another car to hit mine. I would ask if I could please just get a very aggressive and terminal cancer. I would ask for something to happen in some way that would take me off of the earth without hurting anyone else.

Please just take me away.
Please just take me away.
Please just take me away.

I have a lot of shame about this, so there's no need to shame me or lecture me about it. And I want you to know that I KNOW that life is a gift, that I am blessed, that I have children and grandchildren and a husband who all love me unquestionably. I was so exhausted and saw no relief in sight.

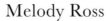
Melody Ross

There was so much going on in the background that no one else could see. Life was unbearably heavy with unrelenting responsibility and problems that seemed to have no solutions. I was drowning in all of it. I also felt the acute sting of an old belief installed in me like some kind of metal-spiked torture device, a belief that I was bad and rotten inside, a belief that had been with me since early childhood. And then around the same time, some information had come to light in my world that shattered my heart and made me question just about everything. And I was just worn to the bone and felt like my family would be better off with my life insurance money than with the remnants of the vibrant person I once was. I was in despair over my husband's relapses. I felt deeply betrayed by some things that were happening and I was battling massively with what was TRUE and what was solid, and what I could count on and where I even belonged.

Yet if you were to take a quick glance from the outside, it just might look like I had a perfect life.

I wasn't sleeping well, but I had been having this recurring dream where I was at a big beautiful gathering on a beach with the people in my life I loved most. We went out to the ocean to swim and somehow I got pulled out into a riptide. Everyone else went back to the beach to prepare food and continue on with the party. I was in the ocean alone.

I kept getting pulled out further and further into the sea. I was waving my arms frantically, and screaming and yelling for someone to help me.

I was drowning.

In the dream, I could see people in my life on the beach, and they thought I was out swimming and having fun. Some of them were even saying "I can't believe she's out there swimming and having fun and we are here preparing the food." or "she is so rude to be late for the party while she's just out there swimming." or "I can't believe she's not even going to show up."

But I wasn't swimming, I was drowning. I needed help.

This recurring dream went on for months and into years. And one night when I had it, I was so far from any land that I could hardly see the shore. And then I could just see smoke, like my whole old life was burning down and even if I was able to swim back to shore, it would be gone.

The dream eventually resolved itself in a beautiful way that I will talk about on an upcoming road but I wanted to begin here because when I was having this dream . . . I so desperately wanted to be found. I wanted someone to see that I was drowning, I wanted someone to help me.

I wanted to be found.

But then after a while, I didn't want to be found anymore. I wanted to disappear.

And so I would ask in prayer….
over and over…
PLEASE TAKE ME AWAY.
PLEASE TAKE ME AWAY
PLEASE TAKE ME AWAY
PLEASE. JUST. TAKE. ME. AWAY.

In the summer of 2017, I was really battling these feelings and on a night that I couldn't sleep, I wrote a song and started singing it as a prayer. I even recorded it in GarageBand on my computer. Just me and my guitar and my quiet voice that I wish I could get to be louder, but I can't. I'm going to be vulnerable here and post the first verse, my prayer to God, asking to be taken away. I had started to lose the deep trust I had in God, but I still prayed, just in case. I tried so hard to stop believing in God, my friends. I tried so hard. But when I sang this song to God, God sang back an answer so profound that I have only started to understand it this year. It's been almost 5 years since I first sang this in prayer, and just these last few years did the answer I was given start to manifest into my life.

On the next road, I will show you and let you hear how God answered back….but for now, here's my prayer to God, asking to be taken away….

> *I lift my head to the sky*
> *I am not here to ask why*
> *I think I know what I need*
> *I'm all used up, set me free*

> *Take me away*

Melody Ross

I don't think I can go another day
I did my best, oh how I tried,
but here I am dried up inside

So take me - please take me away
I know I said I would stay
Got my white flag held high
Can't find the strength to fly....

There are a zillion things that led up to these feelings and to this desperate plea. Some of them I can talk about and some of them I cannot. What is striking to me is how easily I was able to hide it, and it makes me wonder how many others hide it too.

Well, I asked God to take me away, a God I wasn't sure I believed in anymore. And then, God did it, God took me away . . .

. . . but not in the way I expected. He took me somewhere that I couldn't be found for a while, but where I would finally find myself.
And then God taught me the importance of taking myself away from a life that is killing me when I want to be taken out of life. There is a better way to live than merely working to tolerate your existence. There is a beautiful way to live. I promise.

So, Dear Soul,

Has there ever been a time when you wanted to be taken away from life?

AND

Have you ever wanted to be found, or lost or both?

Thank you for walking this vulnerable road with me. It is going somewhere good, I assure you. But first, I want to tell you about what happened when I experienced The Road Where God Sang Back.

I love you. If you're struggling, life will get better!
xo
melody freebird

23

The Road Where God Sang Back

The very word "God" has become such a loaded word, and I want you to know that I know that. I wish it wasn't so. I feel like as a human family, we need a shared benevolent parent now more than ever. But we won't talk about that today.

I feel like I know God, and I feel like God knows me. We've traveled way more than 50 roads together. That's why I have struggled with feelings of deep confusion when it comes to what I thought I used to know about the nature of God, and the way life works, and how if you are just a good kid who does all the right things, everything will work out.

I lost my faith for a while. And then I got to experience the way others sometimes treat you when they think you've got a horrifically contagious disease called a "faith crisis."

This is the road where I earnestly asked God a question, not sure if I even believed in God anymore . . . and then God answered. And I can never ever ever deny that, even though I've struggled with the way things have happened between God and I. We are working it out, and it's something that's too private and sacred to discuss.

We are very good, close friends. And we are having some very honest and difficult conversations, currently.

Melody Ross

And goodness gracious do we ever live in a time when saying GOD causes so much inflammation in the collective human psyche. How did we get to the place where God has been weaponized? I refuse to participate in what I believe is the actual definition of "taking God's name in vain."

Because we are all very different as individuals, we all have different ways in our relationships, including our relationship with the Divine. But I believe we are all one big family, trying to figure out how we got here and who put us here and who in the world is in charge of this family. I think on our deepest level, we are all trying to figure out who our Divine parent is, and where our Divine parent is and how we got so divided from each other as a family.

At least I am.
I am homesick for the mutual love of our human family.

I'm going to tell you upfront that I have a hard and fast rule, generally, that I don't discuss the sacred nature of my faith journey with anyone but my husband and on rare occasions, I will be knee to knee and eye to eye and heart to heart with someone, and when it feels appropriate, I will share my thoughts, my experiences, my faith, my personal values and what I have hope in being true – what I put my faith in. But generally, I allow others their journey to figure things out in the way that feels most true for them, and I respect that right deeply.

And I ask others to grant me the same respect for what I'm trying to figure out on my journey.

My journey with God at the moment is really just too tender and complicated to put out on a community table. We are bound together at this time as we work to figure things out pretty much 24/7. It's a wild time that some DO call a "faith crisis" — as if you could label something this multidimensional and personal. It is not a crisis at all, it is a homecoming. I have no need to defend it or define it, thankfully. It is not open for public scrutiny. I hold it in the deepest recesses of my heart. I guide my life by it. It's between me and God. And it's right for ME, it's pure and it's raw and it's honest. AND I would never assume that just because the kind of relationship I experience with the Divine is right for me, that living it out the way I do is right for everyone.

There is no way that is even possible.
We all have so much complexity.

I really have no business asking you what you believe as some kind of qualifying question to see if you are worthy of my time, and you have no business doing that to me, either. Most religious people belong to an organization that professes to be rooted in love and care. Qualifying another human being through questioning their belief system doesn't feel like love to me. So I don't do it. And I don't allow others to do it to me. And frankly, when I see others do it to each other, I speak up.

And if you were to try to explain the multidimensional experience you have with the Divine, I would tell you the same. That it's none of my business and that I know you're doing the best you can and you're going to get it figured out exactly perfectly. I'd tell you to go straight to the source and don't involve anyone else. It's just too personal.

And….I'd tell you that I love you no matter what. I just do. And I ache for you to love me no matter what. I know you are on your own journey and you are finding your way as best you can. I know that you carefully think through what you believe and how you live your life. I know you are always trying to do the next good and right thing. I know that you are good. I KNOW that you are valuable and precious beyond any quantification, and you don't ever have to do a single thing to earn that value. I know you are different from any soul who has ever walked this earth, so your journey is different too.

And the same is true for me.

So with all of that being said, I want to tell you about what happened on this road. And like I said, I usually use the word "Truthteller" but I'm going to make an exception as I share this road with you. Just know that this is not where this book turns to some kind of tool to convert you to my belief system. This is definitely not that. In fact, the things I thought I knew for sure shattered to pieces like so much of the rest of my life and I am currently in a relationship with my Truthteller that has been stripped away of everything but He and I. Yep, these days it's just me and Jesus, trying to find our way back to each other. At least that's what I'm doing.

I started having visitations in the night from Jesus when I was a little girl.

Melody Ross

I don't know if it was in dreams or if I was actually awake, but it was very real. It extended into my life as an adult, just little visits here and there. But then when Marq had his brain injury, it happened more times than I can count, and it sustained me. I can never deny the existence of Jesus in my life.

I don't talk about it publicly, like I said, because these days, it just seems to cause a deep canyon of division. And besides, I only know for sure what happens between He and I. And for me, for 45+ years, Jesus has been telling me that it's pretty simple, it's all about love. Just love each other. And then love each other more. And then love each other no matter what. It might seem childlike and simplistic, but I think we can all agree that as simple as "love each other" is, it seems to be the most difficult task we've ever had as a human family.

But I'm not gonna talk about that now. I'm gonna tell you about what happened when I sang that plea to Him on the last road…the plea to TAKE ME AWAY.

He answered.

And He said, SURE I will take you away . . . I've been waiting for you to ask….

Here was His answer (you can find the whole recording of this song on my YouTube channel if you'd like to hear it . . . Take Me Away by melody ross)

I hear your heart
I hear you plead

Rest assured
I know what you need
It's easy to see
What your burdens weigh

So I'm gonna take you away.

First we will heal up your eyes
You need to see

50 Roads To The Middle Of My Life

The beauty of the sunrise

The starry sky
Cloudy blue or gray

With your eyes
I'll take you away

Look up and see

The way the trees sway
Let's heal your ears
So you can hear what they say

Feel the wind blowing on your face
I'll take you away to this place

I'll take you
Take you away

We're gonna have
Such a good time today

You have forgotten how to play
So that's how I'll take you away

I hear your heart when you pray
I know you think that you don't wanna stay

You're tired and worn day after day

You need to take yourself away

I'm always here,
I'll never stray
I watch you suffer
Every day

You're not meant
To live this way

173

Melody Ross

Come with me
it's gonna be okay

I'll take you
Take you away
Cuz this whole world
Needs you to stay

And love your life,
Let's start today
Close your eyes and
Take yourself away....

I don't know that there's anything more personal that I could ever share with you. In fact, just a few weeks ago, I shared this song/prayer with my husband for the first time, when my friends D'Laine and Kat came to visit. They flew across the country and drove almost 4 hours up into the mountains to see us for a few days.

And because it had been years since we'd seen each other face to face, we got really deep and personal, and I finally shared this secret with them. And I sang them this song.

We sat in the tipi and cried together. It was love.

Somewhere in my life, I cut my voice box out and sold it for ransom. I lost my voice. I'm getting it back. If you know me, you know that I wish I could talk and sing loud, but my voice just won't do it. It's soft and quiet and I've struggled with that for years. I'm working so hard to get a strong voice.

This song/prayer is the most powerful way I have ever used my voice, but it's been 5 years since this song first came to me in the night, and since then I've written countless songs like this and never found the courage to share any of them. I am working on that with my Truthteller, and maybe the songs are just supposed to be between He and I for now.

This is a miracle to me, friends. And that's why I wanted to share it. God cannot be put into a neat little box, God meets us where we are and how we will best hear and learn and heal. God talks to me through art and songs and through nature. So that's where He took me . . . to beautiful, remote places where I could hear Him and hear myself and hear US, our conversations with each other.

I wanted to put this song/prayer and this road near the middle of this book because the second half of this book is about what happened when He took me away, and when I learned to take myself away, like the song says. And you just wouldn't be able to understand what happened next without hearing what I asked for, and what the answer was....

Here was my final verse..........just a little proclamation of where this took me.

And it's miraculous to me that this song was given to me in 2017, but I didn't hit the road until 2019. It took a while for me to be able to TAKE MYSELF AWAY.

Wide Open Eyes
I don't know what to say
I think I'm gonna be okay

I'll think and feel and hear
it all today
my open eyes will take me away

I'll take me
I'll take me away

I'll always come back
Come back to stay

But right now I'll take me away

Melody Ross

....

So, dear Soul Siblings,

Do you ever long to be taken away?

AND

How can you heal your eyes and ears and let that take you away to REAL LIVING?

Next, I can't wait to share with you The Road To The Mountaintop.

I love you. Thank you for being a safe place for me to share.
I hope you'll sing your songs too.

xo
melody freebird

24

The Road To The Mountaintop

Sometime in early 2020 I decided I wanted to climb 100 mountains. On Mountain #6, I fell down a 12 foot cliff and landed on an even higher cliff and just about fell to my death.

It started out innocently enough, I mean I was so experienced after climbing the first 5 mountains that I chose a really ambitious one for my 6th.

We had just gotten to St. George, Utah and everywhere you look there's another mountain. Kami had started taking me to some of her favorite places and Marq had been scouting out remote locations he wanted to see, mostly recommendations from his mountaineering and canyoneering friends. He loves to go places that aren't marked on regular maps.

The first mountain I climbed was about a 2 mile hike and at the top we ended up at a place called "The Vortex," an enormous hole that looks like it was carved with a giant Dremel at the top of the mountain. I mean, this hole is huge, as big as a house. The entire mountain is made of red sandstone and people from at least 100 years back have climbed up to the top, then down into the hole and carved their names in sidewalls.

I remember on this particular day, Marq and I woke up early to hike it. It was chilly in the morning but quickly got warm. It was sunny and gorgeous, the way St. George is in the winter.

And of course, Marq had packed my backpack for me. The 10 essentials, trail mix, water. I was just excited that my backpack matched my hiking boots. I had gained a lot of weight after we left Idaho, I'm sure my body was trying to protect me from all that was happening. I was not in the greatest physical shape. But I was determined.

So we climbed on a sandy trail that turned to slick rock for the first mile or so, and then we started climbing up toward the top. It was exhilarating the way new experiences are. I couldn't stop smiling.

In St. George, you'll find red mountains, white mountains, black mountains and brown mountains. Often all in the same place. I don't know what exactly happened there millions of years ago, but it was something spectacular and breathtaking. Volcanos left behind black cinder cone mountains and all sorts of rivers of black rock made from cooled lava. These rivers of rock run right through the middle of red iron rock formations and white sandstone hills. Petrified sand dunes and enormous monuments of rock outcroppings.

My heart just beat faster and faster every time we'd turn another corner and see how these combinations manifested into magnificence. Cactus grew through cracks, water would be settling in surprising places. Somehow plants were able to grow flowers in the harsh desert environment.

Within days of being in this magnificent place, I was madly in love. And after climbing up that first mountain. I was addicted.

Just beyond the site of The Vortex at the top of that mountain were 3 big humps…like little mountains on top of the top of the mountain. I ran over and tried to climb the highest one, and I did it. I was able to do it because of my cute matching hiking boots, they gave me climbing superpowers.

Marq kept saying… "Be careful! The sandstone is not like the granite mountains in Idaho! It's slippery and it can break off!"

But I made it to the top and that's when I knew I wanted to do this at least 99 more times. I was going to climb 100 mountains.

I stood on the top of that first little hump and I yelled over to Marq…

50 Roads To The Middle Of My Life

"TAKE MY PICTURE!" And I put my index finger high in the air to make a NUMBER ONE.

Something you need to know is that while this was my first mountain, this was probably Marq's 1000th mountain. And if you asked him, he'd probably say it was a walk and not a hike, and a hill and not a mountain. But for me, this was my Mount Everest.

We actually went back to the house (we were "visiting" West and Kami at their St. George house) and we asked them if they wanted to come back and hike it with us. So we actually climbed that mountain twice that day. And on thet second hike, the sun was setting and after we got back up to the Vortex, we looked over and saw something we'd never seen before, a huge city of cairns up at the top of another mountain. I think I cried when I first saw it . . . it was so magnificent to me to see an art installation up there in the middle of nowhere. I don't know who did or how long it took, but it was the beginning of my quest to find magical things in the middle of nowhere that would extend into the remaking of my life.

So that was Mountain #1. And the second time we climbed it, when Marq and West climbed down into The Vortex, I asked Kami if she wanted to climb 99 more mountains with me. And she said YES.

So Mountains 2, 3, 4 and 5 . . . I climbed with Kami. We had such a blast and she took me to some spectacular places. On #5, The White Rocks of Snow Canyon, I saw the one I wanted to do for #6. Marq and West had been on a multi-day horse ride and when they got back, I asked Marq if he would take me to this mountainI wanted to climb.

We got our backpacks and drove back to Snow Canyon. By now of course, I was an expert. I took him down the same trail that Kami had taken me on the day before, I showed him the mountain we had climbed and then I turned the other direction and pointed to the one I wanted to climb that day. I think it was about 4:00 in the afternoon when we started.

He looked at the mountain and then he looked at me. He walked closer toward it, looking for a trail and then he said "Babe, there's no trail, I don't know if you're ready for this."

Okay, for me, those are fighting words. No one tells me I'm not ready. No one tells me I can't do something.

So I said, "Can we just walk over and see?"

So we trudged through cactus and rocks to the base of that mountain and it was STEEP. It was mostly made of boulders of all sizes, and there were big cracks that sort of looked like trails. I said…"Can I just try?"

And he reluctantly said he'd follow behind me, because I needed to make my own route that I felt like I could handle.

So I started climbing up those boulders and through those cracks and he was genuinely impressed. It felt really good to impress him. He's a certified rock climbing instructor, a canyoneering instructor and a record-breaking repelling guy, among other mountaineering things I can't remember.

So, impressing him was pretty awesome. And I was getting over-confident.

He was right behind me and he would wait and see where I would put my hands to climb up. A few times he would say, "Why don't you try that hole right there instead, that's a better hand hold," but almost always he kept saying, "that's the route I would have chosen, you have good instincts."

He also said several times, "I don't think I would have done this one without climbing gear." and a few of the routes I wanted to take, he just flat refused and said "We can't do that one without being harnessed and roped up, it's just too dangerous."

So I'd pick a different route. Man, I felt like a badass though.

I was falling in love with this kind of hiking because it was THE ONE THING in my life that made me forget every other thing. When you're hiking in the desert you've got to be so present. You have to watch exactly where your feet and hands go next or you'll get poked by a cactus or slip on the myriad incredible pebbles and rocks and sand that are everywhere. I had never experienced this kind of peace in my mind, where I was only thinking about ONE THING instead of millions of thoughts swirling through my brain.

I was learning why Marq did this as often as he could. Especially after his brain injury recovery. It was the thing that brought him peace and calmed his brain down. He'd taken our boys to so many hundreds of places and always invited me, but I was always too busy. After I climbed the first few mountains, I started to understand why he never took photos. I always asked when they got home from trips if there were any photos to look at. My boys would show me a few, but very rarely did Marq take any photos. When I'd ask why, he'd say, "You'd just have to be there to understand."

After having the full sensory experience of being on the top of a mountain that you'd climbed with your own two legs, I understood. There is NO WAY a photo could ever adequately capture that experience. Trying to do it is almost disrespectful.

Being present to all of it without feeling like you have to memorialize it is its own beautiful gift.

So when we got to the top of that mountain, tears just streamed down my face at the view. There is something so unexplainable about being at the top of a place and seeing life from up there. I could see the entire Canyon, which is actually a state park and I could see the city of St. George beyond that, as well as a few other surrounding towns. I could see all of that but none of it could see me. There is nothing in the world like being so small on something so big that you disappear in its majesty. It was the ultimate disappearing act, yet I felt part of that mountain at the same time.

I climbed to the highest point and Marq took a picture of me holding up 6 fingers. We ate some celebratory trail mix, drank some water and then he said we better head back down because the sun was starting to set.

So again, he let me pick the route. I decided to go down a different way than we came up, almost on the other side of the mountain.

I made it about 20 or 30 feet down when we got to a cliff. I looked up at him to see what he was thinking and he was looking all around at the natural resources we had to draw from to get down safely.

I spotted a rock column that extended almost to the bottom of the 12 foot cliff and I said. "what if I just hold on to this and shimmy down it?" and he said "that's exactly what I was thinking…"

Melody Ross

It was about half the width of my body and made of grippy sandstone so I could easily grasp it.

I wrapped my arms around it and started to sort of slide and shimmy down it and then suddenly I felt it separating from the rest of the mountain and I was falling backward down that cliff.

Everything went into slow motion at that point and I could hear Marq yelling, "MELLY!!!!" I could see this rock column that was once part of the mountain was now a boulder. I felt myself falling, falling, falling and then I hit the ground.

I looked up, breathless, and Marq was scrambling down behind me, making his way to me.

I looked down at my leg because suddenly it felt hot and burning. I saw that it was bleeding profusely and I was trying to catch my breath from having the wind knocked out of me. I saw the blood, I saw Marq and then I looked the other direction and saw that I'd landed on another cliff. I also realized how high up we were and how much further we had to go and that it was starting to get dark. All of this overwhelmed me and I passed out.

Everything just got very black.

Marq had just made it down to me right when I started to fall over from passing out and he grabbed me — just in time before I fell down the second cliff.

I woke up and he was so calm. He's trained in this kind of stuff. But he said . . . "you've got a stick stuck in your leg at least an inch, and you're bleeding pretty bad. You need to lay down for a bit, I don't know if we will be able to get back down."

So he made me a little pillow and bed with our backpacks and he gave me some water and he started trying to figure out how we were going to get down. He found a little cave and asked me to climb over and crawl into it so that I had shelter while he climbed down to get help.

I sat in the cave for 20 or 30 minutes with him until I had my bearings and then I said "I think I can do it, I think I can climb down."

He said "Babe, you have a stick in your leg and we can't pull it out because it will just bleed too much. If you climb down, you have to do it with this stick in your leg."

I said "I think I can do it."

So we started the climb down, and I led the way. There were a few spots where I had to do full-on ninja moves to get across deep cracks in the rocks and steep parts of the mountain. But I did it. And he was so encouraging and so impressed. He let me figure it out and he helped me when needed, but I did it.

Once we got to the bottom, and back to the trail that took us to our truck, he started telling me what we were going to have to do next. He said he might be able to clean out that wound, but we were probably going to have to go to the hospital. I said "can you just try to do it so I don't have to go to the hospital?"

We got back to West and Kami's place, where we had the whole upstairs to ourselves and we went in the bathroom and I put my leg in the shower and Marq ran water over it and then took his Leatherman tool, opened the pliers and pulled out the stick. Turns out, it was an enormous thorn. And I had another wound right next to it. When the stick was out, it looked like I'd been bit by a giant snake with those two holes in my leg.

Then he got a syringe of some sort and told me he had to irrigate the wound because it was at least an inch deep. He first pushed water into it and then alcohol. It was excruciatingly painful. But I felt like such a ba-dass.

The look of pride and awe on his face that night did it for me. I was addicted. I was gonna climb every mountain.

But that night I also started learning respect for nature. Respect for things we are not quite ready for. Respect for things that are "no respecter of persons" that will allow you to learn from the natural consequences of your lack of understanding for what is possible in nature.

When I laid in bed that night, I started thinking about all the times I'd decided I wanted to do something gargantuan and incredible in my life. A big art project or event or whatever. I thought about all the times I'd put myself and others in harm's way that I didn't even know existed because I just wanted to get to the top of that mountain.

I knew I was about to learn some enormous lessons on this quest to climb 100 mountains, and I did. Never have I learned so well and rapidly, the way life works, than what happened over that year of mountain climbs.

I learned just as much in the lowest places as the highest places.

So, Adventurous Soul,

When have you "climbed a mountain" that you weren't well-equipped for?

AND

What happened when you fell?

Next I will take you on The Road to the Lowest Place and we will learn together how different and the same the gifts are at the top and the bottom.

I love you.
melody freebird

25

The Road To
The Lowest Place

As I mentioned on the last road, there are some things you can only see if you climb up high enough for the view.

The same is true for the things in the lowest places. There are some things you can only see if you are willing to go down instead of up. There are things you can only experience in the lowest places.

It's become stupefying to me how much we, as a culture, seem to always think that more is better than less. Or that higher is better than lower. Or that bright light is better than darkness. Or even that health is better than sickness or death is better than life.

My feelings about these old beliefs have changed so much. There are so many gifts in less. There are so many gifts in the lowest places. There are so many gifts in the darkness. There are so many gifts in both sickness and death.

And whether or not a person ever gets to a place of embracing the other side of delight — these things are always going to be a part of life.

In fact, I have been trying to train myself to stop saying "I just want to do the best thing." Instead, now I say to myself, "I just want to do the next good thing." Then I don't have to chase around making judgements about things I don't understand yet. We miss out on so many incredible experiences in life when we are always trying to find the best thing. What I know down to the marrow of my bones is that every good choice we make might not look like the best choice, but every every EVERY choice we make can turn out for the best. Every single one. Life is just magical like that.

On The Road to the Lowest Place, I learned that what I interpreted as a punishment, or unjust results, or just flat-out crummy actually ended up turning out for the "best."

A few years ago, several of my artist friends and I traveled to Ghost Ranch in New Mexico, where we got to teach for a week on the same property where Georgia O'Keeffe lived and painted. It was my 3rd year teaching there, and this time, I got to teach with my friend, Pixie.

We taught a self-portrait class together where everyone was assigned to paint themselves as something from nature that felt like who they are. After much deliberation, I painted myself as a river. It felt so true, it still does.

But when we went around the circle and explained why we chose what we chose, something came out of my mouth that I had never said, that I didn't even know until I said it — that I chose a river because it's never the same, it's always flowing, and it always flows to the lowest place.

I am certain I looked puzzled after I said that. Because I was.

I went back to my room and really thought about it and then I started to cry a little. I said to my Truthteller.....WHY DO I ALWAYS END UP IN THE LOWEST PLACE? And I started to have a little pity party, like I do.

Until I got schooled.

I sat and had this conversation with the sky for a long time, and as I would talk, I would also listen.......and here's what I got told....

That it's actually wonderful to be a river because you get to experience everything and be just about everywhere. Top to bottom. Top to bottom. Top to bottom. You aren't always in the lowest place, you just end up there and it's actually exactly where you're supposed to be. Sacred things happen in the lowest places...in the trenches of life.

But where did the water originate from? A mountain river used to be a high mountain lake, which used to be cloud. So if you're a river, you started at the highest place and then flowed down…and all the way down you watered everything in your path, and in the end, you brought the water where it was most needed — to the lowest place.

I love water. I love rivers. I love lakes. I love the ocean. I love the faucet. I even love puddles.

But I am a river.

There was a time when everything felt so dead and dying in my life, much the way the whole world feels right now. Sometime in the last 10 years, I wrote this poem about what it felt like to see a dead and dried out field of flowers that once used to be so beautiful and vibrant. That's what my life felt like. That's what I felt like inside. I desperately needed to know that something was going to stay alive no matter how horrible the conditions.

Then I had a vision of a green place…far far far away, and it was green because of the water that flowed there through the dried out death.

In Spite of Everything

I see something green so far away
Out the window I look at death and pray

I need to see there's something still alive
In spite of everything, it has survived

Flowers used to cover up this place
Flowers everywhere, they fell from grace

I need to see there's something still alive
In spite of everything, it can survive

I hear water trickling down the stream
Running to the lowest place, it seems

I need to know there's something still alive

187

Melody Ross

In spite of everything it has survived

Plant the seeds and hope that they will grow
There really isn't any way to know

People tell you nothing can survive
People tell you love won't stay alive

I need to know that good things are alive
In spite of everything they can survive

We'll plant more seeds and ache for them to grow
Something in this seed already knows

Art we the ones to keep it all alive?
In spite of everything, we will survive

We journeyed here to see with our eyes
They swore it was dead…but here it is alive

Well be the ones who keep it all alive
In spite of everything….
In spite of every single thing…
In spite of everything….
We will survive

In spite of everything
We are alive.

I found myself in my lowest place after I realized I was disassociating from myself and leaving myself there in the lowest place to try to be in the highest place. I left myself there, so I had to go and find myself there.

And guess what? When I let myself flow down down down down down the mountain of all that I had worked so hard to achieve, I ended up where the water was. I ended up where my parched soul could drink and drink and drink from truth. It just kept flowing.

It can feel so painful and unfair when you worked so hard to get up high and suddenly you are being carried by some strong force, stronger than you are, down down down down. But the pain comes largely because of the perspective. What if it's the best thing that could ever be happening? What if being up high was good and being down low is good too? What if all of it is good?

I'm learning to trust where the river goes. And then I have to remind myself that the river is continuously flowing all the way from way up top, to all the way to the bottom. Simultaneously. Sometimes I am the water that is flowing and sometimes I am the thing that is floating on top of it that makes me believe I am at the mercy of where it takes me. When I forget that I am the river and not the paper boat, I suffer.

You are a river too.

So, Ever-Flowing Soul

What does it feel like for you to be in the lowest places?

AND

Where did you start? Where did you flow from to get there?

I love you and I love doing life next to you, and with you. I hope that when you're flowing to the lowest place, you can see and feel the gifts in it.

Next, we will go down The Road That Forked Wildly.

I will see you there.

Drink from the river of truth, okay?

I love you.
melody freebird

189

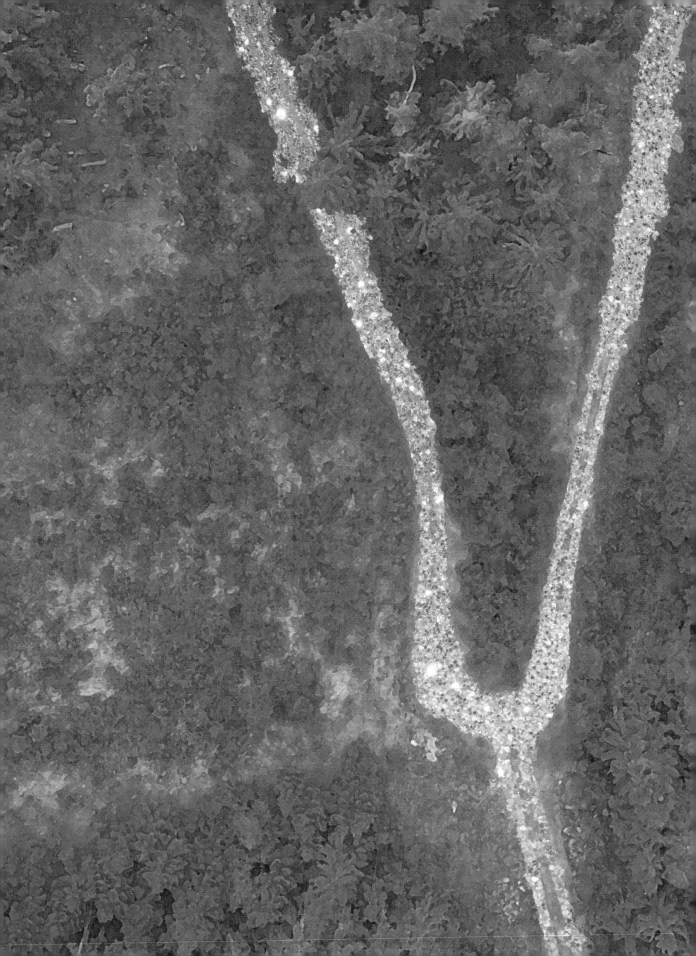

26

The Road That Forked Wildly

Making choices is one of the most gutsy, brave things you will ever do, and not everyone is up to the task or up to the consequences. When you reach a fork in the road, all you have left in that moment is choices. You can choose to choose or you can choose to do nothing.

And all of it has a consequence, or lots of consequences.

This is a bumpy, gravely road. One that gives you road rash from time to time because when you're brave enough to make choices, you're going to fall on your face every once in a while, it's guaranteed.

I used to want other people to make my decisions for me. For lots of reasons. But I got dragged behind a truck so many times because of my decision to not decide for myself that I just don't do that anymore.

I decide to decide. I choose to choose. And sometimes I wish I would have chosen differently, so I choose to choose again. FOR MYSELF.

I try not to even ask for opinions anymore. I have found that the freedom I have been so desperately seeking requires me not just to make all of my own decisions, but to OWN the decisions I make once I make them.

And all of the consequences that come with them.

You can gather up every good and wonderful thing in the world and feel totally safe and secure. You can do all the "right" things. But there's always going to come a time when you're traveling down a calm and predictable road that's headed in the exact direction you want to be headed, and then suddenly it hits what seems like a dead end —but it's actually a fork in the road.

What was once one predictable road is suddenly two, or three, or four . . . and you have to choose which one you will take.

A dead end would actually be easier, I think.

This is a defining moment, my friends. At least it has been for me. And for nearly 50 years, I've witnessed a pretty consistent pattern in both myself and other humans concerning what happens at these forks in the road.

Human beings, when faced with choices that must be made, will either freeze and do nothing, submit to someone else to make the choice, or put on their big-kid undies and make the dang choice for themselves, come what may.

I realized on this road that there's something repulsive I've done in the past — and in just the last few years this realization has stared me blank in the face without blinking. It's this: I don't want to decide, so I let others decide. And then I feel either really disappointed or really frustrated at the consequences of the decision made.

What a mess, and what a cop-out.

I've also been on the flip side of that situation — where someone wouldn't make the choice that needed to be made, so I had to make it. Then sometimes the consequences were dire and suddenly I was in the hot seat for making a choice that others didn't like — even though they weren't willing to make a decision at all.

These days, I am dedicated to doing all I can to make sure neither of those scenarios ever happen again in my realm. This is a tough commitment to make because when you have to make your own decisions, life can really kick your bootie. When you own your decisions, you've got to also own the consequences.

And that, my friends, is one of the great lessons of adulthood and one of the great skills of becoming a person of integrity and wisdom . . . when you don't try to find a fall-guy for the decisions you make or the way you behave or how your life has turned out, everything changes for the better.

Making decisions is essentially putting yourself on the line. So most people try to avoid it at all costs. It's just too risky, too uncomfortable and there's too much accountability required.

When you choose to do things that require putting yourself on the line, you're also going to be responsible for whatever happens next. When other people do things that end up putting you out on the line, you're gonna be the one who is responsible for the choices you make next. And the choices that you make after that. And after that. And ALL OF THE CONSEQUENCES that come from those choices.

Lots of people put themselves in positions where they either don't have to make choices, or where they are hidden from the consequences of their choices and instead put someone else in the line of fire to live the consequences of those choices.

The most destructive consequences come from people who are in positions they accepted and chose, positions of leadership and accountability, yet they do all they can to make sure they are never responsible for any of the decisions that get made. And when poor decisions are made, they search endlessly for the fall-guy and let them fall on their sword.

That is the opposite of badass.

I learned this on The Road That Forked Wildly. And I learned it in ways that left me with road rash so severe that I'm still picking gravel out of my elbows.

It's human nature to point your finger outward when you've made a choice that didn't turn out in the most advantageous or beautiful way. Lots of times our choices end up with inopportune and ugly consequences. Sometimes even devastating consequences, but if you're gonna be a badass, you better own the choices you've made. Or haven't made.

I've handled this both ways, unfortunately — with my finger pointed outward and with my finger pointed right at my own self. It always feels more honest and powerful to point the finger back at yourself when you're the one who made the decision. Or didn't make the decision.

Because bottom line — it's becoming more and more rare for people to own up to what has happened in their life and the role they played in it. It's becoming more and more rare for people to take responsibility for their choices and own up to them. When someone does own a poor decision, I don't even look at the poor consequences of unfortunate choices, I just give them a standing ovation for owning up to it.

I want to be that kind of badass person.

Because sometimes you have a whole bunch of wonderful things to choose from, and the worst thing that can happen is that you wish later that you would have chosen one wonderful thing over another.

And then sometimes all you are left with is a whole bunch of really awful things to choose from, and all you can hope for is that you'll choose the decision that is least awful.

And there will be opinions, oh so many opinions. Both as you're making the decision and after you've made the decision.

What I have learned on this road of owning my own decisions is that if you are indeed going to be brave enough to make and own your own decisions, it's critically necessary to go on an opinion fast. Because unless someone is going to be sharing the responsibility of the consequences of the decisions that must be made — it's not only useless to ask for their opinion, it's actually dangerous.

I hope to NEVER EVER EVER EVER again put the future of my life in the hands of another person who will never have to live the consequences of what must be decided.

I will sail my own ship, I will be my own captain.

I will live the hard consequences when I wish I would have chosen differently and I will live the beautiful consequences when I've had the courage to make decisions that yield beautiful results.

Going on an opinion fast was one of the scariest things I ever did. It was essentially breaking a very relentless addiction.

But you can't really own your decisions unless you're the one who made them.

What I learned on this road is that I was the one scaring myself. I was the one making it scary. When I realized I can pivot anytime I want, I learned the power of deciding.

Because **NOT DECIDING** is often the most destructive choice of all. If you're at a fork in the road and you just decide to build a house right there in front of that fork, in this place that you really don't want to be — just so that you don't have to decide which road to take — you just imprisoned yourself.

We have to keep moving forward, and that requires making decisions. We are all going to make decisions we wish we would have made differently. So then, we decide again. You just have to keep deciding and moving into that decision and then deciding again and moving into that decision. Over and over and over.

And own all of it, it makes the next decision easier when you own the last one. And for heaven's sake, please stop asking everyone what you should do next. ASK YOURSELF. AND THEN ANSWER YOURSELF. AND THEN OWN THE ANSWER.

Did you ever see the video of the little boy who thought he was drowning? He was holding on to a bar and his legs were floating in front of him and he couldn't get his footing…he just kept crying in distress and kicking his legs in the water in front of him. Then a loving person came and just moved his legs down and he realized the water wasn't even deep, that he could stand in it easily.

That's what it feels like when you stop asking for opinions as you're making decisions and start owning every decision you make. Your feet get put underneath you and you realize you're totally okay, you can totally stand on your own two feet and nothing is there drowning you after all, you just thought it was.

I had a severe case of fork phobia, but on this road, I learned to embrace and APPRECIATE the myriad choices we all are able to enjoy. I learned to expect that the more decisions I made, the more risks I was taking. And the more risks you take, the more odds are that you'll both love some of the decisions you make and you'll learn from the ones that you wish you wouldn't have made.

And if there were a book called "1000 Things Not To Do," it would be every bit as valuable as the book called "1000 Things TO DO That Guarantee Success." But there's not a manual like that for the whole human family, because all of our lives are way too different. So we have to write that book ourselves. That means you've got to make at least 2000 decisions that either yield "TO DO" or "NOT TO DO."

It's all valuable. All of it. So get to it. Be brave. Keep deciding FOR YOURSELF. Don't ever give that responsibility to someone else. Unless you love road rash.

So, Beautiful Soul,

When have you been so afraid to decide that you either didn't decide or you let someone else decide?

AND

What have you learned from making your own decisions?

I loved walking this road with you. Thank you for deciding to walk it with me. Next we will set off on The Road I Didn't Take.

I love you.
Be brave and make the choice. Just do it.
xoxo
melody freebird

27

The Road
I Didn't Take

Regrets suck. They just do. And when I say this, what I mean is that they
suck the life out of you.

I wonder if there have ever been as many choices in life available as there
are now? When I think about that, of course there have always been myriad choices since the beginning of this earth, but have they all ever been
blaring right in your face all at once the way they are now?

It's hard to imagine more information all screaming at us at once than
there is at this time in history.

So let's keep that in mind as we walk this road about the roads not taken.

Sometime in the last 10 years I had an idea to make words out of fabric
trims and fabric scraps and as I sat down and sketched out what words I
would choose to "write" with fabric, I wrote the words I most needed to
hear; that what I do is never going to matter more than who I am becoming. Because I was addicted to doing, and it was killing me.

I just pulled this piece of art out of the trailer where it is stored and hung
it in the "kitchen" of my studio where I have been working the last few
winters. These words have never meant more to me than they do today.

When we think of the roads we've taken or haven't taken, it is so important to remember we can learn, grow and become on just about any road.
No road is wasted. No experience is wasted. And what we do really IS
NEVER going to be more important than learning, growing and becoming — neither is the road we do it on.

With that in mind, it's often still hard to be standing on the road I'm on
and look around at all the other roads that I could have taken. And to be
honest in knowing that I am at least halfway through my life and there are
some roads I will never have time to explore and experience. There are
just too many roads to choose from.

Did I make the "best" choices?

I have a problem these days with the word "best," as I mentioned on the
last road. I believe there are countless good roads that always have the
opportunity to work out for the best. Always. No matter what road it is.
We get stuck when we keep waiting for a "best" road. YOU ARE THE
ELEMENT that makes a road the best road for you. YOU ARE THE
COMMON DENOMINATOR on every good road you can remember.

YOU WILL CONTINUE TO BE on every road you take. So you don't
have to worry that the best thing is on some road you're looking for. Look
in the mirror, the best thing is YOU. And as long as you take yourself on
your own journeys and don't leave yourself behind, every good road will
be your best road. Your best road is not hiding from you, waiting for you to
find it. Your best road is the one you firmly plant your feet on and decide
to grow on.

The biggest risk when this realization is made is that we spend WAY TOO
MUCH TIME lamenting over roads that felt like a colossal waste of time,
and we get bitter for time "lost" that could have been spent on a road we
could have experienced had we chosen "better." This is a risk because it
steals life from TODAY. And life is a terrible thing to waste on things we
have absolutely no influence over, and never will. The past is one of those
things. Yet, we give so so so much of our most precious resources to something that doesn't even exist anymore.

Here's what I've learned from observing The Road I Didn't Take, and
that's truly all we can do — observe it. Which means we can't ever truly

know what those roads we didn't take even are. We can only make up stories about what they are, because we are observing only the outside layer.

Anyway, what I am learning from "observing" these roads is that the only thing useful about spending any time thinking, feeling, wishing or wondering about these roads — is to mine the wisdom from the observation. But to be very very careful with that too. Because "time" is always moving and we can fail to remember that we know more now than we did then. We can punish ourselves in very unfair ways if we tell ourselves the story that we have always known as much as we know now.

Please don't spend any time assuming you know everything about something just because you are observing it. It's really such a waste of your life. BE ON THE ROAD YOU ARE ON NOW — even as your feet are taking the long walk OFF of a road you're ready to be done with. BE ON THAT ROAD while you're on it. Mine the wisdom and experiences from it, because you're never going to be able to do more than observe it and tell yourself stories about it once you're off the road you're on now.

So what about the roads we don't take? Why didn't we take them?

Maybe it was too scary.
Maybe we procrastinated for too long that the opportunity is gone now.
Maybe we allowed ourselves to get tricked and coerced onto other roads.
Maybe we got there too early and it wasn't open yet, so we moved on.
And then when we circled back, it was too late.
Maybe we gave up too soon.
Maybe another road was a lot longer than we thought it would be, and it took years to get off of it, and now we can't even find the road we thought we wanted to take before all of that happened.

I could go on for days writing "maybes."

And unless it's to mine the wisdom from all of it, it's a pretty destructive way to invest the time of this day and this road and this moment. Regret is a particularly violent form of punishment if you let it go past the wisdom-mining stages.

Here's what I wish for us, that we can learn from every road and then let that road go. Let it go so you can go. Give yourself a head start on the next road by untying yourself from the last road once you've mined the wisdom.

Only look back to be grateful.

Because there are roads that have expiration dates, too. There are roads that may have felt so right and we still didn't take them, so now the memory of those roads ARE TAKING FROM US. There may have been a tiny little window in "time" when a road would have been a perfect match for us. And then not only did the window close, but the road went away. We can REALLY tell ourselves tragic stories about those kinds of roads. And how could the story ever be right? We have no idea what would have happened had we chosen that road at that time. We really don't even have any idea if that road even existed in the way we thought it did. It could have been another story that we told ourselves.

I put TIME in parentheses because time is tricky. We make up time and time feels different to everyone and it seems to stretch, expand and contract. It comes and goes and we give it WAY TOO MUCH CONTROL. Without sounding too cliche, I hope I can express the importance of understanding how THIS MOMENT IS REALLY ALL THAT MATTERS RIGHT NOW.

And that means THIS ROAD IS THE ROAD THAT MATTERS MOST RIGHT NOW.

Regrets and comparisons steal our ability to make the next decision, and none of us really have time to waste with that kind of nonsense, there are too many decisions to be made.

Staying or going. Holding on or letting go. Leaving it there or taking it with. Trying one more time or putting a stop to it.

Every day we have to choose between those things and more. And guess what? As long as we are making a "good" choice, a choice we are making with the heart, mind and soul all showing up as best they can — those choices will turn out for OUR BEST. Because it's about learning, growing and becoming. And having the grit to keep choosing new roads when old roads end is how we learn, grow and become.

50 Roads To The Middle Of My Life

Grit is a regret eliminator. The more you have the grit to try in life, the more you fall, but you also let feelings of regret go. The only regret you're really left with is that you didn't have more grit to try more things.

Regret, jealousy and comparison are the things smeared on a pair of dirty glasses that cloud every beautiful thing that's happening right now. No matter what road you're on right now, or that I'm on — there is ALWAYS so much beauty to be found. Even if the beauty we find is our own courage to keep going on crappy roads.

It's so tempting to call certain roads a big mistake. And sometimes we get 100 yards down a road and we know we would have chosen differently had we held more information. Sometimes it's a good decision in not-so-good company, making it look like a bad decision. Sometimes it's a crummy decision in good company, making it look like it was a better choice than it actually was.

There are a million ways of scrutiny to shame ourselves with. It's useless, though. MINE THE WISDOM AND CUT THE CHAIN THAT'S KEEPING YOU IN CAPTIVITY.

There may be a lot of redirecting to do but once you move into an all-consuming shame or bitterness or jealousy or regret, you've moved into making a lesson into a prison sentence.

Don't SHOULD on yourself, okay?

Wisdom comes from experience and sometimes the best experience comes from knowing you didn't take that road, but this one — and you own that decision, and you let it grow you. There are so many gifts of experience in that lesson.

As we all look at the roads we didn't take, let's let the road we are on right now grow us, because it's the only thing that CAN grow us in this moment.

So, Beautiful Traveler,

What roads that you ARE NOT ON are distracting you right now from the road you are on?

AND

What are the greatest gifts that came to you from NOT taking certain roads?

Thank you for observing this road with me. Next we will expand on this observation by experiencing as best we can The Road Sparkling Next To Mine.

I love you, I believe in you, and I know whatever road you're on right now is an opportune place for you to become more than you have ever been.

xo
melody freebird

28

The Road Sparkling Next To Mine

Jealousy is a beast. So is pity.

It's tough to walk next to someone who seems to have zero problems and plenty of fortune. It's tough to walk next to someone who has an abundance of problems and lots of needs, too.

Seems like we want to just walk next to those who make us feel comfortable in our existence and circumstance.

I have felt jealousy and envy plenty in my life, and it's never been a pleasant feeling. I have compared myself to my perception of someone else's life experience and told myself all sorts of stories. Again, it never led to pleasant feelings. Until I walked away from most of society for a while, I didn't realize how much I'd been comparing my life to just about everyone in my view.

I remember when Marq had his traumatic brain injury and all those long years of recovery, nearly a decade at its worst. There was a solid 5 years, maybe more, when I wouldn't go to weddings or any other events where couples were celebrated or invited. It was just too painful.

I remember not wanting to go much of anywhere at all after I'd gained 50+ pounds and I just looked like grief and sorrow embodied, because I was. I couldn't bear the way I felt when I saw happy and healthy people walking around without a care in the world.

I remember watching people on social media going on vacations, buying new cars and decorating their homes and I actually "snoozed" the worst offenders because I couldn't bear seeing their fortune when mine was out back in a burn barrel.

And I remember stalking Britney Spears when she melted down, trying to find every article I could find to prove that she was even worse off than I was. And then searching "movies about mental breakdowns" just so I could see someone else who made my breakdown look like a hangnail.

Comparing.
Comparing.
Comparing.

Things changed for me massively on this road once I was alone for months at a time and had to sit with myself. What I learned so permanently is how desperately I wanted people to see me beyond my outside layer. There were questions I desperately wanted to answer that no one ever asked, and there were questions I was sick of answering that were so irrelevant to who I am. I wanted people to see past the clothes and the success or failure and the neighborhood and the job and the relationships.

I wanted people to see WHO I ACTUALLY AM.

And then when I started to emerge back into society, back with people in our human family, it was one of the first stark realizations I made as I stood eyeball to eyeball with other souls.

They all just wanted to be seen AS WHO THEY ACTUALLY ARE.

Here's something I've noticed a lot over the years — people's eyes light up in a way that cannot be faked when they talk about things that matter to them. And often, the things that matter to them are hiding so covertly in the plain sight of ordinary life that we never even talk about it.

But when you find that vein of gold in someone, and you can get them to start really talking about it, their whole inner solar system aligns so perfectly that the sunshine in their eyes will light up the darkest place.

It is so beautiful. AND — it is the antidote for comparison, envy and jealousy.

The best thing we can do for each other is bring out the sparkle in each other's eyes without assuming we know what will bring it. Without making judgments about what SHOULD put the sparkle in each other's eyes. I've found that the best way to do this is to first realize that every human we meet is an opportunity to feel extraordinary AWE. If we just ask the right questions, and then we listen, and then we feel what that kind of listening feels like. If you ask the right questions with the right intentions, and you wait in a way that helps another to feel safe — you will be met with a feeling of extraordinary awe at what happens next.

What do you wish for when you're blowing out your birthday candles?
What still hurts after all these years?
What costume would you have made for you if an epic tailor wanted to craft the most epic costume of all time for you?
What do you wish you knew for sure?

Ask. And then listen. And then feel.

Listening without interrupting is stoking the fire, igniting the light, making it bigger, repeating it back…letting them really talk through what they're excited about. Feeling their words bounce into your heart and ricochet back to them with your undivided attention. Holding eye contact is like billows on that beautiful soul fire.

Tell me more about that.
What's your favorite part?
What's the hardest part?
What do you wish you knew more about?
What would you love to turn this into?
Do you know how incredible you are?

Let them talk until the light is coaxed back into their eyes. That bright light melts away every chocolate-covered layer of narrative you were jealous of, envious of or felt pity for. All of that comparison is a pile of fondue on the floor.

And now you're just soul to soul. And it's AWE.

Ask. Listen. Be genuinely interested. Let every answer weave into the next question. Let every question open the room-darkening shades that have covered their life and yours. Ask and listen until the window of their soul is so clear and open that both of you can see for miles. You'll see it in their eyes.

And by the time we are done with the conversation, the sparkle will be back in your eyes too.

When I remember to do this, my heart swells and all I want is to keep stoking that fire. Any hint of jealousy is suddenly gone. We are both just lit up. We are stoking the same fire at that point, rather than comparing fires or looking at each other's fire longingly. The fire is inside my heart and their heart and in all the spaces between us.

That is awe.

Doesn't that sound so much better than silent comparison, silent jealousy, silent pity and very loud inner dialogue that leads nowhere good?

Bringing out the light in another's eyes will burn away the stories that made you feel divided. Their light will merge with your light and — wow. AWE.

Awe, from my perspective, is a mixed state of gratitude, curiosity, wonder and humility. What if we made it a habit to approach others in that mixed state? What if each road sparkling next to our own was an opportunity to experience awe, and to make sure we do all we can to make it a shared experience?

Of course, we can't MAKE someone else feel awe, but there is a whole lot we can do to help someone to feel seen, heard and valued. And the magic of it is that those are shared experiences by their very virtue. We are the ones who get to SEE and HEAR and APPRECIATE.

What is the downside? I fail to see one.

When I felt my life consumed by the addictive habit of comparing, I knew I had to make some changes.

I decided to start by seeing, hearing and valuing my own experience. But not spending much time there — because too much time spent thinking about our own experience is almost always the first culprit leading to comparison. And that leads to the addictive inner-drug of either feeling envy or feeling pity. Both of these feelings create chemical reactions in our body that can be very addictive. And both of these feelings cause us to feel "other than." Othering causes separation. Separation causes horrific loneliness. And loneliness leads to despair. And despair leads to a kind of soul death that tricks us into thinking it's too hard to recover.

And it all started with spending too much time thinking about our own experience — rather than seeking out the AWE in the shared experience of finding AWE in both others and in ourselves.

It's simple to fix. But not always easy. Just like with you, there are things people wish others knew about them; rather than the way they get pigeon-holed. Be the one who finds out what those things are.

I bet other people wish someone would ask them what book section they'd go to first if they were at the library right now rather than some empty question about their outside layer. People long to be truly known.

They want to be seen as who they are behind the things society teaches us all to hide behind. When we keep trying to put up facades to protect ourselves by impressing others or scaring others, we miss out on each other. We miss out on AWE.

I wish we could stop comparing and start truly seeing each other.

It will never be a fair comparison, no matter which 2 or more people you're lining up in a row. There is so much we can't know. There is so much behind everything. There is so much that cannot be seen. There is so much that cannot be heard. There is so much to learn about each other and that is a far better goal than trying to pick each other apart in order to feel better or worse. We use each other to numb our own feelings. No one wants to be used, only to be known and valued for what and who they actually are.

Find the rare things, the unique things, the things that are not obvious. Find them in others and then find them in yourself, and you'll have no need to compare, because it's useless and it's throwing away a magnificent opportunity to feel WHAT IS REAL in each other's presence.

We can focus on bringing out the light in each other's eyes by finding little starlight glimpses of what's REALLY inside of a person. And suddenly, the darkness of this world becomes a starlit sky.

It works. Try it.

I have learned on ALL The Roads Sparkling Next to Mine that when we walk next to each other in all of our glory and all of our pain, each of us feels profound gratitude, purpose and determination to not just stay on our own roads, but to MAKE THE VERY MOST of every step we take.

And we never again want to be on the road of another, only our own.

So, Gorgeous Soul,

When have YOU longed to be on the road sparkling next to yours, rather than your own?

AND

What questions can you ask to coax the light back into the eyes of someone you've been comparing yourself to?

I love you, fellow soul. Thank you for walking this road with me and putting the light back into MY EYES. I hope for the opportunity to do the same for you.

Next, we will carefully step over to The Road I Walked With Monsters

Just be you. Let them be them. It's all perfect.
xo
melody freebird

29

The Road I Walked With Monsters

I have known some monsters, let me tell you.

And I used to think they were real.

My biggest monsters have been big old bullies. And I have never quite known what to do with bullies, or about them. It's been a struggle for most of the years of my life that I thought would go away as I got older. This road I've walked with monsters has taught me that even after I was a powerless child, I was still essentially feeding my monsters a very balanced diet that kept them alive and well.

Yes, I was actually giving power, energy and life-force to my monsters & bullies.
I was the one keeping them alive.

I know the path of the bully quite well, because the most heinous one was living right in my head, taunting me day and night. Shouting or whispering, whichever was most effective at the time. They both have their uses.

I almost always shrunk in terror and did whatever I had to do to keep the bullies from getting even meaner and scarier.

But then the reckoning came. With all the bullies in my head, I suppose my soul was ready to get this figured out once and for all in my thirties and forties— and my very soul led me right to the master class of overcoming this old habit of feeding the monsters that vexed me — by giving me the opportunity to learn from some of the meanest people I could ever imagine. Adult bullies.

Thank you, life teachers. Thank you, thank you, thank you.

This can be such a triggering topic for people, so I want you to know that this is going somewhere very good and you'll be glad you read it, even if you are cringing right now.

I also want to tell you that I know bullying is typically a trauma response. I understand this and I wish no one ever had to be traumatized, especially children. A bully is usually someone who has been mercilessly bullied themselves in some way. It's typically someone who feels powerless in the world so they medicate themselves by trying to dominate and crush the spirit of others. It starts in childhood and you hope it will go away, but adult bullies are even more brutal in my experience. I send them love and healing, and I also get to talk about what it's like to be bullied by them.

In my half a century of being alive, I've noticed something about we human beings — we all have to find ways to expel the energy inside that comes from big feelings, especially scary ones. The monsters. And, what I've noticed is that people either lash outward or lash inward.

What is unfortunate about this fact is that it often becomes 2 toxic puzzle pieces that fit perfectly and make a pretty destructive picture once they are put together. The ones who find temporary relief in lashing outward somehow find the ones who have a habit of lashing inward.

People who lash inward are already bullying themselves so much on the inside that when a flesh and bone bully comes along to lash out at them, the lashing is exponentially damaging.

It's a vicious dance. And I suspect that a bully doesn't love how they feel after they've self-medicated their powerlessness through fear, intimidation, insults, accusations, taunting and domination. This is just a losing game for everyone all together.

50 Roads To The Middle Of My Life

Now let's get to the part where this road became one of the greatest blessings of my life . . .

I had a dream one night during a time when I was smack in the middle of dealing with someone I didn't know how to deal with. A bully, a lasher-outer. It was affecting my health, my creativity, my relationships, my sleep, everything. I was also keeping it a giant secret from people in my life who could have helped me.

Well, in this dream, I was walking down a road that was lined with monsters. The monsters were moving their arms and heads and bodies in creepy ways that were very intimidating. It was foggy and scary. But I had to keep going even though I was terrified.

As I got closer to the monsters, I saw what they actually were.

They were those blow-up dancing guys that often get installed in front of car dealerships. The ones that are made of a big tube of fabric for the body and head, and 2 more tubes of fabric coming out the sides to make the arms.

And what was giving them life was air being compressed into them.

So . . . I was giving my entire life over to a bunch of blow-up dancing guys that weren't even real. This realization was both hilarious and horrific.

In the dream, I saw the big extension cord that led to the air compressor that filled them up and made them do their scary dance, and I realized I had the power to unplug those cords.

And then I saw that the cord was actually plugged into ME. I was the power source.

I'm sure you see where I'm going here. That dream was a whopper, but it didn't immediately fix my problem — it just started to reveal it. I was a woman in my forties who had done so many powerful things, but I was utilizing a large portion of my energy and life-force blowing up a bunch of fake monsters.

And all I had to do all along was unplug them. Easier said than done, but pretty simple all the same.

I am probably someone else's blow-up dancing guy monster thing and I don't even know it. Life is like that. We get to play all sorts of teaching roles for each other and we are changed and strengthened either way. So much of what we think is real is simply an illusion, but it teaches us just as effectively as if it were real.

You can blow up your fears and inner bullying thoughts and make them so enormous, you can also do that with others who are bullies. They'll plug right into you because you are the electricity for their compressor.

It's a bad match, someone addicted to hurting others and someone addicted to being hurt. And almost always, this dynamic will not end without one or the other putting a stop to it.

So I started imagining these bullying words and actions that either originated in my head or came at me from a real live person as blow-up arm-flailing tube men, and it shifted everything. It made it kind of funny and it also took the wind from those monsters.

Have you ever been driving through your neighborhood during the holidays and seen those giant sad blow-up snowmen who are laying on the grass at a neighbor's house early in the morning because the compressor got shut off for the night. All in a pile?

That's what we've got to do with our inner-monsters, inner-bullies and inner-meanies. And outer monsters and outer bullies. Unplug them and see them for what they are, a pile of outward shell that has no ability to frighten us without us giving it the power to do it. We have to deflate them, all of them.

Our thoughts, beliefs and attention are the air that fills up those monsters. We are literally PAYING them to fill up and be scary, with our attention. I decided to stop paying attention to their dance.

I decided to put my attention elsewhere.

So now I walk right through them, and by them, even when they're dancing. And sometimes I will do a funky little dance with them just for fun before I do what must be done — I then unplug them.

And there they are, in a very revealing, sad little pile — just like a deflated giant fabric snowman on the neighbor's lawn.

We can do that with the bullies in our head and also with the real life bullies.

But we have to remember something important about real life bullies — they were never the scary monsters we thought they were or the fabric blow-up things, that's not really who they are either. It's just who they were pretending to be. And when I don't engage, maybe it gives them the opportunity to figure out their own magnificence, their own value and their own inner power. Maybe if I unplug them from me, it can help them realize they don't need to be plugged into anyone at all. Maybe they'll learn that they're not powerless at all, they've got their own power source right inside, that it's safe just being who they are.

Maybe they'll learn that it's even safe to be kind.
Who knows.

These days I only have the energy and strength to unplug them and walk away, not much more.

The Road I Walked With Monsters has taught me more lessons than I can count. I don't intentionally entertain monsters in my head anymore, and when they arrive unannounced and uninvited, I lead them back to the door. I pretend they're just little kids going trick-or-treating and I give them a dumdum sucker and wish them well. Some of them are pretty cute.

It's a beautiful thing how our walk through healing can shine a big light and expose things that were paralyzingly scary in the shadows. We have to remember that sometimes the things scaring us most are filled with air and not much else.

Our power is sacred and meant to be used in sacred ways that grow us, build us and teach us. It's not meant to be squandered away in front of a car dealership.

So if you've gotta dance with your monsters, dance with them. But don't be afraid of them. And when you've had enough of the dance, just unplug them. You have all the power.

So, Mighty Soul,

What monsters have you been airing up?

AND

What would life be like if you stopped giving them life?

I love you, I believe in you and I thank you for walking this road with me.

Next, we will travel The Road I Walked With Angels. Some of these roads are pretty exquisite, and that's one of them. I will see you there.

xoxo
melody freebird

30

The Road I Walked
With Angels

A pretty common thing that happens when life falls apart and you fall apart and breathing is your number one goal for the day is that your life just gets really small, really contracted and really self-centered. I hate that it's true, but sometimes when you're healing you get so centered on your own suffering that you can't/don't see the miracles happening right in front of your face. You just get really selfish.

I need to say that this is true for me. I thought I was so alone, but the truth is, I was surrounded almost all the time by earth angels and angels from other realms too. I wish I could have recognized it while it was happening.

The Road I Walked With Angels was a long and crowded road, actually.

I have been loved deeply by others who were brave enough to sit beside me when I wasn't a whole lot of fun to be with. It is one of the errands of angels, I believe.

One of the greatest acts of love I know of is sitting with a person during times when you'd really just like to avoid them until they're in a better state of mind. There is something very angelic about running toward the places everyone else is running away from because you know there's someone in there that needs help getting out.

Melody Ross

I was a mess for a while there . . . a blubbering, crying, hopeless mess. And I couldn't move because of the mental and emotional paralyzation I felt. So if you wanted to see me, you had to come and sit by me. And I pretty much had nothing to offer anyone during this time.

I don't know why anyone showed up, but they did. I needed help getting out.

They helped me.

Today I started making a list of all of the angels who showed up for one minute or for days and weeks and months. And the list is long and incomplete. I know I have missed some of the names and I know they will come to me later but I was astounded at how long the list was. The acts are not enormous if you just looked at them on paper, but if you could see the impact that just showing up and sitting, or sending encouragement and reminders has on a person . . . I think we'd all see that we are surrounded by angels all the time. And that we have opportunities every day to be an angel ourselves.

We have opportunities to truly help others to literally stay alive another day. And it's easier than we think.

I know I cannot list every single one, but I want to tell you about a few — with the hope that you'll both see how often YOU have been an angel and how often angels have shown up FOR YOU. And that's what this road is all about.

My friend September bought a plane ticket to Idaho when I was packing up to leave. She didn't even ask first, she just showed up because she knew. These were not good days. I was not a fun companion. I will never forget the way she came and helped me pack up my beautiful life and give some of it to Goodwill, throw some of it in the burn pile, and sort through the rest to find things tiny enough to fit in our RV. She helped me in very practical ways, but it was the sitting with me that mattered most. The showing up. The not being afraid of the grief and sorrow oozing out of me like a putrid infection. She just sat with me and loved me exactly as I was, where I was.

216

50 Roads To The Middle Of My Life

It was sort of a tag-team as I look back, because Hilarie, who had been beside me for 10 years of running retreats and making courses and making art and just general sistering, sat beside me every minute of every day . . . and sometimes spent the night on the worst days just so I wouldn't be alone. She continues to be the most sparkling example of angelic sisterhood I could ever try to describe. You just have to know her to understand what I mean. She has never, ever stopped showing up.

And Shannon would drive for a large portion of the day to come and visit me before I left — so many times. I know it wasn't fun for her, but she just kept showing up anyway. We'd sit in my RV and I would just cry. And she would hold my hand and tell me about the days when she had to leave her beautiful life behind and all of the complicated mess that went along with it.

And my sister Lynda would drive out to the country from the city, in her beautiful business clothes. And sit next to me in my RV for hours and hours and hours. Like it was a hospital room. She just kept showing up.

And my friend Vicki who listened to more tearful accounts of what had happened since the last time I saw her, and my excruciating crisis of faith. No matter what a mess I was, she just kept returning. Never giving up.

And Kolleen. Always always always, no matter what. Sweet love and tough love. She's the one you'd want beside you if you were on a long journey and you wanted to quit. She's a cheerleader and truth speaker. She won't let you drown but she will also remind you of how strong a swimmer you are. She'd send songs and notes and the dorkiest GIFs she could find. Because she is a master at medicinal laughter.

And Jenny Gray. Ohhhhhhh, how I wish everyone had an angel in their life like she is. Perfect timing. Perfect words.

And Lori always knew when I was slipping down. She'd send care packages and record her voice saying motherly words and reminding me of what I needed to remember to stay afloat.

And Terry, and Maria and Shelley. I remember for months that went into years, Shelley sent me messages and texts EVERY DAY from her home in Canada— beautiful, encouraging words. And though I didn't write back nearly enough, she never stopped sending me reminders that everything was going to be okay. Every single day, without fail.

Terry has been doing this for more than 10 years all the way from Texas.

Maria has been doing it for even longer, no matter where we both end up and how long it's been since we've seen each other face to face.

And Robin. My Anam Cara. Even when she was sick and struggling, she'd always send a life preserver. She still does. Soon I will take you on The Road to Anam Cara and you will understand.

And my nieces, my beautiful nieces who have been my very close friends since they were just little girls. A text, a casserole, a sweet reminder.

And Mary-Anne, and Orly, and Lisa. And Lisa Lisa. And D'Wana. And Janet. And Joelle. And Lavi. And Tamara and Keesha and Nancy and Trina and Angela and Amy and Amy and Amy and D'Laine and Kat………….

And EVERY SINGLE BRAVE GIRL. Deep in my heart, deep in my soul.

Glenda is the name of the good witch in Wizard of Oz…but I have a real-life Glenda who consistently reminds me of the value of my work.

And Ann….she's become one of my very best friends. She took my courses for years and years and when my life fell apart, she contacted me and told me that she's a computer wiz and she'd help me rebuild my website and my school. She'd help me unearth my work that had been lost. And she has. She still does. She helps me unearth MYSELF the most. She is the angel of angels.

And of course Pixie and Flora and Kelly-Rae and Katie and Lynx and Anahata and Shanny. Ohhhh the ways they've sat with me and I've sat with them.

Rebecca and Lex and Rose.

There are so many others. The list goes on and on. And on. YOU are probably on this list.

…and now West and Kami and my kids…and of course, Marq. Every day they are angels to me.

I tell you this because you never know how 10 minutes of your time when you feel prompted to reach out to someone just might save their life. I've told you on other roads how good I have been at smiling and waving when I'm falling apart inside. So the ones who can see past that dog & pony show and aren't afraid to look behind the curtain are truly angels.

And if you believe in world peace, it's a great investment to make. Because now that I am on the other side of that long nightmare, all I want to do is show up for people. It's just what happens once you're nursed back to health . . . you want others to heal too.

I once gave my keynote speech at Symposium about the dream I had where a giant pair of hands showed up and made a sort of boat. And asked me to get in the boat and just flow down the river. The hands asked me to rest. They just kept saying SHHHHH, JUST LET ME HOLD YOU.

Be still and know that I am here. Rest. Just let me hold you.

SHHHHH, just let me hold you.

I hear the angels saying these words. I will sit with you, they say . . . for as long as it takes. I am not going anywhere.

The stillness, the quiet, the willingness to do everything that matters by expecting nothing, the patience, the gentleness, the respect, the love. It's unforgettable and medicinal even if it only lasts a few minutes. It's what we need so much from each other. It's angelic.

I will spend my lifetime looking for opportunities to pay it forward, to repay this time in my life when so many good angels showed up. It kept me alive.

And even as I am rebuilding my life, as Marq and I are rebuilding our shared life and ourselves . . . so many of the same angels have shown up.

Melody Ross

And so many new ones.

On The Road I Walked With Angels I learned about those miraculous minutes of lifesaving love that might have seemed so small to the one giving it, but were everything to the one receiving it. The way we look at a person at the store matters. The way we touch the arm of someone who feels alone matters. The way we save a seat for someone matters. The way we love others in their darkest hour matters.

We are indeed surrounded by angels, each other.

So, Wonderful Soul,

When have you been in the presence of angelic love?

AND

What was a small act that someone performed for you that was SO BIG in the grand scheme of your life?

Thank you for walking this road with me, it was a beautiful one.
Tomorrow we will travel to The Road Where I Got So Sick of Myself
I love you - thank you for being an angel.

melody freebird

31

The Road Where I Got Really Sick of Myself

I guess there has to come a big moment when you're so sick of the stories constantly rolling through your head that you'll do just about anything to get rid of them.

Because it's the stories we tell ourselves that end up molding our life.

This moment of being sick of yourself is a crossroads that pokes at you like a kid in line with you at the grocery store who is eye-level with the m&ms and won't give you a moment of peace until you put them in the cart.

This moment is the gateway to the turnaround. Life is about to change, big time — if you let it.

I remember Jenny Gray telling me to keep talking about "it" until it is so worn out that I don't want to talk about it anymore. "It" being whatever story is stuck in you like a sliver.

So I did. I did and I did and I did. If I could choose the most accurate inscription on my tombstone at this time in my life, it would say . . ,

"she lived and she lived and she lived, until all that was left was her story"

In fact, that used to be my title photo on my personal facebook page for years and years, and it was true. Still is. But man I am so sick and tired of some of my stories and what I've learned on this Road Where I Got So Sick of Myself is that old emotional wounds are a lot like physical wounds.

Think of that last bit of healing on a burn or a cut or scrape or even an internal wound. It aches and it aches and it aches until that last bit of healing when it just starts to itch so annoyingly. That's when you know the healing is almost done. It feels like an old, tight wool sweater that you've totally grown out of and you just want to pull that thing off and put on something comfy. Or just wear nothing for a while.

That's what it feels like when you get sick of your old stories and sick of yourself. At least that's what it feels like for me.

Big life transitions can make you feel crazy. They can make you feel outside of your own body. They can make you feel trapped inside of your body too. Everything feels surreal and weird and like you got dropped in a place akin to Alice's Wonderland. You stop recognizing yourself and you feel like a stranger to your own life. You feel drifted further and further away from everything you once knew. Weird characters show up to teach you. It freaks you out lots of days. And there's this excitement at the same time, that something is coming that you can't name yet, something that is meant just for you.

This summer I got to help Kami raise some monarch butterflies. We ended up with 10 of them in total. But each of them started as a tiny little caterpillar barely the size of a stick pin.

And then they grew. And they grew and they grew and they grew. We had this amazing photo illustrated "instruction" book that told us every stage the caterpillar would grow into, by the day and some of it by the hour. So we would camp out in the barn where the caterpillars munched on fresh milkweed we collected up the mountain every other day or so.

We had 2 magnifying glasses and we would watch every day to see what changes they would make. It was one of the most sacred, satisfying and fascinating experiences of my life to witness these transformations by the hour.

50 Roads To The Middle Of My Life

In the book, it said the chemicals change in the caterpillar's body and they just know it's time to do what they have to do next. I think 3 or 4 times before they climb up the branch and hang for a few days and then become a chrysalis, they actually turn sort of this grayish black transparent color outside of their black and yellow stripes and then suddenly they crawl out of their own skin and they are vibrant and beautiful again, and there's a lump of grayish black skin laying there like a discarded pantyhose. They do that 3 or 4 times!

Because I got to watch this happen with 10 different caterpillars, it became one of my life's greatest lessons. I would watch them just start wandering around, stop eating and turn that weird color. I related to that feeling so much. If I could humanize it, I would say that if it were me I might think I was dying, but I was really just ready for new skin — and even more importantly, I was ready for my old skin to go.

These caterpillars lost that skin 3 or 4 times but it is the final time that blows your mind. And it's pretty disgusting. Once they grow as big as they can be, they stop eating again and just start wandering around. They climb all over the place and sometimes just sit in the same place for hours, it looks like they are doing nothing but I suspect they are testing a place to see if it's where they will make their final hang and become a chrysalis. As they're searching for a place, they reach to the sky….it is incredible!!! A few of their feet stay on the branch and the rest of their body extends into the air, searching searching searching for something they can't quite reach.

Over those months, I would sneak out to the barn at all hours and watch them. And sometimes it would just make me cry because I could totally relate to what appeared to be happening. It's like they knew they were supposed to do something, so they just kept moving awkwardly, uncomfortably. They seemed restless and agitated a bit. They were searching and searching.

And then they'd find a good spot and build a little silky pillow on the branch, grab onto it with the very back of themselves and hang in the shape of a J, sometimes for a few days. How did they even know what they were doing? And did they know why? And did they know what was to come?

Our human brains are bigger and have higher functionality for reasoning, and we don't even know, so I don't think they do either. They just do it instinctively.

As I watched them go through this whole process, it taught me so much about trusting what seems useless and tedious and like a big waste of life. These times when we ourselves are wandering around looking for something and shedding our skin here and there and just waiting for something we can't define.

And pieces of us are on the floor like a used pantyhose.

If the caterpillar could think and reason the way we can, I wonder if it was sick of itself the way I was. The way I still am in so many ways as I navigate this whole new era of myself, of this time in life, of this time as part of our human family in the world. I had to get so sick of myself that I would be willing to let that part of me die and become whatever it is supposed to become next.

That's where I'm at right now.

Well, after the caterpillar is hanging in a J shape, you'll know something is about to happen after a day or two when its antennae starts to droop. That means it's getting really close to shedding that black and white stripey skin one last time. And you better stick around or you will miss it.

Again, if it were human, if it were me or you, I have to say that I would feel so insulted and defeated by what happens next. One last time, the skin literally splits and a big old green blob smashes its way out of it. It looks so much uglier than a caterpillar and definitely nothing close to a butterfly.

That's the part I related to most. Taking this long journey and thinking you're going somewhere good, knowing that you will evolve past this caterpillar stage, but then suddenly you're just this big green blob of grossness. That's how it felt to me, anyway.

That's how I've felt so many times over the last few years.

And then before you can even blink, a hard shell wraps around the green blob and encases it. And then GOLD SHOWS UP. It's the most incredible thing….a stripe of metallic gold and several dots cover the chrysalis.

50 Roads To The Middle Of My Life

And it's silent.
And dark.
And still.
Just hanging there with absolutely no movement.
For weeks. Nothing.
Sleeping? Dying? Being Born?

Who knows.

People do this. I am doing this. From the outside we might wonder where a person went when this happens in their life. I literally disappeared from just about everyone's radar. I went black into the darkness of that cocoon as a big old blob of green. And what happens inside of that chrysalis is that you liquify. You have no shape and no form and no ability to move, you're just slime.

And for me, it felt and feels just fine because I WAS SO SICK OF MY-SELF.

They say that teenagers start acting like bratty, selfish jerks sometime before they're ready to leave the safety of the family nest SO THAT it's not such a devastating experience for mamas when they do. The mama and the kid start butting heads and cutting apron strings so that they feel ready when the time comes for the child to fly the coop.

For me, that's what all of this has felt like. I started to butt heads with myself and just got so uncomfortable in my own life, my own skin, my own world that there was nothing else to do but let it shed.

They also say that right around the age I am now, that a woman stops making the hormones that make her want to take care of everyone else while she essentially forgets herself. I felt that happening. Suddenly I feel myself going inward, and retreating from so much outward effort. It is happening more every day. It is strange and disconcerting and uncontrol-lable. It makes sense that at this age we start keeping our own blood and our own milk. We used to give it freely at younger ages. Our body just knows when it's time to bring all of our resources back inside.

So that we can grow our wings.

And maybe we don't just get sick of ourselves, but we get sick of how most things are in our life. And maybe that is what is supposed to happen, because if we didn't get sick of it, we'd probably be trying to glue our skin back on when it sheds off and we wouldn't be able to experience what is supposed to happen next.

I am still on this road, in large part, but I am learning to trust it. Instead of thinking that there must be something terribly wrong with me because I am feeling so sick of myself, I'm seeing it as a rite of passage to help me cut my own apron strings from my old self and fly my own coop.

Because I want to fly. I really do.

But if I cut myself out of this cocoon/chrysalis too soon, I won't make it. Just like a butterfly. These things take as long as they take. We can cry and moan and call the management and tell them that this timeline is absolutely unacceptable, but none of that will speed up the process.

Growing wings takes as long as it takes. And getting sick of yourself is the first step to letting it happen.

So, Becoming Soul,

What does it feel like for you when you start to feel like you're growing out of your own skin?

AND

What could it mean if you're feeling sick of yourself?

Thank you for sauntering on this unsure road with me. Next I will take you to The Road Made of Messy Middles.

I love you and I hope you'll trust the process.
xo
melody freebird

32

The Road Made Of Messy Middles

I know I wrote about the journey of the butterfly on the last road, but not all middle places are as magical as the one of the caterpillar turning into a butterfly. Some of the middle places feel more like a dumpster fire.

I don't have a car anymore so when I drive somewhere, I have to drive the giant pickup truck. It is enormous. I don't love parking it, or passing people in it or getting groceries in and out of it. So usually Marq drives, or I will ride somewhere with a friend.

But every once in a while, I have to drive it. Last year, my son came to visit in the deep of winter, where we spent those months in the desert in St. George, Utah. He and I went to run some errands together and I had to drive the great big truck because he hates driving it even more than I do. When we were turning the corner on one of the busiest intersections in town, going uphill, the truck totally lost power. Rather than continuing to turn the corner, I just went straight through the light and got as far as I could while we were coasting. We made it almost all the way out of the intersection and then we hurried and got out and started pushing to get the rest of the way out.

Luckily, the road we ended up on was sort of a dead end going into a Motel 6 and so we just sat in that giant truck and tried to figure out what to do. The back of the truck was sticking out further into the intersection than it should have been but we did the best we could.

I started to laugh and then my son started to laugh. We didn't even talk about what was so funny, because I don't know that you could put your finger on it or if it would even be funny out of the context of the 2 decades we'd spent doing life together. It was funny because OF COURSE I was the one this would happen to on the ONE time I decided to drive. And it was just a weird time in life all together with one thing after another happening — those times when you'll cry if you don't laugh.

It was the messy middle.

Again, people tell me all the time that they cannot believe how resilient I am. I wasn't born this way, I don't know if anyone is born resilient. it's just something that happens over time, and it's not something you set out to learn because it's really not something that can be learned in a book. It's experiential, and it takes a LOT of experience. You just keep doing hard things until they're not hard anymore. You keep doing impossible things until they are possible. The same way most of us can walk with our own two legs even though we couldn't walk when we were babies. We don't even think about the fact that we can walk and we couldn't walk at one time. We don't think about it because we just do it now without thinking about it. It's easy.

That's how almost everything in life is. It's hard to do until it's easy. That's not to say that everything that is hard to do becomes pleasant to do, but if you do it enough times, it just doesn't feel as difficult to do anymore.

Unless, again, you tell yourself stories that make it more difficult than it has to be.

When we are not where we were anymore and we are not yet where we are headed, we can seriously let ourselves believe we are never going to get to where we most want to be. We can also just lose steam and motivation when we can't see the end and we can't see where we started, either. That's how we get stuck. That's when we start to numb ourselves so we don't have to think about any of it...not where we started, not where we are headed, and certainly not where we are stuck.

It's the messy messy messy middle of the journey from here to there. Or there to there. Or where to where.

I don't love this place on most journeys, I have to say. It's like having some-one watch you while you are part way through a painting. You know that if you keep going, you'll eventually get the painting where you want it, but sometimes it's awful and ugly and such a mess. And it makes it worse when others are watching. It's humiliating and it makes you nervously clumsy. It makes you feel like you have to explain all your steps out of the ugliness so THEY KNOW that YOU KNOW how ugly it is.

That moment in the truck in that busy intersection felt that way too.

I have been in situations like this before, but I was so much younger. And for some reason I figured that as I got older, the middles wouldn't be messy anymore. Seems like you should have enough experience by now that you can just ACE all the journeys inside of the journey. But these days, I am much more surprised at minimally messy middle parts than I am of mas-sively messy middle parts. Seems like that bigger mess is par for the course — especially when you're reinventing or rebuilding or restoring.

And there's a tremendous temptation to feel humiliation and embarrass-ment. And I do struggle with that sometimes when I get stuck in the mid-dle of the story and keep re-reading the same middle chapters over and over again, pretending they are the end of the story.

I would have loved for my son to come and visit and see that his mom was incredibly successful and healthy and passionate and put-together and joyful and wise and impressive. With millions of dollars in the bank for retirement. And an epic guest house for him to stay in. And a sensible car for me to drive that I can actually parallel park. Maybe even a pool for him to take selfies in with hashtag #hanginwithmycoolmom.

But that's not what it looks like in this messy middle. So we laugh.

My kids and I have already been through a lot together. Marq's brain in-jury happened when I was 33 years old and the kids were 3, 4, 8, 11 & 14 years old. We figured out lots of messy middles together, and we made it fun. But now the kids are all adults and I thought by now I'd be helping them through their messy middles and I would have it all figured out.

But life is just not like that.

Every morning when my son was visiting, I would make him a green smoothie from the fold-up table that held our blender. I think about all the years I made them Eggo Waffles with a bowl of fake maple syrup, and the way they'd move to the next seat at the kitchen bar when too much syrup was spilled at their place, until the entire kitchen island/bar was covered in syrup. I'd be getting ready for work and taking care of Marq and I'd give them their waffles, cut into strips, with a little bowl of syrup to dip them in and I'd head upstairs to get ready. I'd come back downstairs and have to clean up all of the syrup. In my luxury kitchen.

I realized that I AM doing better when I put kale and oranges and avocados and all sorts of supplements in the blender and gave him that for breakfast instead of a million grams of simple carbohydrates and liquid sugar. I am making wholesome green smoothies on a very un-luxurious folding table.

So maybe our messy middles are like a spiral going up and up and up and up and around and around and around. And just because we are in the same general place on the round and round, we are up a little higher than we were before.

As long as we are alive and as long as we are moving, I don't think we are ever going to make it from where we were to where we want to be without a messy middle. And that is okay. I think about all I've learned in those places over the years and I guess the very best thing I can really do for my children and grandchildren is to NOT be so embarrassed and humiliated by them, but be enthusiastic and grateful and determined. And laugh instead of cry.

Because they are going to have plenty of messy middles too.

The messy middles feel like an insult when we think we should be somewhere else, or that we should have gotten to where we are headed by now. Or things should have turned out in a way that let us stay where we were so we didn't have to go on another hard journey again (or what we are telling ourselves is "hard.")

Sometimes you do need to sit in the middle of the intersection and cry.

And sometimes it feels better to laugh. It makes the memory of it sweeter. It's been many months since that happened, and the best part of it was that I was with my son, and we had learned together how to laugh and stay calm in situations like this. We learned it BECAUSE we have been through so much of this kind of thing together.

And let's be honest, The Road Made of Messy Middles is the one we are all on, folks. Forever and ever. It's not just one messy middle, it's the soft squishy place inside of every new experience, every goal, every relationship, every tragedy, every historic event, everything that is growing something.

And the messier the middle, the more it's true that the thing that is growing is US.

I love for things to look beautiful all the time. But I've learned that there are so many different kinds of beauty,. The beauty that captivates me most is the beauty that comes from patina and layers and cracks and chips and rust and life. That's the stuff that happens to something in the middle of where something begins and where something ends. The parts that are the most exquisite take time. And it seems like a big old mess during that time, a useless and ridiculous and meaningless mess, but it's not.

It's what makes us all so gorgeous. In the best way.

I am learning, and will continue to learn until my dying day, that The Road Made of Messy Middles is a road to be held with awe and gratitude — even reverence. Because getting there means we are still alive. Getting there means we've got grit and fortitude and determination. If we were only ever at the beginnings and the endings, it would be a very shallow experience. If we went from the beginning of a great trip to the very end of a great trip and skipped everything that happened in-between, I think we'd remember that the meatiest experiences of life don't happen at the beginning or the end of those experiences, they almost always happen somewhere after it all started and before it was over. There are parts that simply cannot be skipped.

It is hard when you think a rough experience should be over before it is. It's even harder when you think it never should have happened in the first place. I've learned that when we can exercise the mindset of BEING ALL

IN whatever experience we are currently in, the gifts are countless. There are a lot of really rough experiences in life that last way longer than we think we can bear, but we do bear them . . . and then suddenly what was hard isn't so hard anymore. And we get to the other side of it. And we are different because we made that journey and we stuck with it.

It's okay to cry, and it also feels really good to laugh. Life has room for all of it.

So, Resilient Soul,

What are you in the middle of right now?

AND

What gifts might be hidden under it all if you look a little harder?

We are all gonna get through this! Thank you for being on The Road Made of Messy Middles. We will all be on this road many times in our life!

Next, we will travel to The Road Where I Got Called On the Carpet . It's a doozy!

Thank you for being in the human family with me.
xo
melody freebird

33

The Road Where I Got Called On The Carpet

Marq and I were watching a movie a few nights ago where a woman and her husband and teenage daughter were driving in the middle of the night and started getting heckled and taunted by a carload of do-no-gooders on the freeway, out in the middle of nowhere with no cell service and no passing traffic. (by the way, I would not recommend this movie, it was terrifying)

Anyway, the bad guys kept ramming their car and eventually ran the family off the road to the point that their car wouldn't drive. Then they demanded that the family exit the vehicle. They then separated the woman and her daughter from the husband and drove away with them.

One bad dude stayed back with the husband and drove him to a remote place and dropped him off, only to come back a few hours later to get him.

That was the scene that did me in . . . the one where the husband had to hide and decide if he was going to get in the vehicle with the bad guys and gamble whether he'd end up back with his wife and daughter or if he should just keep hiding, knowing that if he were separated from the horrible kidnapping situation, he'd have a lot better chance to do something about it than if he became one of the kidnapped again just so he could be with his wife and daughter.

Marq and I paused the movie there, and discussed what we would do in that situation — we both decided that we would keep hiding so we could be on the outside of the situation and observe it, above it so we could observe it, away from it so we can have our full faculties and mobility to move into it in the safest and most effective way to help the ones kept captive rather than being a prisoner inside of it.

Ugh. What a choice.

It was a tough choice and it choked me up. Marq then went on to explain to me why he does a lot of the overprotective and on-guard and super prepared things he does. Because he always wants to be in a position where he can have as much mobility, choice and sovereignty as possible. So he can actually be of service and not mired down in the thick tar of situations that can arise when one steps into any kind of oppressive situation.

These are the choices we have to make sometimes when we love someone and when we value life.

And often they are split-second choices. Sometimes they are well thought out and strategic — this choice to stay outside of thick tar-covered life situations. But either way, they are hard choices that others are quick to judge who have not been in dire situations like these.

I have to thank my lucky stars for the ones who refuse to be part of tarry situations or who didn't get pulled into the tar. Maybe they didn't choose, they were just fortunate this go-round. But the ones who are on the outside of the tar are in incredibly opportune positions to throw someone a rope. And they are the ones who can stage really effective interventions.

That's where I'm going with this. To my intervention that happened unexpectedly in the kitchen of my dear friends, West and Kami. By unexpectedly, I mean that I DIDN'T EXPECT IT. And I guess that's how interventions are supposed to go.

I want to start by saying that you can't call someone on the carpet effectively unless you have a track record of loving rapport, trust and respect. If someone calls you on the carpet that you don't feel safe with, that you don't respect, or someone you feel like PUSHED YOU into the tar, it doesn't work. It just feels like another hit.

But when someone who you know loves you and wants the best for you, an intervention can be one of the best things to ever happen to you. And it can simultaneously feel humiliating and uncomfortable. And like a relief. And like a punch in the gut. And like love. Yes, all of these at the same time.

I am so grateful that we all, in our human family, have different personalities and different gifts. All of them are important and all of them matter.

When someone is spiraling down, I have seen several different ways those around them handle the spiraling down. There are the ones who only sympathize with you and let you be as sad and pathetic as you need to be. They listen and hug and empathize and sympathize and comfort. Man, this is so needed and I am so grateful.

There are also the ones who accuse and find fault, often passive-aggressively. They seem to want to give you a quick solution based on all the things you did to get yourself in this situation. And they seem to know exactly how you can RIGHT NOW get yourself out of it and never have it happen again. These ones often have a list of the things you've done in the past that they didn't approve of and they've done the math on all of it and you are always far more in negative numbers than you can ever see yourself working your way out of. It's accusations, faults and pre-made solutions that are so far off the mark that the only result of the interaction is more division and more shame and more frustration. Because almost never have these people been through something like what they are professing to be an expert at. These are the times we need to turn on the Charlie Brown adult voice filter WHA WHA WHA WHA.....

And then there are the ones who call you on the carpet and show you all the sides they can see, including the ones you don't want to see for yourself. They make you aware that they are aware and that they want YOU TO BE AWARE of what it seems like you are doing. It's not an accusation. It's an intervention, and it's rooted in CHOICE. They want you to make the choice that keeps you alive.

They are coming from a place of WANTING YOU TO SEE SO MUCH GOOD IN YOURSELF that you are willing to STOP DOING THE

THINGS THAT ARE DESTROYING YOU. So like I said, these people are effective because of the rapport and trust they've built. They have "earned" the credibility to speak some harsh truth to you about how you're destroying your own life. It's not an accusation and it's not a criticism. It's a loud and booming yell at you as you run toward a really high cliff that will mean a fall to your death.

It's love, actually.

So I walked straight into an intervention. We rent the top of West and Kami's house and that's where we stay in the cold months. That's when this happened. We have to go down the stairs to get out of the house and when this happened, I don't think I'd been down those stairs in several weeks. I made myself a little place to hide and I'd covered myself up with a permanent blanket made of Cheetos, m&ms and shame.

And it was a short intervention, but it was potent. It was effective. It was to the point. I don't remember exactly the chronology of the conversation but it contained the following elements:

"Melody, we can't stand by and be part of this anymore and we can't keep it from Marq. You are in an abusive situation"

"You could put a stop to it today and you're the only one who can do it."

"We wish you would do it because we love you, but if you don't do it, we can't be part of it any way and we are stepping away from this situation today."

"We have watched you slowly die, hide, gain weight and wither away in spirit every week since you got here. You are not okay. We are here to support you but we can't support what you are doing to your life by staying in the situations you are in."

"You're allowing things that we cannot allow and all we can do for you at this point is not participate in it any longer."

"We have seen, we know now. Now you know that we know. And so now you have some choices to make."

"And…..we are going to tell Marq everything we know, because we love you."

So here I stood in the kitchen, naked as a jaybird in all ways pertaining to the soul, and I was speechless. I was exposed. I was humiliated and relieved. I could not run and hide. I didn't have an argument because I knew these two well enough that my default arguments of "But……" would always be met with….

"Melody, where is your accountability?"
"Melody, this does suck but you are the only one who can put a stop to it."

I knew that arguing was futile. I knew they were right.

Well, then Marq entered into the conversation, and the details of what had been happening for months that had turned into years became new knowledge to him. So he and I went upstairs and had to have some very honest conversations.

I have only made my husband cry a few times. And it was out of sheer frustration. This series of conversations was one of those times and I did it again just about a month ago. He gets frustrated when I behave as if I am powerless, when I forget what I know to be true, and when I go into my stubborn default martyr mode. He has been reduced to tears by this because he does everything he can possibly do to help me without taking away my choices and my freedom and often I just keep doing the thing that is killing me, which in turn, kills us. He was tired of a million vicarious deaths.

So after this intervention, I made some choices. And I made them swiftly. And it was hard. And the early consequences were dire. But the consequences always come around anyway and often the longer you wait, the more extreme the consequences are.

I wanted it to be someone else's responsibility.
I wanted someone to come save me, but not in a messy way.
I wanted to go to sleep until it was over.

But I was submitting to things I'd NEVER allow someone else to participate in and endure.

I was hiding it.
I was participating in my own slow death.
I was isolating and putting myself deeper and deeper into a cave so that no one else could see what was really happening.
I was ignoring offers of help and encouragement.
I was building more walls and digging more holes and weaving more heavy blankets of tar and fat and busy-ness and stories to cover myself with so that I could disappear.

So I had to look at myself in the brutal mirror of truth again. I was aging in that distinctive way that self-betrayal ages you. I was feeling old and chubby and I looked like someone who was trying to die by being crushed or smothered or smashed — or just by disappearing.

And now, I was exposed. I was in a corner with nowhere to back into but back into myself.

I see myself as someone who, when I've made it to an age old enough that I know my time has come, might go out into the woods and die alone just so that I don't have to do it in front of others. So if you're like this and a part of you is being killed by something that you're allowing, it makes sense that you might try to go and do that in a dark corner, alone.

And you might think that's what you're actually doing, but others really can see it. Sometimes it doesn't really matter that they can see it because we can't control what others can see and they can't control what we do when they DO see. But we also can't wait for it — we can't wait for some-one to finally see and stage a big intervention.

Sometimes we have to stage our own intervention on ourselves.

So I set off to give MYSELF an intervention and I wrote down all the things that were happening, and the role I was playing in all of it. I wrote down what it was doing to me and what it was doing to my marriage, my health, my children and my future,

And I did the hard thing and put an end to it — and the consequences were devastating. A lot like pruning most of the branches from a favorite tree . . . branches that might look healthy and strong from the outside but are diseased and spreading disease to the inside.

50 Roads To The Middle Of My Life

When you put a stop to something that's killing you, it really is often a lot like pruning a favorite tree and then having to put the branches in the fire.

It's something that's best done right before winter. Because it's about to get really cold in your life when you prune a lot of disease from your tree.

So you can put those branches in the fire and let them warm you or you can keep trying to pull them out of the fire to glue them back on — and be burned by that fire every time you try to pull a branch back out.

Because it's going to be a long and cold winter of gaining your nutrients and exercising the discipline required to not submit to a story that you are dying or already dead. And not submitting to the story that you should never have cut those branches off and you can somehow glue them back on, even if they are diseased.

That's what winter can feel like to a severely pruned tree, and especially to the pruner.

But it's actually healing time. And this kind all starts with hearing a hard truth that someone had the courage to tell you. Sometimes you, yourself are the hard truth that needs to be told.

When we think there's some way we can beat our shadow, and we think we have…then we hide it even more when it shows back up. The thing is, our shadow is inextricably part of us and we will never be able to make it go away. And why should we? The ramifications of thinking there's some GOOD THING we can do to never struggle in life again are devastating because we need community more than ever when we struggle. When we retreat in the darkness to hide our struggles, there IS a sweet spot of isolation where you get the message and come back. But it can start to smother you like tar if you stay there for too long. There are so many things that are medicinal when the timing is right and then go toxic when they start to rot. Isolation is this way.

I wish we didn't hide our struggles and our need to go into isolation for a while to figure things out. Why can't we say, as if we were trekking into the literal wilderness; " I am gathering some intel in my shadow, will you come get me if I haven't returned by this time?" And not shame each other for having to do it,but support each other in going there "to get what needs to be got." Sometimes you've got to do it alone and other times it's nice to have a friend come along. But no shame is needed, ever.

It's a tarry place. There's the starry sky and tarry cellar. I was closing my eyes and pinching my nose and slowly letting my body sink into that immersive black tar - it was holding me and I just wanted to be held. Sometimes we will settle for anything that is holding us, even if it's like quicksand.

That's why we need others to intervene sometimes and call us on the tarry carpet.

And they've got to stay outside of our mess to be able to do it. That's where they can be most helpful. There's only so much others can do before it turns to codependency and mutual paralyzation. At some point, someone has to decide to climb out or stay out or get above it all so they can be the one to throw the rope.

This can look like callousness and dissociation but it's actually mercy and accountability and sacrifice. If everyone is drowning, everyone is dying.

Just beware of the ones who push others into tarry pits in the secret dark and throw them a rope in the public light. But that's a conversation for another road.

On The Road Where I Got Called On The Carpet, I learned the valuable lesson of WISDOM. The wisdom it takes to know that being in someone's mess is a great place to help them — but making sure you're on solid ground outside of a tarry mess is probably the best place to be able to help everyone OUT OF those places. I think we need people in both places.

So I am practicing that, and trying to unlearn what I used to think was true about being right in the middle of the messes. It can look the same because being WITH SOMEONE on solid ground next to their mess, while they are in their mess is right next to ENTERING INTO THE MESS with them.

I am learning to be powerful by learning to throw a rope to others from a solid place rather than throwing myself in, where now we have two people to save. And I'm learning to take the rope when someone throws it and not expecting them to jump in with me.

It's a hard lesson to learn, but I'm here for it.

So, Beautiful Soul,

When have you been called on the carpet?

AND

What could have happened in your life if someone would not have shown you the kind of uncomfortable love it takes to have that conversation with you?

Thank you for staying next to me in this awkwardness. Next we will go even deeper in, on The Road Where I Remembered My Sins.

I love you,
melody freebird

34

The Road Where I/They Remembered My Sins

When things happen in life that look like destruction and everything is stripped away, you feel naked. And lots of days life feels like those awful dreams where you're somewhere public (usually at school or work) and you look down and you're naked. And everyone is just right there with you, looking at you, and you're naked. And they're laughing and taking photos and whispering and talking about you. And you're naked.

Did I mention YOU'RE NAKED? I used to have that dream a lot.

And life feels that way sometimes. You think everyone can see how naked you are, and everywhere you go, you think people are either pretending they can't tell you're naked, or talking about how naked you are. Add to that a feeling that you are committing some sort of a "sin" if you show your naked body and this dream can really start messing with your head.

That's why I write so open-heartedly, vulnerably and transparently. Sometimes it makes others cringe how much I share. Sometimes it makes ME cringe how much I share. I do it for a few reasons. One is so that I'm not a big surprise later on . . . so that others will always know that I am flawed-and-trying and I won't have to live with the heartbreak I've felt too many times when others found my flaws and threw them in my face. I want you to know that I know I am flawed. And I know that I am magnificent too.

I want you to know that I know that's true about you too. I want to help you feel the freedom of showing up as WHO YOU ARE. Flawed and magnificent. It is the thing that makes you so gorgeous..

And what is a flaw, anyway? I don't like that I used that word so many times. I think flaws are one of the things that make us unique and interesting. They are the raw material of our greatest creative expression, the clay that we constantly get to dig our hands into and smooth away the bumps (if we want to!) What I dislike most is when flaws get framed as SINS. Because the word SIN actually got framed.

A lot of words have been hijacked throughout history and one of those words is the word "SIN."

This word brings strong feelings out in me, so when I think about it, I have to remember what it actually means. Because like I said, over hundreds of years it has been hijacked and most people don't even know what the true meaning of it is. And the "new" meaning of it gives it a whole lot of power to control and manipulate and shame someone into giving themselves up and to essentially be squished like a bug.

If you grew up in or around any kind of a religious culture, it might have happened to you. It was never supposed to be this way. This word might immediately bring feelings of fear and shame. But when I started studying ancient Hebrew a few years ago, one of the first words that blew my mind was SIN. Because it actually doesn't mean anything shameful after all, it's just part of the human experience. It's simply what happens when we get off of our own Soul Road. We miss the mark, we get off track.

I'm not going to go into any kind of religious direction here, but here's a quote from a famous Hebrew website, and it's important:

"The Hebrew word for "sin" is hhatah (Strong's #2403) and literally means "miss the mark." From my understanding of the Bible, there are two types of sin, accidental and deliberate. I explain it this way. The Hebrew people were a nomadic people and their language and lifestyle is wrapped around this culture. One of the aspects of a nomad is his constant journey from one watering hole to another and one pasture to another. If you are walking on a journey (literal or figurative) and find yourself "lost from the path," which is the Hebrew word rasha, (Strong's #7563), you correct yourself and get back on the path. This was a "mistake" (accidentally missing the mark), but not deliberate. Once you are back on the right path, all is good. However, if you decide to leave the path and make your own, you are again "lost from the path", but this time, being a deliberate act, it is a purposeful mistake (missing the mark on purpose). In the Bible God gives his "directions" (usually translated as "commands") for the journey that his people are to be on. As long as they remain on that journey, they are tsadiq (Strong's #6662, usually translated as "righteous," but literally means "on the correct path"), even if they accidentally leave the path, but return (this is the Hebrew verb shuv, Strong's #7725, usually translated as "repentance," but literally means "to return") back to the correct path."

There are a few more words there that have been hijacked too, like the word REPENTANCE. Which, as it states, means "TO RETURN BACK TO THE CORRECT PATH." In my estimation, this means to get back on your own Soul Road. Because each of us have different life circumstances, different strengths and weaknesses and a different sense of purpose built into us, based on what our gifts are, what our desires are and the time and place we are born and raised and choose to settle in.

On The Road Where I/They Remembered My Sins, I learned a lot about what happens when we mistake the meanings in words and meanings in mistakes and meanings in life. I mostly learned about what can happen when you tell yourself the story that EVERYONE IS REMEMBERING MY SINS. Especially if your definition of sin is wrapped up in shame and dirtiness and punishment and deep soul debt.

We are fantastically self-centered when we are afraid, hurt, desperate, and trying to heal. For some reason we think everyone is talking about us, thinking about us and having long conversations not just about our nakedness but about every inch of cellulite, moles, lumps and bumps that can be seen in our nakedness.

Here's the truth though, and I know you know this . . . almost no one is having these conversations. And if others ARE having these conversations about us, they're not the kind of people we want in our life anyway and it's a gift to know about it when it happens because you find out who to steer clear of.

The bottom line is that people are thinking about us and talking about us FAR LESS than we lead ourselves to believe.

AND!!!!! When we think that others ARE talking about our nakedness and we believe they have some kind of list of our "sins," it's an enormous opportunity to identify the most painful stories we fear they are telling.

And then heal them. It's a great time to tend to the fear hidden in our own "sins." When we believe others are remembering our sins, we are the ones who get to redirect the situation back to REMEMBERING the times we got off our own Soul Road. The times we betrayed ourselves.

When we can remember where we've turned away from our own path, and what it did to our life, we can make better plans for the next turn we take. When we can remember what happened on any of the paths we've been on that hurt us, we can tend to our own wounds. WE MUST remember our "sins." BUT WE HAVE GOT TO STOP USING THIS NEW AND DESTRUCTIVE AND SHAME-FILLED definition of the human condition. We have to stop weaponizing a word that seems like it was created to communicate something helpful pertaining to the human condition and not something destructive.

And that's what it is. The human condition. Sometimes we get off track, and we learn A LOT. And then we get back on track. And then we are on track for as long as we can be, doing the very best we can do. And then sometimes we get off track again. And then we get back on. And IT IS SO PERSONAL.

No one can see our Soul Road the way we can. In fact, no one can see it at all except our own self and our Truthteller. So it does not matter IN THE LEAST when/if others are remembering or talking about when we got off track. Because they can't even know what our track is.

That is why I've learned it's so critically important to:
1. Not care what others think or perceive about our path
2. Make sure we are paying attention to what WE think and feel and know about our own path

People aren't thinking of us as much as we think they are.
People aren't talking about us as much as we think they are.

But if they were, what are we so afraid of?

I have found there's another weird thing humans do both to themselves and each other, and it's this generalized sorting. We sort ourselves and others into piles and then we have to prove that we're right, or that they're wrong.

We sometimes want to prove someone should be in the bad pile who everyone else thinks is in the good pile. Or we go to the ends of the earth to help the underdog or the accused and prove they should be in the good pile and not the bad pile.
I really don't like sorting humans. I don't like piles. I don't like generalizing.

On this road, and on the next one about REMEMBERING MY MAGNIFICENCE, I want to share the lessons with you I've learned from the excruciating pain of being sorted into a pile, or the painful sting I've felt after I've sorted someone else into a pile.

Here are two sentences that are truer than true for me and for all of us, especially when we are being sorted into piles of GOOD or BAD:
1. I am probably not as good as you think I am.
2. I am probably not as bad as you think I am.

They're both true, depending on the context, depending on who is doing the "thinking," and like I said, others are not thinking about us nearly as much we think they are so we HAVE TO tell ourselves THE TRUTH if we're wrapped in a belief that we have to be perfect everyday, lest we commit THE sin that will finally make us COMPLETELY worthless and unlovable.

It would be really great if we made merciful room for each other to figure out how to get back on track and if we cheered for each other instead of ridiculing and scrutinizing each other.

Oh, here I go….talking like others talk about each other more than they do. So let's reword the sentence: It would be really great if I made merciful room for myself to figure out how to get back on track instead of ridiculing and scrutinizing myself.

247

It would be really great if you would do that too, beloved.

Two more things that are truer than true, and a much more productive way to look at things:

1. I don't NEED TO BE nearly as good as I think I need to be, it's okay if I'm flawed and doing my best simultaneously.
2. There's no way I could ever be so bad that I am not worthy of love and belonging, and there is NOTHING that can take my value away.

I learned on this road that when I sort myself into a pile of being either MAG-NIFICENT or HORRIBLE, I suffer so greatly. I suffer so greatly when I think that it's the point of life, to always be magnificent. Sometimes we learn and grow the best in the most horrible situations. Sometimes we grow the most during the temporary periods when we are totally off-track. And then once we get back on track, we are millions of miles ahead because of the growth we experienced. AND we are SO HAPPY because we now appreciate the peace that comes when we are walking on our own path.

This doesn't mean it's a good idea to deliberately get yourself off track, it just means that it's never wasted. Finding yourself off your own road is a devastating and terrifying experience. It can quickly put you to sleep in such a powerful way that you don't even remember your own road anymore. BUT it is an experience that's never wasted. The pain helps you remember it forever.

It helps me so much more when I remember my own "sins" than when I focus ANY amount of attention to wondering if others do. Because there's really no way they can ever be right. They don't know my soul road, they don't know what happened on the road where I got off track, they can't see where I'm headed, they don't know much of anything at all as a mere observer.

My Soul Road is between me and my Truthteller. Yours is between you and yours.

So friends, as crazy as this might sound, I love to remember my sins. Because it means I was moving forward. It means I was LIVING. It means I was DOING SOMETHING. And I always did my best. I always got back on track. I love re-membering my own sins because I can see how much help I got from my Truth-teller and all sorts of other unexplainable help from other sparkly divine places.

I also love remembering the pain of those times because it makes the exquisite feeling of peace on my own Soul Road even more exquisite.

And it sure beats hiding it. It sure beats pretending it didn't happen. It sure beats hiding behind a blinged-out perfect cardboard cutout of the person I want to be seen as. This road, every time you travel it, reminds you not to hide your true self behind anything at all. Just show up as you are as you make your way back to your own Soul Road.

I am dedicated to staying on my own path. But sometimes I miss the mark. Sometimes I get off track. So I get to try again. Isn't it amazing that we get to try again and again and again? I will live into my next try at hitting the mark, staying on the path, acing the plan, and getting to the destination as best I can. I have no idea from day to day what the destination will be, but as long as I'm on my own Soul Road, and not the path of another, I know it will be breathtaking.

I hold hands with my Truthteller and trust the whole journey as I focus on staying on my own path. When I miss the mark, my Truthteller hands me another arrow and says "wow, you're getting better and better at this!"

When I keep my eyes on the path of another, or the target of another, that's usually when I miss my own mark. You gotta stay focused on the mark to hit the mark. And the mark you're focused on has got to be your own.

So, Daring Soul,

When have you gotten off your own Soul Road and sorted yourself into the BAD PILE for it?

AND

What did it feel like when you got back on your own path?

Thanks for going down yet another awkwardly beautiful path with me, next I'm gonna take you on The Road Where I Remembered My Magnificence.

I love you. You are good. So good. Believe it.
xo
melody freebird

35

The Road Where I/They Remembered My Magnificence

I don't know if it's harder to know that we're not perfect or if it's harder to know we are also more magnificent than we could ever quantify.

Which is scarier?
Which is more uncomfortable?
What is vanity?
What is pride?
Could we be in a dysfunctional relationship with how proud we are of how broken we are?

I have a fluctuating relationship with all of this. I bet you do too. I hop between my fear of disappointing others, my fear of impressing others and my fear of being labeled as any ONE thing. I want to be lots of things!

So I often set out to prove myself. But not TO MYSELF, to others. Ugh.

I have been a millionaire a couple of times. The first time, I was only 27 years old. The thing that shocked me about it most was how it didn't fix everything.

I have 2 books published with Simon & Schuster and hundreds of products I've developed and designed and licensed to other companies. I have

Melody Ross

won awards from the US Chamber of Commerce, The National Association for Women Business Owners, The Craft and Hobby Association and BEST NEW PRODUCT from several magazines.

I've self-published more than 25 books and written more than 50 courses. I have designed and manufactured THOUSANDS of products for my own companies.

I have had an epic bikini body. I've had a perfect marriage. I've had a house full of perfect and beautiful children. I've driven beautiful cars and lived in beautiful homes.

And none of it ever made me feel like I was enough. None of it led to me seeing my magnificence for any sustained period of time.

Having most of that stuff stripped from me, however, did the trick.

It started when a majority of my life's work got deleted from the internet. And my "following" that was in the hundreds of thousands. And my writing and my inspirational quotes and photos I'd posted or been tagged in that showed the amazing places I'd been, the things I'd done and who I was with. I didn't even have my email list anymore to go find my people.

My proof of value was gone.

Suddenly, I was a weird kind of lost where I didn't know how to be found. Suddenly, I had no proof that I was "somebody." Or that I did "something."

And worst of all, suddenly, I was not in my own community anymore. There was no way for me to find them and no way for them to find me. So…again, I told myself stories that got me off my own Soul Road. And they were NOT stories of the magnificence that is our birthright. They were deadly stories.

I've talked about this experience a bit on other roads but this time I want to tell you what finally showed me where I fit, who I am and that every single one of us is absolutely magnificent . . . even me.

It was Lillie, the little old one-eyed dog who became not just a true friend

252

to me, but one of my greatest teachers.

Ugh, I cry as I write this because she died about a month ago. As it turned out, only Marq and I were at the ranch when she died. So I got to bundle her up in a blanket and hold her until she took her last breath. Marq and I buried her together and surrounded her with flowers from the field before we covered her with earth. She was old and crippled and for a few days she kept hiding and sleeping. We couldn't find her. Then when we did find her, she was just acting so strange, and we knew she was getting ready to cross over the rainbow bridge into doggie heaven.

I miss her. But I want to tell you about the 2 summers I got to spend with her.

Lillie was little, but not as little as she was expected to be. When Kami got her, she thought she was going to be teacup size and that she could keep her in her purse. Well Lillie grew and she grew and she grew and she grew. She loved to eat, and she had really short legs. So she was a very roly-poly old gal. She was old so she had arthritis or something that made her a bit crippled. She waddled when she walked or ran and she had the face of an Ewok.

And then she lost her eye.

So you might think she'd lose her zest for life, but man SHE DID NOT. Lillie was THE HAPPIEST and MOST GRATEFUL creature I think I have ever experienced. She was constantly wagging her tail and looking at you excitedly with her one good eye. It's as if she always expected something magical to happen. And so it did. Because she was so magical.

She was just SO HAPPY and SO EXCITED about EVERYTHING.

Every morning when I came out of the trailer, she would be waiting next to my step. It was the most wonderful feeling to have someone waiting for me who was so happy to see me. Admittedly, it's probably because I always gave her doggie treats and I'd rub her belly. When she'd see me she'd often roll over on her back because she knew I'd kneel down or sit on the ground and rub her chubby belly for as long as she'd stay put..

So we had a nice relationship. But I learned the most by just watching her.

Melody Ross

She was small and mighty but she held her own with the bigger creatures, albeit her lost eye that was the result of a run-in with a predator. She made friends with any dog or cat that came to the ranch as if she just assumed they knew how magnificent she was. She MADE THE MOST OF HER ONE BEAUTIFUL LIFE with her one eye and her waddly walk and her crippled features . . . as if she was saying, "what I have is just perfect!"

SHE. WAS. MAGNIFICENT.

And I've tried to figure out what it was that made everyone fall in love with her, and it was this: She was gonna be happy and love her life no matter who liked her, no matter what happened to her and no matter how many eyes she ended up with. Her love for life made her magnificent. She knew she belonged and she didn't care if you knew or not.

Part of her magnificence was that she waddled around like a beauty queen. Like she was the MOST magnificent creature that had ever been created.

It started to rub off on me. Here I was, living in an old RV and having lost the things I thought gave me a chance at being magnificent — and she would wait outside my little aluminum door as if it were Buckingham Palace. She'd wag her tail and breathe excitedly at me as if I were the Queen herself. She knew she was magnificent and she treated me like I was magnificent.

There wasn't anything weird about it. No one was trying to cut anyone else down who were acting "too big for their britches" and needing to be put back into their place. It was just two battle-worn gals being magnificent together.

Sometimes it's easier to be broken, or to focus on our missteps, our "sins" and our brokenness than it is to claim our magnificence. We live in a world that has a scorecard for such things. We need to burn that damned scorecard. Magnificence is our birthright and to make qualifiers for it would be like scoring the starry sky.

Every living thing is magnificent. People step on magnificent stuff all the time, just because it's on the ground. Some of the most magnificent things are in the most unlikely places.

50 Roads To The Middle Of My Life

Nothing is less magnificent than anything else, either. We too often use the world's scorecard and put ourselves in the box where we feel most comfortable...less magnificent, more magnificent - and then we look for proof that others are putting us there....or we even try to get others to put us there......but really , we are the one who put us there and we are the only one who can take us out of there.

Lillie taught me to take myself out of those kinds of boxes. She taught me to see my magnificence just by being magnificent herself..

That's the great lesson I learned on The Road Where I/They Saw My Magnificence.

I learned that even though I have done some pretty cool things like we all have, and I have had some absolutely disastrous failures, none of it has anything to do with how magnificent I am. None of it. None of it can add and none of it can take it away.

I learned that I want to keep trying new things and dreaming new dreams and even doing epic things again, but for different reasons. I might even be a millionaire again someday but I don't need to pay for my place in the human family and neither do you. I don't need to buy my magnificence and neither do you. I don't need to prove myself. I was born proven. So were you.

So we get to have experiences of all sorts. And it is AWESOME! Sometimes we are in a skyscraper in New York City and sometimes we are on the other end of a shovel, burying our beautiful canine friend in the middle of the desert mountains, with not much to our name but a whole lot in our heart. All of it is magnificent.

There are not prerequisite titles to go with being magnificent. Titles are not my thing anyway, so I'm so relieved to know this. We have to be brave enough to be unlabeled and unboxed too. No piles to sort each other into, no labels and no boxes. You just get to be magnificent and free, like Lillie.

And we get to be ALL kinds of magnificent. The bright and sparkly kind, and the sad and grieving kind. You are so magnificent when you are being magnificent. You have so many facets and you are pretty darn good at all of them. Which one feels best today? Which one feels truest today? Which one serves your life best today? All of them are part of you and all of them are magnificent and all of them yield different results in your life. The joy, the sorrow, the awesomeness, the need for rest, the quiet times, the rowdy times, the times when you're surrounded by others and the times when you're very much alone.

There are infinite possibilities inside of our magnificence and so there are infinite combinations. It's just a big experiment of combining and experimenting with your gifts and your traits and your circumstances. Trying every good thing. Learning as much as you can. Experiencing as many good things as you can. All of it has different results and all of it is magnificent. Even when it's not. And there's nothing you have to do to earn your joy and your peace. It just comes naturally when you stay true to your own path, when you realize how very much there is to be grateful for and when you burn that dang scorecard.

It's been more than 2 years since I've had a dishwasher, or a washer and dryer, or a car. I'm currently wearing a t-shirt from Walmart and thrifted jeans. I haven't won any awards in a really long time. I haven't made another million and I don't know if I ever will. My hands are definitely not manicured but are almost always dirty from making and cleaning up creative messes. I am one of the messes I'm cleaning up.

But I have never felt so magnificent.

So, Magnificent Soul,

How has your definition of magnificence changed?

AND

What unnecessary things have you done in the past to try to prove your magnificence?

I love you. Next I'm going to tell you what I learned on The Road Where I Got Left Behind

See you there.
xoxo
melody freebird

36

The Road Where
I Got Left Behind

Feeling left behind is part of a slippery story we tell ourselves.

I'm speaking generally of course, but at the least, it's an incomplete story that just leads to suffering if we aren't careful. I learned on The Road Where I Got Left Behind that there are millions of ways to interpret the moment you see someone walking away. Or lots of people walking away. Or driving away. Or drifting away.

Or maybe it just seems like you're getting left behind when everyone around you is moving so fast and you don't know which way to go yet.

I grew up in a culture of what would, these days, be considered very large families. Six kids, eight kids, ten kids. And just about every big family I knew had a story of accidentally leaving one of the kids at the store, or at church or at a rest stop on a road trip. Yep, they left their own kid behind.

And the way every person tells the story is different.

The one left behind had totally different feelings than the ones who never would have left them behind on purpose.

We all have experiences to draw from that might start to look like patterns and they can really mess with us. For example — I have never been a competitive or particularly coordinated person, so as I remember it, I didn't get picked in P.E. class until there wasn't much selection left.

I told myself stories about that. It kept me from doing lots of things in my future that I really wanted to do. And it was all because of a story I told myself about what it means when you don't get picked in P.E.

There are 2 other stories from childhood and teenagerhood that colored the way I've looked at being left behind. I've had to work hard to change the narrative of what those stories mean about me and about life and about the whole human family.

Just a few months ago, Kami and I went to the mountains for the afternoon and we decided to do some soul work and journaling. I'm not sure exactly what led to the question we asked each other, but it had something to do with extracting a moment in time when we each developed a belief that hasn't ended up serving us.

The first story came from remembering moving to a new town the summer before my Sophomore year and feeling so scared and alone. I met a very nice girl at church and she asked me if I wanted to go to High School registration with her. I was so relieved and so excited. I had worked all summer and had several new outfits to show for it. I spent hours getting ready. Then she called me an hour before we were supposed to meet to tell me she couldn't go with me — or maybe she said that I couldn't come with her. She didn't tell me why, but I sure made up a lot of stories about it. It left me feeling so rejected and left behind that I actually stopped going to that school and drove 45 minutes every day to my old school.

Maybe that nice girl was sick. Maybe she had to work. And maybe she just didn't want to include me in her friend group. No matter the reason for the cancellation phone call, it was not worth what I did to myself.

The other story was when I was maybe 8 or 9 years old. I was a little wild child. I was always outside and going on adventures and I wore shoes as little as possible.

We had 9 kids in our family and I was #6. The kids across the street had 9 and then they kept going. I think by the time their family was complete, there were 11 children and 2 parents.

50 Roads To The Middle Of My Life

I was friends with a few of the girls. We played together a lot. I have always LOVED my friends, since the very first one I made in that neighborhood. The girls across the street were a big part of my childhood but my wild ways and tender heart often ended up getting me into situations that left me feeling left behind; and emotionally devastated. These girls had very different personalities than I did. I was sensitive and had my head in the clouds. I believed in fairies and unicorns and just about anything else anyone would tell me. So I was really easy to play jokes on and tease. And honestly, these girls were kind of mean. Girls I probably wouldn't have allowed my daughters to spend time with unsupervised. They played jokes on me and teased me but I just wanted to be with them, so I allowed it. It happened a lot, and I never seemed to get the jokes. I fell for them over and over again.

I was also clumsy and awkward and I asked a million questions. I was probably really obnoxious to the graceful and elegant ones. But I LOVED ADVENTURE, so if I got asked, I usually said YES!

I had a yellow bike with a big long banana seat. I ran those tires bald with all the miles I rode that bike. On the day this memory happened with the girls across the street, I'm thinking my yellow bike probably had a flat tire.

I was out in the front yard, babysitting my little brother, who was probably 4 or 5 at the time, which would have made me 8 or 9 years old. The girls across the street rode up on their bikes and asked if I wanted to go on a bike ride with them. I told them my bike was broken and I was babysitting my brother. So they offered to give each of us a ride on their bikes. I wasn't wearing any shoes, but that was not a rare occurrence, so I got on one girl's bike, and put my brother on the other. I don't think he was wearing shoes either.

We rode to a place we often went — it was probably about a mile away from our house as well as I can remember. Could have been more, could have been less, but it was long enough away from home that I wouldn't be able to hear someone from home yell for me and they wouldn't be able to hear me either.

There was a little pond where we liked to look at tadpoles and up a little hill was a site where a house had burnt down a long time ago or something, because we would always find burnt up treasures in the dirt.

Melody Ross

That day it was SO HOT that you could see heat waves coming off the asphalt. We got to the pond and I had to be careful to walk in only the softest dirt and plants because my feet were bare and the ground was scorching hot. We got off the bikes and I was either holding my little brother's hand or giving him a piggyback ride because the ground would burn his feet otherwise.

Then the unspeakable happened. It still feels like yesterday. My two friends got on their bikes, started laughing and rode away. They left my brother and I there to walk home. No bike. No shoes. Scorching ground in every direction.

This memory is so fresh that it still makes my feet hurt. It even makes my heart hurt after all these years.

We lived in the high desert. When it's hot in the desert there are very evil thorns called "goat heads" all over the place. They grow on low vines that spread out across the ground like vengeful monsters, ready to pierce the bottom of your feet, leaving behind a poison that aches for days.

Walking home with my brother on my back on the hot road covered in thorns and rocks was one of the most heart crushing, humiliating and confusing experiences of my life. I know it was just a couple of older girls playing a joke, but it crushed me and stained my childhood in lots of ways.

So as I told this story to Kami, as a nearly 50 year old woman, and isolated it out of the rest of my experience, I started to see how I could learn from it, even now. I also saw similar patterns that have carried through all these decades. I want to learn from this.

For starters, I will not get on someone else's "bike" ever again. I will fix my own bike and ride my own bike.

And I will put shoes on first.

And I will not go to any place without knowing what the plan is, and know how I will get out of there if I need to.

And for goodness sake, if someone does something like that to me ever again, it will be the last time we adventure together.

50 Roads To The Middle Of My Life

I started thinking about this pattern of feeling left behind and I decided to toss it out. I stopped making these stories mean something about me and who I am.

And after 5 decades, these stories still surface like ancient shrapnel that was once embedded somewhere deep in the body; and suddenly there are sharp and angry pieces right under your skin, ready to be removed — these stories we tell ourselves about our experiences secretly go toxic and poison so much of our present life experience.

I just don't want any of them anymore.
So I'm doing the painful work of pulling them out.

The truth is…those girls were young and they were just acting like jerks at the moment. So I got to learn that I will no longer get on a bike with someone who is kind of a jerk. I will learn from it and get my own bike. Or stay home. Or walk.

I just won't get on someone else's bike again in a spontaneous action, with no shoes on and no plan.

This transcends into so many other parts of my personal history, and I can look and see that I have been foolish and went on to do this sort of thing a few more times in my life, even as an adult. Getting on someone's proverbial bicycle, only to be left behind without a plan for how to get back home.

And…I've also had to be honest with myself and remember that many things have happened in my life where others could feel like I WAS THE ONE who left them behind. That's been a sobering thought.

This road taught me once again how we can allow experiences we've had in our history, some that only last a few moments, to stain the rest of our experience. We can allow these experiences to define our value, our possibilities and our self-respect.

Or we can learn from them.

In my course called SOUL RESTORATION, one of the activities we do is to write, in what we call a BURN BOOK. In that book, we write-out past experiences that caused us to go on and create a big narrative around what happened. We created a story and called it truth, and it then traveled with us to the present. When it happened, we put a defining label on ourselves that continues to hold us back.

In this Burn Book exercise, we start by writing . . . "I am a beautiful soul who experienced _____, and that experience hurt and it was terrible. Some of the lies I've told myself about that experience are _____ "

The Burn Book exercise is so effective because we put our experiences back where they should be, **AS ONLY EXPERIENCES.** Not as moments that got to burn labels into our skin with a hot iron. We all get to have myriad experiences throughout life, and hopefully we get to learn something very valuable from every one of them. Not a single one gets to define us permanently, though. Not the good ones and not the tainted ones.

Feeling we are being left behind is some kind of primal fear that is deeply embedded in our DNA. We truly believe we will not survive if we get left behind. So we do all sorts of things to belong so we don't get left behind.

Those behaviors are what need to be examined . . . why we allow others to mistreat us so that we can belong. We don't need to label ourselves by the unkind deeds of others, **OR** even by the unkind deeds we've done to others. Or the unkind deeds we've done to ourselves.

We get to be free of labels.

I pull these stories out of my skin because I want to live as an unlabeled soul.

What I learned on The Road Where I Got Left Behind is that the only variety of being left behind that can truly hurt us is when we leave ourselves behind.

And I am committed to never doing that again.

I am my own ride-or-die. And that feels really good.

Every day, I check and make sure I am bringing myself along. And then

I try to behave like the kind of travel companion you'd want to have on a long journey.

I've learned that this is what makes life constantly an epic adventure.

And I'm here for it.

So, Valuable Soul,

When have you felt completely left behind?

AND

What stories have you embraced about yourself because you thought you'd been left behind?

Tellling ourselves damaging stories can continue to damage our lives until our life is over. Let's tell ourselves the truth.

Next, I'll tell you all about The Road Where I Hitchhiked.

I love you, dear one.
melody freebird

37

The Road Where
I Hitchhiked

Right smack in the middle of a spike in the Pandemic, I picked up a hitch-hiker somewhere in rural New Mexico.

I say "I" instead of "we" because it was my choice and Marq didn't really have any say in it, because I agreed to it before he could even know about it.

We were on a very long road trip to see a dear friend and while he was in the bathroom at a truck stop, all masked up, I saw a young woman and her dog sitting outside, distressed. It was late Fall and the world was reeling from another spike of Covid and it was probably a very dangerous decision to even talk to a stranger up close. But I couldn't say no. I walked over and asked her if she or her dog needed food, and she said she had food, but what she really needed was a ride. I looked deep into her eyes to see if there was any glimpse of deception or ill-intent and all I could see was exhaustion and desperation. And myself.

So I took her over to the fill-up gas tanks where the truck was parked and I offered her some fresh fruit . While she was eating it, I went to tell Marq that we were taking a stranger and her dog a few hours down the road so she could get picked up by someone who could take her home.

He just stood there and looked at me silently for what seemed like several minutes, but was just a looooong few seconds, our eyes were locked but neither of us were saying a word. We've been married long enough though, that he knew what my eyes were saying and I knew what his were saying. So he said . . . "okay, babe." And then he walked over and very kindly loaded her things into the truck and laid out an old blanket for her dog. He made her feel really welcome and like this was all no big deal. I fell in love with him for the 1 millionth time in that moment.

There are SO MANY reasons why picking her up was a bad idea. She could have had Covid. She could have been dangerous in a lot of ways that could easily have ended us all up on a Dateline episode. But none of those reasons were bigger than the reason it was a good idea to pick her up.

She and I talked nonstop for the few hours we were with her. I adored her. I admired her. I was in awe of her. She was brave and resilient and smart. Her dog was adorable and well-behaved. Turns out she was an artist. She made jewelry and sold it at shows out of her van, the same van she lived in. She had been traveling around to shows with friends, but then a deer jumped in front of her van and totaled it, and it wasn't fully insured. So she had a business that kept her going, and then it was gone overnight. Then her friends ditched her too after there was no longer a place to sleep or to get to other places. She'd trusted that someone was going to come and get her in her time of need and they never showed up. So here she was in a strange place, sleeping behind the gas station, trying to figure out how she was going to get to the truck stop where someone had agreed to meet her and take her home.

I believed her then and I still believe her now. I've grown to understand how traumatic it can be when a person tells you their most vulnerable story and you treat them like you don't believe them. I believed her. She was truly doing the very best she could do, she had done the best she could do all along and she'd built a life she loved. Then something happened and now she was out in the world, hitchhiking.

I wanted to give her a safe ride with no strings attached. Because I have been a soul-hitchhiker too. Not wanting to call home because I wanted to prove I could do it out there on my own. Sometimes not even having a home to call home to, or not one I felt like I could call. So then I'd put my thumb out and take whatever ride was available. From whomever was driving.

I've put myself in countless dangerous situations, far more dangerous than the last road where I got on the back of some trickster girls' bikes.

I say this all figuratively. I have actually never stood on a road with my thumb out and actually entered the car of a stranger, but I HAVE put all my golden eggs in one basket and handed that entire basket over to others because I didn't know how to get the eggs to where they needed to go. And I have often put myself in that basket right along with the eggs.

Naive? Risky? Irresponsible? Desperate? Too proud to ask for the safe thing? Or too tired to consider other options? What made ME into a soul-hitchhiker?

Whatever it was, I'm at an age now where it would be ridiculous to ever count myself a victim. I know by now that a person should be very careful who they go for a ride with, and really shouldn't be soul-hitchhiking at all. And, the last few times I've put myself in these kinds of dangerous situations, there was a part of me that knew I was taking a big risk. There was a part of me that knew I was copping-out and that I could rise up and get my own car somehow and take my own self where I needed to go. I was just so so so so tired. Too tired to care what car showed up.

Like that young woman, I have often been in very desperate situations. But I wasn't young anymore, and it's not as romantic and charming and acceptable when a middle-aged woman is hitchhiking as it is when a boho hippie young woman with a handmade backpack and a bottle of kombucha is hitchhiking. I had too many years behind me to not know better. But when I looked into her eyes the first time at that truck stop and saw the desperation, it was another mirror. And I started to forgive myself for what had put ME sleeping behind the proverbial gas station, trying to figure out not only how to get home, but where home even was.

I'm still trying to figure out why I've done this so many times, but I'm learning to forgive myself. And I want to talk about what I learned when I was the "soul-hitchhiker," thumb outstretched, on the road(s) where I got picked up.

And before I begin, I need to say that THIS is a road I've traveled way too

many times. It has brought me more than any other road to a place of recognizing my patterns of being a martyr. And my definition of martyr, as
I've probably said before somewhere in this book . . . is someone who says
yes when they want to say no, and then behaves like a victim and punishes
many of the people they love most because they "had" to say yes instead
of saying no when they knew they should say no.

I have said yes when I knew I should say no — and many times that act
left me without my basket of eggs, on the side of some shady road with my
thumb outstretched, soul-hitchhiking, getting ready to say yes once again
to something I should say no to. AND PUTTING MYSELF THERE.
And then crying because of what happened next.

I need you to know that I know that. And I need to own that. I need to
own it and feel it and change it. So that I can stop doing it.

And I also need to say that not everyone who picks up hitchhikers has
good intentions. And when someone is desperate enough to have to hitch-
hike, it's a damned shame that others take that as an opportunity to exploit
them.

I have always been pretty darned gullible, and until the last few years, I
have been tragically trusting of pretty much every person. When I started in therapy, I learned that there were parts of me that sort of stopped
maturing at the ages where specific trauma took place as a young kid. So
I started learning about some of my erratic and impulsive and confusing behaviors. And what's cool is that our brains have so much elasticity
that we can change our behaviors and we can stop doing the chaotic and
destructive things we do. We can heal into adults who can take care of
themselves, and that's what I'm finally doing.

But it's been messy. I've learned that there was a part of me that just had
no clue that I could take care of myself, though I've been given every opportunity imaginable to prove that to myself — as if I've got an exasper-
ated guardian angel who keeps guiding me to new chances to rise up into
the warrior I've always wanted to be, shaking her head every time I put my
life in someone else's hands after I've been given the perfect situation to
show myself what I can do. She shakes her head and says "we are gonna
have to try AGAIN, this is gonna be painful AGAIN."
Until my therapist and I started to discover this scared little girl inside

of me in therapy, one that I thought I'd healed with art and journaling and words, NO ONE has ever been able to get it through to me what I am capable of. It was never for lack of trying. Countless times, I have looked dead in the eye someone who was trying to talk me "off the ledge" in one of my fear spirals and I got the same familiar look I've gotten so many times, from whomever was looking at me in the same confused way, communicating the message "WHAT IN THE WORLD ARE YOU SO AFRAID OF, WOMAN? YOU HAVE ALREADY DONE SO MANY THINGS!"

And I've never been able to answer. But the fear has been SO REAL and SO BIG.

This might be a big shock to the people who have watched me from the outside. I've been a successful CEO, I've done so many of the things that would make me look like the ultimate boss-babe. I've raised 5 stellar children and had the most epic marriage filled with triumph and tragedy. I've done strong and epic things, but inside I was always terrified and looking for the person who was going to save me, protect me, or give me a ride to the next destination. And often, I picked the first person who was willing. Often I didn't even know where we were going when I got into someone else's "car" but I was just relieved to have a ride for a little while.

I have been so reckless in so many ways.

I got married at age 18 to someone who did take care of me, protect me and take me everywhere I wanted to go. It was the fairy-tale ending that I always wanted as a little girl, and it was that way for a long time. When he had his brain injury when I was 33, that's when I started soul-hitchhiking. I had 5 small children to raise and a big company to run by myself. I had several large baskets full of golden eggs. The first thing I did was put my thumb out and look for the next person who could save me and take me where I needed to go. I handed over my basket. It never occurred to me that I could do it myself. And that I was responsible for protecting my own golden eggs.

Often I behaved like a kid and wanted to be taken care of. Then I was devastated when I got treated like an adult. Sometimes I got treated in good ways and sometimes I got treated in really crappy ways, but either way, it often felt like the child part of me was being abandoned and abused when it was really just a jerk bully adult treating another adult in a crappy way. AND all along, I WAS AN ADULT who didn't know how to behave like an adult — with self-respect, self-protection, boundaries and self-account-ability. I didn't know I could look a bully in the face and tell them to "stick it where the sun don't shine." I didn't know I could take care of myself. I didn't know how annoying it is to other adults who are taking care of themselves to have to work with someone who doesn't believe they are capable of doing the same. I didn't know what I was capable of. I know I annoyed a lot of people while I was out conquering the world, terrified inside.

I'm just learning now, at 50 years old, what I am capable of. And it's both a humiliating and phenomenal realization. There's a road up ahead called THE ROAD WHERE HE TOLD THE TRUTH that happened just before my 50th Birthday, where everything came full circle and I start-ed to scratch the surface of my pattern of soul-hitchhiking; and made a profound commitment to get my own wheels, my own wings and stay on my own Soul Road.

And to hold on to my own golden eggs.

And that right there is one of the biggest lessons I've learned from soul-hitchhiking. That we can't blame others for what they do when we offer everything we've got — and they put their hands out and take it. We have to be careful about what we offer, even when we have hopes that others will do what we believe to be the right thing. It's another way of being a martyr when we put everything we've got out on a table like we are some kind of yard sale, and then we weep when they give us a handful of quarters or dicker down to a handful of pennies. We've got to name our own price, or not sell-out at all.

We each are the sole steward over our own golden eggs. And a basket full of golden eggs is worth so much more than a ride to a truck stop.

When we can't get somewhere as fast as we need to get there, or we can't seem to get there at all, it might mean we need to step back for a moment and assess the situation. It might mean we need to stay where we are a little bit longer and think about where we want to end up.

There are lots and lots of ways to move through life. And there are also a lot of good things about slowing down and letting the river of wisdom inside of us be the only thing that's moving for a while.

Either way, I'm done hitchhiking.

So, Life Traveler,

When have YOU soul-hitchhiked and found yourself somewhere you didn't want to be?

AND

In what places do you find yourself behaving as if you can't move forward without someone taking you there?

I hope you're done hitchhiking too. Next I will take you on the Road To Anam Cara. It's a good one.

I love you and I believe in you.
xo
melody freebird

38

The Road To Anam Cara

I worked hard to find the right place to put this road in this book. And this as good a place as any. I wanted it to be the right place, because this road means a lot to me. So here it is, the perfect place. Because on Road #37, when we picked up a hitchhiker, we were actually on a very long road trip to see my dear friend Robina, where Marq would be doing some remodeling projects on her house in Malibu, California.

So for 4 months, we ended up going from living in our RV, to living in the same neighborhood as the people you see in the movies and on television, in a beautiful Spanish home, surrounded by palm trees, orange trees and ocean breeze. We lived in a small neighborhood filled with famous people who needed privacy. In fact, we lived right next door to a man who shaped a large part of my childhood though the characters he played in so many movies, and on his own multi-decade television show. Now well into his 90s, the real life version of him did not disappoint. He was so kind and so real. For those 4 months, when I was sitting outside at the pool, there were countless times I could hear him singing over the fence . . . with the same jolly holiday voice he used to sing to Mary Poppins.

I'm not going to talk much about how my beautiful friend made her way to where movie stars end up, because she would hate that and frankly, it would be an insult to who she is. But it was a wild experience to see this beautiful bird in flight of a human being and what she was able to build out of not just sheer grit and determination, but a commitment to beauty and art that rivals the greatest creators of our time. I deeply understood her, for I was a bird, too.

I read a book many years ago by John O'Donohue called Anam Cara. It means Soul Friend. It can also be spelled Anamchara . It is wonderful to have a soul friend, isn't it? I am one who feels more comfortable relating to life as a soul than I do as a human being. Being a human has often been very confusing and very painful and very scary to me. I know it feels this way to lots of people. So I am always in search of breadcrumbs to show me the way back to my soul, and to my soul's road. After our time together, Robina and I realized that she is an Anam Cara to me and I am one to her. We are soul friends. We see each other beyond the things that label us as humans. We can be stripped of our labels together, and that is a wonderful experience. But she and I are so similar that when we are together, we can see the labels on ourselves that have to be stripped off if there can ever be the kind of freedom that a freebird needs.

She is an artist in every sense of the word. She is more magical than I could ever use words to describe. She is a very successful clothing designer, interior designer and big dream designer. But all of that pales in comparison to her giant, beautiful, pure heart. She is the embodiment of love.

She is my Anam Cara. She calls me Songbird. I call her Birdie. But she is my Anam Cara.

So let's talk about the origin of this word. Anamchara is traditionally used to refer to one's confessor or spiritual advisor. Originally, it was used to refer to the spiritual advisor a young monk would be assigned when he joined the monastery.

What is extraordinary is that Robina's home was at the base of a mountain that held one of the oldest monasteries in the United States. Almost every day, she and I would walk the winding road up to the top of that mountain where we could see the ocean and the islands and the hills surrounding all of it. She would stand up next to the cross that was lit up at night and we'd talk about Jesus and what He'd think of all of this. One of our strongest connections was the way we both felt about Jesus. And the way we knew He felt about us. We'd walk around that monastery and cry at the statues of Jesus being tortured and crucified. Then we'd smell every different kind of flower on the property. We'd laugh and skip and dance and sing. We were both goofy girls and when we were alone together, we were suddenly 9 years old. We proudly claimed that we were deep and dorky. We talked about poetry and philosophy and fashion and food and heaven. We'd finish each other's sentences.

And that's why our friendship is painful too, because when she and I are together, we are a full-length soul mirror to each other. And that can get very very very messy — when suddenly you see yourself unobstructed.

We had talked and dreamed for over a decade about what it would take for us to finally spend some real time together. And because she and I were both running companies, there was never time. In fact, there would be months and years where we would hardly even check-in with each other. But it was always okay, and we always circled back to our friendship. We made so many plans that had to fall through, but the summer of 2020, she finally got in her motorhome and drove all the way up to the ranch to see me. Almost 20 hours of driving from Texas to Utah. And for 10 days, we made up for lost time. Of course she fell in love with Kami and West, and they fell in love with her too. She was able to connect with the horses and learn so much from West about it all. But mostly we all just sat around and talked in the tiny town where less than 100 people live. We'd sit in the sun, and sit around the fire and we'd pile on her bed in her motorhome and watch movies. We'd drink green smoothies and eat blueberries.

And then it was time for them to go. But they needed some help in Malibu with their house, so Marq and I planned to get there by Fall. And we did.

I have rarely spoken of this friendship in any kind of detail, so for anyone who knows me, it might be a surprise to hear all of this. I have held this relationship close to my chest in an effort to protect it. I cannot bear the thought of anything destroying it. Some people may not even know about our friendship at all. Our friendship has been like the place in the forest you don't tell anyone about because you want to keep it to yourself so that when you can finally get back there, no one will have had the chance to ruin it or name it - there won't be trails and signs that meant some of the trees had to be ripped up. People ruin so many things just by trying to name them and label them. There are so many things to keep holy and without labels. You have to protect those things. It is the same way with my children and my grandchildren, I just don't talk about them. There are things I rarely speak of in detail

Melody Ross

because of the sacred nature of them. And the risk of them getting sullied.

But I asked Robina if it was okay if I wrote about us in my book. Those 4 months together in Malibu shaped my life experience in ways that I'm still trying to make sense of. And it was the same for her.

There are people who don't have to say a word to you, and they teach you with every breath of their being. That's how it is with us. And it's not because either of us are wise and sage, or even trying to teach. It's because we are a mirror to each other. We see each other in ourselves, and that's why our relationship is so complicated and why I'm grateful we had 10 years to prepare for our time together.

Robina and I have been friends since the moment we were introduced to each other, and we have the most complicated bond I have ever experienced with another human being. When I asked her if I could write about it, we started to talk about what this has been like for both of us . . . to know someone who is so much like you that you can't run from yourself anymore. It sounds wonderful in theory, but it gets complicated and can be very painful for both parties. She and I were friends for over a decadebefore we even got to be together in the flesh. We were introduced because we were both in the issue of the same magazine and after the publisher had flown to each of our homes, interviewing and photographing us for days . . . she said the same thing to both of us. That she had never met two people who were so much alike, and that it would be tragic if we never met and made friends.

We became instant friends the way so many of us do . . . over the internet and the phone. We'd send words and art and love to each other. We are both artists, free spirits and magical thinkers. We both want to save the world from all suffering. We have both had our share of trauma. We have both ended up on a fast-moving train after our art ventures were successful. But both of us would rather be sitting up in a tree in a forest, talking to the animals and the sky and making castles out of mud and sticks and moss. We did all of that together in Malibu, incidentally.

So we create as adult ladies with child hearts. And when we are together and I see the way she is, I see the way I am. And that is a difficult reality and a beautiful reality. I see her go through things that she can't talk about and it brings up the things I can't talk about. I see the crushing weight of all her responsibilities and labels and it's a mirror of my own. I see her big, generous

276

and beautiful heart getting misunderstood and crushed while she balances being a successful and epic businesswoman and it's like watching those life reviews that people talk about when they have a near-death experience. That's what it's like when we are together — it's like we've died and gone somewhere in the ethers where everything is truth. And Love. Experiencing technocolor love like this can make the rest of life a dull experience if you let it. That's what makes it complicated.

I am certain she and I have been together and known each other for millennia, however that works. This feeling is so real that it is painful to be apart and it is also painful to be together - simply because we know we will have to be apart again. And the way we know each other so well creates all sorts of feelings and situations that you can't run and hide from. So you have to be ready to be seen that way to be able to be together.

These relationships that can't exist on a surface level make us grow the most. They are so reflective, like a mirror. You can't pretend anything. So you better be ready to be real or it's just going to throw everything into a tailspin. Sacred things are like that. That's the way it feels with my children. And my grandchildren, and with my husband when he is well and when he is sick. So I hold these relationships in a little pouch around my neck that hangs right by my heart. And I don't talk about it.

I hold all of my friendships sacred this way. But Robina has a very public life. She's a famous designer. She works with celebrities and big names and she's so much more than all of that. We are all so much more than the way we get labeled.

Anam Cara means soul friend, and although I would truly say that I have at least 2 handfuls of friends who I would count as deep soul friends, there have been none quite like Robin. Because she is so much like me that I have to face all my demons when I'm with her. Because I see the same ones vexing her. I have to face the ways I often treat myself and allow others to treat me, because I see the same experiences happening to her. From the first connection we made, it has felt like we were conjoined twins, separated at birth. This leads to very complicated, difficult and blissful feelings. And I write this road to try to explain things that happen in life that feel so beautiful and good that they will hurt for the rest of your life because they can't always be just like they were.

This road was otherworldly. And sometimes when you've had otherworldly experiences, you spend the rest of your life feeling homesick for a place that simply does not exist on this planet.

But you get glimpses, and that has to sustain you. That's what I had during my 4 months with Robin. Glimpses so potent that the entire quarter of a year felt like one long near-death experience. Like I said before, the kind you read about where a person's body dies, and they go to a place in the ether and they see a review of their life, they see things as they are, they learn what life means . . . and then they come back down to earth and feel an edict to live out what they learned. Robin and I had an experience like that together, and then we both had to go back to our lives and live out what we learned.

They say that when you have a near-death experience, you often feel jealous of people who get to cross over to the other side where they're not on earth anymore. That's how I feel sometimes, and I know Robina does too. Because we both got to see a glimpse of what is truest and what is most real. We walked with angels and we saw the horror and the beauty of what life can do to a person. In each other's eyes and in each other's stories, we got to see a sort of life-review.

We both had to learn about finding something you've always wanted to find and having to exercise the disciipline to be happy that it happened more than sad that it's over

Coincidentally, Robin just finished her memoir, and I hope you'll read it. The working title is Carving Your Own Sun and that's just what I've seen her do.

And I know what it takes to do something like that. I've done it myself. I know what it takes to pull yourself up and out of your trauma, over and over again. And to pull your dreams and plans and ideas up and out of your mind and heart. . . for all the world to see and to judge, too. It's an incredible honor and a beautiful experience. But it can leave scars. When we'd sit together, I saw her scars like I was at a 3-D movie and I was the only one who had the glasses to see them. It was the same for her. She could see my scars. We didn't have to talk about what gave us our scars and that was such a relief. We just sat and loved each other. We reverted back to who we actually are, just idealist little girls, here to love and play and create with whatever is in front of us. We saw each other beyond the "dream life" we'd each worked so hard to create over and over again.

50 Roads To The Middle Of My Life

When our 4 months was over, it was an incredibly painful experience to say goodbye. It was like watching yourself go back out into the mean old world. We'd worked through layers and layers and layers to see the sacredness of each other and ourselves. This gave such a glimpse into each other that touched our hearts in ways I don't know if we will ever stop feeling, like phantom pain

We would sneak away with the dogs and go on walks through the creek bed. We'd go to the ocean and to the horse farm or farmer's markets. I'd look over at her as we were driving in her little open-topped vehicle and her cheeks were shiny like apples on a tree. We'd be laughing and laughing. Telling dorky jokes and talking about the deepest things. She had so much light in her eyes when I looked at her. It was a mirror, because I looked exactly the same way.

And then I'd see her deep pain. And it activated my deep pain. I would cry at night because I wanted to take her pain away. And then I realized it was my own pain talking. Being with Robin made me see where I needed to heal.

We'd sit by the pool and I'd read books of poetry to her while she rested from her millions of meetings. We'd turn up the music and dance all the way around the water with the dogs chasing us. We'd laugh and sing. We'd go out back and pick oranges off the tree. We'd hear our friend over the fence singing his songs and talk about how on earth we ended up where we were in our lives. We'd walk the neighborhood and see famous people drive by . . . they'd wave. And we saw that they were just little kids too . . . trying to find their way just like we were.

We hated when it was over. We still do. But it gave us the gift we both needed. We needed to see our own selves in someone we deeply loved so we'd start treating ourselves with the same kind of love we'd want to give each other.

She got me on a path of using food as medicine. She'd make us all the most incredible meals out of the most beautiful plants of all kinds. She taught me how to make the perfect green smoothie and how to make the most delicious soups. I learned so much from her.

It's still surreal to me to think about those 4 months. Like it was a dream. I'm still trying to process all that happened over that time and I know she is too. It's so difficult when things end before you want them to. But it also makes the remembering really sweet. And my remembrances are sweet.

What I learned on the Road to Anam Cara is that we are all on such personal journeys, but they're also so much the same. Each of us wants to be seen and loved for WHO WE ARE rather than for who we appear to be, or who others make us to be.

I learned that no matter how much success or failure you experience in your life, none of it changes who you are. I know some of what Robin has overcome, and it would take your breath away. I won't give you a spoiler because I really want you to read her book, but this woman has walked through the depths of hell over and over again . . . always emerging with another sun she carved. A sun big enough to light up this entire universe. And that's what she does. She lights this place up. Big time.

It was surreal to be there. I know I keep saying that, but it just was. I was walking around during those 4 months among the "rich and famous" but no one knew I was actually experiencing absolute ruin and feeling like such a failure. It's such an example of how we should never make a final judgement about a person from what we can see on their outside layer.

Robin appeared to be at the height of every American Dream story. But I know the other side of that stick. She suffers while she's giving. Not BECAUSE she is giving, because giving is what sustains her. But she suffers tremendously every day WHILE she's giving. She just doesn't let it stop her. Among many other trials, she also has very crippling headaches and tremendous pain. I'd watch her work and work and work until she collapsed in bed — not even able to feel the relief of sleep. I'd sit on her bed with her and massage her scalp and face and feet and hands. I'd grab my guitar and sing to her. And she couldn't see me, but I was crying. Her pain was my pain.

And I wish this was how we could all be together in this world. I wish the pain of the homeless man on the street was EVERYONE'S pain. I wish when we looked in the eyes of someone magnificent, we saw our own magnificence. I wish when we dreamed up a beautiful world for ourselves, we always included a beautiful world for everyone else.

Because that's what I experienced with my dear Anam Cara, Robina Brown. She and I talk often of the world we are trying to create, and the ways we'd love to be able to work together someday. As life would have it in all of its twists and turns, we have not been able to see each other since the days in

Malibu.

But like every other soul friend, I know we will be together again as soon as it is time.

I think the lesson that sticks most fervently from traveling this road is that we are ALL Soul Family. Sometimes we get to be face to face with soul siblings who are so familiar that we wake up from the afflictions of being human . . . but if we could see things as they truly are, we are ALL soul siblings with each other. We are all mirrors to each other, too.

Robina and I each have a matching bird on our neck holding a key so we can always find our way back to each other. No matter how locked up I get, she'll always have the key to get in and wake me up to go on an adventure. And I have a key to her heart, too. I know that time will come again.

Until then, I will pull out my pocket knife and keep carving suns the way she taught me. And as I think of her, I will see myself in the deep fondness I feel. I will do no harm to myself because I would do no harm to her. I will treat myself the way I want her to be treated.

I love her. And loving her taught me to love myself.

So, Beautiful Soul Friend,

Who in your life is a mirror to YOU?

AND

What is it like to be in their presence?

I learned so much in beautiful Malibu. Next we take a dramatic turn down The Road To The Laundromat.

I will see you there.
xo
melody freebird

39

The Road To
The Laundromat

People who utilize laundromats have their reasons. And something is consistently true, no matter what the reasons are; most of the people you find in a laundromat do not live mainstream lives like the ones you see on tv sitcoms. In truth, laundromat people are generally pretty epic and often society's outsiders.

I have not only met the most interesting and out-of-the-box humans at laundromats, I've also been one of those interesting and out-of-the-box humans; waiting for the washer or dryer to finish. I have been that mysterious person trying to figure out what kind of payment system this particular laundromat has, or finding the place where I can fold my shirts and pants without taking up too much space because everyone else needs to do the same thing.

I'm sure others are people-watching at the laundromat just like I am. And when being people-watched, I'm the aging woman in funky t-shirts and ripped jeans and boots. I'm the one who has way too often left lipstick in my pocket accidentally and ruined an entire load of laundry in the dryer for the whole room of fellow laundromatters to see. That's how I've broken the ice in lots of new laundromat friendships, when they hear me gasp as I hold up a ruined t-shirt covered in melted pink wax . . . and they look at me either very sympathetically or start cracking up in laughter because they've done that before too. It always breaks the ice.

Melody Ross

Marq and I probably go to the laundromat every 2 weeks. We call it a date night. Sometimes it's longer between visits and sometimes it's shorter for some reason or another, but it averages every other week.

The first few months of this lifestyle, I would sit and watch and try to guess what these fellow laundromatter's lives were like, what it could be that brought them to this place instead of doing laundry at home. I did this because I was constantly wondering what people would think if they saw me there. I used to have my own laundry room, with my own front load washer and high speed dryer. I used to have a really nice countertop for folding my clothes, and a big bar above the washer and dryer to hang them. Of course I rarely used either the countertop or the clothes bar, opting for folding laundry on my bed while watching Netflix — in my bedroom, in my house, where I could look outside and see my yard. And now there I was, sitting in a laundromat, counting quarters and measuring detergent and sitting in my car between loads to avoid having to talk to anyone about why I was at the laundromat. I lived in an RV, I had no house, no yard, no washer, no dryer. My life was in smithereens. Like an insecure middle-schooler on the first day of school, I felt like there was a sign on my forehead that said "LOSER."

I'm embarrassed to admit how deep those feelings ran.

Those first few months I rarely made eye contact with the others in the laundromat because I didn't know if they felt as humiliated as I did. But that reluctance only lasted a few months, and it was ridiculous anyway. Again, being in the laundromat made me feel defeated at first, so I kept my head down and didn't make eye contact.

As months went on, it started to feel like a routine, and it started to feel convenient and fast. I started to feel blessed to be there instead of treating it like some kind of ordeal. I got comfortable with being there. I felt like I belonged.

Then I started making eye contact with others, and that went well, so I started talking to them. And somewhere in there, I stopped feeling humiliated and started enjoying the process immensely, feeling a kinship and a curiosity and a unity with the people there. It has caused me a lot of pause to think about why I felt humiliated in the first place, and that's what this road is all about . . . not just the shift in feelings, but the reason for the

284

initial feeling in the first place.

When I started talking to people at the laundromat, I met some of the coolest and most interesting people I could ever begin to imagine. People I deeply respect — almost more than anyone I've ever met. In those moments between loads, I heard so many pieces of so many life stories that I started to fall in love with the human experience again, and with the whole human family. I learned from hearing these stories how quickly things can change in people's lives. I learned how many people choose the kinds of lives that lead to regularly using a laundromat and I learned that other people were there because of things that had happened that were out of their control. Things that left them owning no washer and no dryer — that was us too.

The most important thing I learned was that I had a great big problem in my heart and my beliefs. One that caused me to believe that a person's value is somehow tied to what they own and where they do their laundry.

I also learned that when you've only got $20 left to your name, and you've got to spend $15 of it getting all of your laundry clean, you stop caring so much about what people might think if they saw you walk into a laundromat.

This year, a new series came out on Netflix called MAID. It's about a single mother trying to make it in the world. There's something very compelling about the editing of this show; up in the corner of the screen, there's a tally of the money she's got left and how much everything costs. You can see $17 go to $6 when she has to buy something for them to eat . . . then $6 goes in her gas tank, and then it's $0 - then she gets an unexpected charge for something and the numbers go into the negative. My stomach hurt watching it. I know that feeling well as we've been doing all we can to rebuild our life. I watched every episode of that series and even though I'm not single, and I'm not raising babies anymore, I felt a deep understanding of that young woman as she worked hard to navigate a world that seems to be designed to perfectly fit a perfect kind of sitcom lifestyle, leaving the ones on the fringes to figure out how to get their needs met in very complicated ways. I watched her get knocked down and judged and set-aside. She also got the runaround constantly when she asked for help, or for just a chance.

The me from my old life, while watching that show, would probably have thought about all the things she "should" have done to avoid getting herself in the position she was in. I would have felt bad for her and rooted for her, but still "othered" her by thinking I would "never get myself in that position." The old me would have thought the show was over dramatic and extreme and unbelievable, too. But the new "laundromat me" understood her on so many levels. The "laundromat me" watched situations she endured on the series and could empathize because over these years of not having a home of our own, I have lived out experiences that would have made the old me judge the "laundromat me" pretty harshly.

That's a hard pill to swallow.
And a great gift of awareness.

I have a lot of skills and so does my husband. I have a lot of contacts, I have a lot of friends, I have a lot of prospects, I have a lot of experience and I have a lot of ideas. We are hard workers, we are friendly and easy to get along with. We are resourceful and efficient. We do our best to be good to the people around us and we are both very conscientious about making sure we do a stellar job at whatever we are doing. We have been financially prosperous at many times in our life together and we have been flat-broke just as many times. We are bootstrappers and we've made a zillion wonderful things from scratch. We've always had what we thought were good ideas and good intentions.

But terrible things still happened.
Terrible things happen to everyone.

And rarely do we know the story behind what happened or why someone is in the position they are in.

Over the last few years, I've done a lot of observing — and trying to process what I'm observing. Maybe it's because I'm older and not immersed in mothering young children. Maybe it's because I'm often in new places where no one knows me, so it's easy to observe without being observed. Maybe it's because I'm a little wiser than I used to be. But what I've observed is how quickly a person can fall out of grace. How fast a person can go from being okay to not being okay. I've watched how quickly someone can lose just about everything, when they were just fine the year before, or the month before, or the day before. I've heard so many stories and seen so much human triumph and human tragedy, at the laundromat and everywhere else.

I HAVE PERSONALLY been okay one month and at the bottom of the pit the next. And it's so much more complicated than our culture makes it out to be.

I bring this up because when your life is humming along, it's really hard to see and understand how others' lives aren't. I know this because I had always lived in a house, always had what I needed, always felt part of something somewhere. It was hard to see how others got themselves in the positions they were in, how they found themselves without the security that a home and a place and a community you can count on gives your life

I felt compassion, but it wasn't empathy. It was pity.

I wasn't thinking…"I wonder what happened to them?" . . .
I was thinking…."what is wrong with them?

I was thinking "oh you poor thing…"
instead of "wow, that could be me."

Because I never thought it could be me. I had worked too hard and had too many sure things.

Until I didn't.

Like I said, when your life is humming along, it's really hard to see and understand how others' lives aren't.

So you think . . . if they'd just do this and this and this, they'd be fine. Or you think . . . maybe if they hadn't have done this or that or that, they wouldn't be in the position they're in. And then you go on living your life and telling people you'll pray for them when they express some of the hardships they're living, because you tell yourself that they'll be fine just like you are, because you've worked hard, right? If they'd just work hard, they'd be okay. They just need to make better decisions and work harder.

What I've learned, though, is that it's SO EASY and SO FAST to lose your footing, to lose yourself, to lose your belongings, your confidence, your position. It's so easy to lose LIFE AS YOU KNOW IT overnight. It can happen SO FAST, in an instant sometimes. An accident, a sickness, a death, a betrayal, a truth finally becoming known that was always there but you didn't know it, a nervous breakdown or burnout or heart attack. Humming along can go to the bottom of a pit VERY QUICKLY.

But it is SO SLOW, so so sooooo slow to find your footing after that's happened. To find yourself. To start gathering and rebuilding belongings from almost zero. It's so slow to find your confidence and to know where you fit in the world after you lose it all. It's long and tedious and requires so much more than people know who have never lived it. So people who are living it rarely talk about it. First of all, because they don't have time to talk about it. Most of their time is spent trying to survive and rebuild and keep their thoughts where they need to be to get to the next minute. And secondly, the kinds of ill-informed, judgmental and pitiful responses or suggestions a person is often met with make things so much worse. Even the tone of voice makes things worse. Very often, a person who is trying to get back to a place of "humming along" is very very very quiet and very very very solitary. Every resource has to be carefully managed, especially the resources required to interact with other people.

I have often drawn from an experience I had more than a decade ago. I knew it was a moment I'd always remember, but I didn't know that our lived experiences over the last few years would end up being the time I would need daily doses of this story. It was during the early years of Marq's brain injury, when my children were all home and small.

It was Christmastime. I was Christmas shopping by myself, because I did most things by myself then. Marq was just not well enough to go with me. I was buying gifts for my kids. It was snowing. I was at a popular strip mall and had just emerged from Bath and Bodyworks with a bag of good smelling stuff. I was tired and hungry and feeling a little sad because I was alone. I'm sure I was decked out in a furry jacket and funky boots, with artsy bangles up my arm.

I parked at an Arby's restaurant and went in and ordered a sandwich and sat down and ate it by myself. While I was eating, I saw a man outside on the corner across the street. He had a sign, asking for money. I watched him out there in the snow the whole time I was eating. He looked to be about a decade older than I was.

Well, I had $100 in my purse, it was what I had left after my shopping was done. So I went and ordered him a sandwich and took the $100 bill and walked over like a sparkly good samaritan and offered him the sandwich and told him I was done with my Christmas shopping and had this money leftover. I rehearsed what I was going to say and then my plan was to turn around, get in my car, switch the seat warmers to HOT on my leather seats, and head home.

So I did what I rehearsed, and he was grateful — but then he asked for what he really needed, and I had to make a decision. He asked me if I'd walk back inside to Arby's with him and sit with him while he ate his sandwich. So, I hesitated for a moment and then agreed to do that. He grabbed his tattered backpack and the Arby's bag and we walked across the street and back into the restaurant. Over the course of about 30 minutes, he told me his story. He started with "my life wasn't always like this…" and then went on to tell me about how he'd gotten in an accident, couldn't work, then got very depressed and had to start selling his belongings to have money to live on. Every month he couldn't work, things got worse, until he couldn't pay his rent and got evicted. He told me this between bites and when we started the conversation, he wouldn't even make sustained eye contact. Once he started talking, he looked me right in the eyes more and more earnestly with every detail. He told me he became homeless after he ran out of things to sell and ended up living in his truck. He didn't have any family he could count on and his friends sort of ditched him once he became depressed and especially after he became homeless. He'd tried homeless shelters but terrible things happened there, he said, so he just lived in his truck in random parking lots. He was looking for work but as things got worse, he didn't have anywhere to shower or keep his clothes clean. It was a cycle that seemed endless and he didn't know how to get out of it. He was panhandling to have the money to get cleaned up so he could get a job.

Just like the girl we picked up at the truck stop, I believed every word he said, I could feel the raw truth in his story.

We said goodbye. I can't remember whether I hugged him or not but I hope I did. I got in my car and I couldn't stop crying.

Because this was my husband's story. He got in an accident, he couldn't work, he got very depressed. And THIS COULD HAVE BEEN HIM.

Melody Ross

THIS WOULD HAVE BEEN HIM. Except that he had me. And his parents. And friends. And kids. And a community. This guy didn't have any of that, and so over the months, he was at the bottom of a pit. And it was going to be SLOOOOOW and LOOOOOONG to find his footing again.

I think of that story when I'm at the laundromat. And then I hear more similar stories while I'm folding clothes — when I just look up and say hello instead of burying my face in my own shame or my own self-righteousness or even my own exhaustion. I also hear the stories of adventurers, and people whose washer is broken, and people who just want to get all their laundry done in an hour even though they have a washer and dryer at home. I have spoken to the newly divorced, the ones on business trips, and the ones who finally have a home after living in their car but still love the laundromat. All of these stories have been me, or could be me. And they could be you.

They could be any of us.

We've had a 2 year stretch of living in an RV. And it's been a big learning experience. We are finding our footing, getting back on our feet and even currently living in a house over the Winter. But it has been long. And I hear the veiled meanings in others' comments to me that I feel like I know the intention behind . . . comments meant to be helpful, I think, but that reek of a gross lack of understanding. Comments that essentially mean "maybe if you wouldn't have made that decision, you wouldn't be in this position . . ." or "just do this, and you won't be in this position anymore."

And unless you know the deep complications that first of all lead to losing what you've built in life, and then the even deeper complications that come from starting over, it's not worth it to even respond to those kinds of comments. On the road to the laundromat, I learned when to be quiet and when to speak about our own circumstances. And I learned why so many others who are rebuilding their lives do the same.

Like I said, we are currently rebuilding our life, and I feel like at the moment, we are on pretty solid footing. I am experienced enough to know it's a fragile balance and that we could lose it all again tomorrow. We have what we need, in fact, I can say with all honesty that I feel showered in abundance of a whole new kind.

We don't have a washer and dryer yet. Still saving quarters and checking pockets for lipstick. Literally and figuratively.

We still go to the laundromat for our dates, and maybe we always will. Because I love it there and that's where we learn the things that matter most.

So Gorgeous Soul,

How have you been categorized in ways that hurt because of your life's circumstances?

AND

When do you KNOW you have somehow been spared from the challenges others are going through and how can you be an ally to them?

This is a road I hope to travel for the rest of my life. And I hope you'll try it out too.

Next I will take you to the very personal Road Where He Told Me The Truth.

I will see you there.

If you've made it this far with me, I thank you deeply. And I love you.
xo
melody freebird

40

The Road Where He Told Me The Truth

I mentioned a few roads back that there have only been a few times when I've made my husband cry, and this road is about one of those times. It was only a few months ago.

As I started writing this book, I had great expectations to finish it in 50 consecutive days. I started writing it exactly 50 days before my 50th birthday, planning an epic finish line on that exact day. And I was cruising along just fine until we got Covid about 2 weeks in. First Kami got it, on HER birthday, and then each one of us started getting sick within 2-3 days with a lot of the same symptoms. So we all decided together that we would pack up and head to the top of the mountain and quarantine together in an equestrian campground with the horses in tow. We decided we'd stay at least a week, and take care of each other either around the fire or from our respective RVs.

This campground was above Fish Lake at nearly 10,000 ft. of Utah elevation, and smack in the middle of the largest aspen grove in the world, which I will talk about later. The leaves were changing and it was a spectacular show of color and seasonal transformation. We were the only ones at the campground and for the first few days of cooking homemade soup and sitting together around the fire, it was just a pretty darned magical way to spend our recovery time. Our doctor had loaded us up with all sorts of supplements and protocol and we were diligently doing everything we'd been instructed to do. Within a few days, we were totally on the mend.

The horses needed to be fed and walked and on the 3rd day there, Marq was walking one of the wild mustangs and the horse got spooked and kicked him. I was in the RV resting and writing, keeping up with my schedule of writing one chapter per day and I heard some commotion. I kept writing but then I heard Marq and West talking loud — the way people talk during an emergency. I looked out to see Marq holding his arm close to himself as he and West were inspecting it. So I stepped outside and walked over just as he was pulling up his sleeve to reveal the worst contusion I had ever seen. His forearm was already swollen up to twice it's size in a big strange bump that looked like his bones were popping out. Turns out it was just mutilated muscle and swelling. He had put his arm out to protect himself from the kick. As pain started to sear in his shoulder, he remembered that when the horse kicked his arm, it threw his arm all the way back behind his shoulder.

Although he was fairly certain his arm was broken, we had no idea how damaged his shoulder was until we headed down the mountain to the only medical clinic in the county, where cowboys came in regularly. After the x-rays we learned that his shoulder was very very injured, and this started a long string of drives to bigger and bigger towns, and more powerful equipment to take more intense images through MRI, to an orthopedic surgeon and then ultimately to a shoulder surgery specialist.

Now let me tell you about how the summer went before Autumn came and landed us in this picture. Marq was apprenticing with West to learn Science Based Horsemanship and he had just been hired by West full-time after spending 2 years learning. He had a million things planned because he was feeling so great. He'd spent the summer fixing fences and doing all sorts of beautiful restoration and remodeling projects on the ranch. He was on top of the world. It had been a very long time since his old brain injury symptoms had vexed him because when we are up at the ranch, where the population of the town is literally 99 people, there is not the over-stimulation of modern life that scrambles a lot of people's brains who have suffered a traumatic brain injury. When we have a quiet life in nature, he thrives. So after spending that summer at the ranch, he was not just back to himself, but a version of himself I had not seen in a very long time. He knew and so did I . . . and everything started to feel really good and look really bright. We talked about what this could mean, that I wouldn't have to work so much if he felt good enough to work. I was already wrestling with my fear of reemerging into the world, mixed with my desire to be working and creating again. It was a daily battle. Him working was making it easier and easier for me to procrastinate and even consider staying hidden forever.

This issue with Marq's up and down brain health is something we don't talk about much because like so many of these roads, it's easier to stay silent. Silence is easier because people do not understand the complex nature of it and the conversations often end with us feeling a lot of pain, feeling lost, and definitely feeling harshly judged. One of the greatest miracles of the last few years is the way West and Kami understand it wholly and completely. There's never any awkwardness or explanation required when his brain needs a rest from unexpectedly flipping a switch that takes him down. So Marq having this wonderful opportunity to be the ranch manager and also a horse trainer was a dream come true. And the greatest happy ending to a long story of trying to figure out how Marq can maintain employment when he has no idea how long his brain will cooperate.

Perhaps you can now imagine that Marq breaking his shoulder was heartbreaking on a thousand different levels for a thousand different reasons. As the extent of the injuries became more and more clear, he and I each felt so much defeat and frustration and sorrow. But the actual physical pain he endured was even more than the heartbreak. This pain remained, day and night, night and day . . . with very little help from any kind of medication or device. Weeks of pain turned into months of pain, with little to no mobility. And what had looked like it was going to be the beginning of a really bright future of dreams coming true slowly turned into a very dark episode of depression. Again.

I hope I can find the right way to explain in words what I want to express next, because it could come out all wrong. I will set this up by telling you that Marq and I have had hundreds of conversations over the 30+ years we've been together about MY dysfunctional patterns that were not caused by a brain injury, but by soul injuries. I had old beliefs that came from early childhood trauma and from experiences I'd replicated a bunch of times over my adulthood — in the way that lots of traumatized people do. So I'd have periods where I would shut down because of old soul injuries and he'd have periods where he would shut down because of an old brain injury. And we'd see-saw with each other. It's been exhausting for both of us.

He's not a scared person, he has a very strong sense of himself and he always has. He was already a very honest and straightforward person, someone you could always count on to not only do what he said he was going to do; but to also tell the truth, no matter how brutal. After his frontal lobe brain injury these attributes got even stronger. It's as if all filters that humans create to make it easy to bend the truth were destroyed in him, and he could not bend the truth even if he wanted to. His brain injury made him even more crystal-clear honest. He's honest in a way that intimidates people and makes any situation where the truth is bent very uncomfortable for the truth bender and for him.

So we forge a life where things can be as simple and true as possible. Because his brain goes haywire when he can't make sense of things.

When he has these periods where his brain shuts down, it manifests as what could best be described as a deep depression. I try to ask him questions to understand what's going on with him on the inside and he has a hard time putting it into words. He will hardly talk during these periods. I become invisible to him. He does not look at me or talk to me or even acknowledge me . I don't know what's happening on the inside of him, but on the outside, I lose him. Everyone loses him. He is there, and then suddenly he's gone. And anyone who's around him when he IS there gets to witness the absolute magnificence of this incredible man. His talents know no end. His goodness knows no end. He is the most skilled craftsman, carpenter, welder and teacher. He is funny and fun and incredibly intelligent with an engineer's mind. He's also beautifully sensitive, and loves nature more than anyone I know. He loves people in such an earnest and true way. He's a mountaineering survivalist, a canyoneering expert and he's hiked thousands of miles in remote places. He serves and serves and serves everyone around him. Children love him. Animals love him. Adults who are not chronic truth benders love him. He is the truest person I know.

One of the great challenges of my life is to try to understand how he has maintained his devotion to his God when he has spent a life of serving others and doing good and right things constantly, only to have his body betray him and lock away his life-force to live in some prison that seems to exist 60 feet into the ground where none of us can find him. If I'm honest, the lot he has been dealt in life has many times caused me to scream angry words at my God.

He was a world-class athlete when his accident happened. He was running our business with zero debt. He spent at least 20 hours a week volunteering in the community. He was legendary, everyone in town knew him and seemed to have at least one story of when he'd dropped everything to help them. Because of his lifetime of service and integrity, the stack of letters he has from human beings towers into the air, and every letter says pretty much the same thing . . . "thank you for helping me to become who I am by being the man you are." One guy said what I think just about everyone feels about him . . . "if you were to look up honorable man in the dictionary, you would see a picture of Marq Ross."

I could go on and on about what this man has endured, what he has lost over the years and what he has had to sacrifice and suffer for so many of the days of his life. For a guy who makes meticulous plans, you can only imagine the hell he must feel when he gets these very unplanned brain shut-downs and feels himself sliding down down down down, not able to stop it.

Believe me, we've tried everything to stop it.

With all the experiences others have had with him, what people DON'T know is what happens when he and I are alone, and what he is to ME. Since our first date, this man has seen something in me that I have had great difficulty seeing in myself. He has said in a million different ways and shown me with a million different actions that he would do just about anything for me to see who I am and what I'm capable of. He's said it so many times to me that I could never begin to count them up.

Over these years when so much went wrong, and I finally broke and had a nervous breakdown, he would sit with me and look me deeply in the eyes and tell me that I just need to know who I am. He sat with me the first time I started working with my therapist and said the same thing to the therapist . . . "I really hope you can finally help her see who she is."

This last summer, I was working so hard in therapy. He would tell me so many evenings around the fire that he could see me healing, and he said I never looked more beautiful and it was because I was finally figuring out who I am. I had been working hard that whole spring and the winter before that, too. But I still didn't really know what he meant when he said that.

When my life's work disappeared the way it did, it set me back so far in my healing journey. It was hard for me to even think about putting my work back out in the world because that would mean I'd have to put MYSELF back out into the world. So I made every excuse I could. And when he started to come back alive on the ranch, and then when West hired him, I saw it as a great way for me to stay disappeared. I wouldn't have to face my debilitating fears and I could just stay hidden in the mountains, never to be found. I could fade away into obscurity and I'd never have to face the deep pain of reemerging after so much had happened.

Well, then he got kicked and it was made clear that he wasn't going to be able to work. And I started melting down in a big fear spiral.

When I get that way, everything is so scary to me. Everything feels so insurmountable. Everything feels impossible. I cry a lot. My hands shake. I forget everything good and brave and strong I've ever done.

That's how I got.

One morning a few weeks after his shoulder injury, I woke up in the RV and he wasn't in bed with me. I got up and stepped down the stairs of the bedroom into the rest of the "house" and he was sitting at the table because his shoulder pain had kept him from sleeping.

When I walked down the stairs, he looked at me and his eyes filled with tears. Or maybe they were already filled with tears. I could feel the heaviness in the air. I stood and looked at him. I asked him if something was wrong.

And he said, "Babe, it's time for you to figure out who you are. You've got to figure this out. It's time. Please"

He was literally begging me.

And I said, "what?"

His tone was so sober, it was as if we were in a dramatic movie and he'd been waiting up to tell me he found evidence of me doing something scandalous and he was confronting me. He said that sentence with so much serious conviction.

And again I said, "what? what do you mean?"

I sat down across from him at the little RV table. He went on to tell me about a dream he'd had hours before that rocked his whole being. And before he told me, he said again "there is **NOTHING** I wouldn't do for you to figure out who you are, for you to see yourself the way I see you and the ones who truly know you see you."

And I said what I'd said to him so many times . . . "I don't know what you mean."

And that's when he started to sob. He said in his dream, he first saw the way I grew during the 6 worst years after his brain injury — how when he was taken out of my life for a while, I had to learn to do very difficult things and become very very strong.

And then he started to sob so severely that I could hardly make out what he was saying. He said . . ."and then in the dream, I saw that the only way you would put your work out into the world again is if I got hurt again."

I was silent.

He went on to say, "I would do anything for you babe, **ANYTHING**. But please figure out who you are so you can move forward. So I can move forward, so we can move forward together. I don't want to be stuck anymore. I don't want to be sick. I don't want you to be stuck anymore. I want us to move forward."

I got the message. Big time.

This is a guy who would **NEVER** shift blame, or project or not take total responsibility for himself. But this was a very real moment for us. One where we were both sobbing. Because I knew exactly what he was talking about. I was hiding out, playing small, terrified, weak and trying to disappear in any way I could. And I'd done this **ANY TIME** I felt like I was finally in a place where I wasn't being **FORCED** to show up in the world. I'd take **ANY** opportunity to disappear and never have to be seen by anyone, ever. His illness had always forced me to show up in the world, no matter how scared I was. We had been doing this weird dance for more than 15 years - where I would only let myself be seen if I **HAD TO**.

And he was finally telling the truth about what that was like for him. He'd never said **ANYTHING** like this to me before this moment. I could tell by the way he was talking to me that this was a burden he'd been carrying for so long, that he could see the dysfunction in it but didn't know how to talk to me about it without it hurting me or hurting us. He just kept saying . . . "you need to figure out who you are. You need to see it."

I was desperate for him to be okay. So I said…"I will do it, I promise. I will do it, I will do it for you."

And then he stood up and rose his voice in big gulping sobs, his eyes overflowing with fat tears and said "DAMMIT, Mel, don't do it for me. STOP DOING THINGS FOR ME. DO IT FOR YOU. DO IT FOR YOURSELF."

Never has he spoken to me in such a stern way. That's how I knew he meant all that he was saying. I could clearly see how much he'd reached the end of his ability to carry me. Simultaneously, I had reached the end of my ability to carry him.

And then I started to understand what he meant by "knowing who I am."

I am someone who doesn't need anyone to carry me.
I am someone who does not need to carry anyone else.
That is who I am.

That's what he'd meant all along.

And just like that, we were headed down a whole new road.

So, Authentic Soul,

When has someone told you a truth that changed everything?

AND

What do you need to do for YOURSELF instead of doing it for someone else?

I love you . . . see you on The Road Where I Was Found!
xo
melody freebird

41

The Road Where
I Was Found

These last years, I've been on a quest to find out and remember who I am. On the last road, I explained what a battle this has been. It's such a cliche thing to say, and I know that. But it really is a thing. We can be walking around in a body and look like we are alive, while simultaneously having no idea who or where we are. It's sleepwalking.

So I set off on a quest to find something that was consistently true about me. And the same truth came back over and over:

I am an artist and I always have been. So are you, by the way.

I first figured this out when I was in kindergarten. It was the first time I had ever been exposed to art supplies. It was like being reunited with myself. When I touched and used those art supplies, I dreamt up my future for the rest of my childhood, knowing with absolute certainty that not only was I going to continue on a path of growing as an artist, but that I was actually born to be one. I will never forget those first moments at the easel with a big roll of paper and paint as a 5 year old. I had never felt such a sense of where I belonged — I belonged wherever the art supplies were.

When I learned about libraries and bookstores, I started to look for books about artists. I learned about the really famous ones like Picasso and Michaelangelo, but it wasn't those kinds of artists that inspired me most. It was the ones who illustrated feelings and life's nuanced experiences in ways I could understand. Something sparked in me when I found a coffee table book about Norman Rockwell and I couldn't get enough of his paintings.

I got married at age 18 and actually had access to my own funds and my own house, so I started collecting every Normal Rockwell book I could find.

I loved his style, but it was mostly the emotion he captured and the storytelling he did through his art. He painted so much of the human condition. I think every artist does this to some extent, but after studying Norman Rockwell, I learned that he was not even seen as a true artist. He was considered an illustrator and back then, there were very specific rules for what makes true fine art.

It still makes me angry to think about this.

He would send his paintings to The Saturday Evening Post magazine on canvas, and then they'd photograph them for the cover and send them back to him. No gallery show, no customers waiting in line to buy his originals. Over his career, over 320 of his paintings graced the cover of that magazine. He was epic and prolific.

These days, his paintings sell for millions.

But it wasn't always that way. In fact, his work was so devalued by his own self because of the way art critics wouldn't claim it as real art, that often when his paintings got mailed back, he'd paint his next painting right over the top of them.

I found this paragraph on the Artsper Magazine blog:
"Although his overly empathetic treatment of his subjects was criticized and delayed his recognition by the art world, the Guggenheim Museum eventually organized his first retrospective in 2001. Since then, his works have sold for millions of euros. His painting The Problem We All Live With was exhibited at the White House in 2011 when Barack Obama received Ruby Bridges. Today, Norman Rockwell is no longer just recognized as an illustrator by his peers and the public but is well regarded as one of America's greatest painters."

He was recognized properly in 2001. He died in 1978.

I could go on and on about him, but I bring him up because what struck me with the most impact about his story was the fire that destroyed his studio. Inside were countless props and costumes and tools . . . and countless original paintings. Everything in there burned. Total loss.

I'm certain I gasped when I read about this in my 20's while deeply studying his art. He even did a work of art about the fire. It was devastating to look at. If I didn't shed a tear on the outside, I know I felt it on the inside. Even to this day I have a stomach ache when I think about that fire and how it destroyed so much of the blood, sweat and YEARS he poured into his work.

Then I watched the movie called BIG EYES, about artist Margaret Keene. She painted prolifically for decades. But she got conned into giving credit for all of her paintings to her husband. He literally went parading about the world claiming he was the painter, while she sat in her studio 14 hours a day and painted one picture after another. He lived lavishly. He did interviews and hung out with celebrities. She sat in her locked studio and painted while he lived off of her gifts. She kept the curtains closed and the door locked because her husband didn't want anyone to know. He even asked her to teach him to paint like she did, and he literally thought it was possible for him to learn in a few lessons. She tried, and of course, he couldn't do it. But he convinced her that she'd never make it without him being the one others believed to be the artist. She kept painting and painting and painting. This movie displays disgusting abuse. Eventually, everyone found out she was the one painting the pictures. But it took a lot of years and a court case to prove it. And she proved it by painting right in front of the judge. The judge asked both she and her ex-husband to paint a picture. He claimed his shoulder was injured and he could not paint. She painted a painting exactly like the ones her husband had taken credit for. And she did it in less than an hour. Because she'd been painting and painting and painting and painting for decades. He just SAID he was.

I watched a documentary recently and learned what happened to our beloved happy painter, Bob Ross, and how an investor found him to be as captivating as we all do. In the end, he was (in my opinion) severely taken advantage of. And his estate was, from where I stand, stolen from his own posterity by a very greedy, jealous and evil woman he trusted. The bile rises into my throat.

If you've never read the story of one of my favorite singer/songwriter/poets, Jewel, it's so much the same story. She worked and worked and worked and created and created and created and gave half of her empire to her own mother so she could manage it. Only to have her not only squander it away, but leave Jewel millions of dollars in debt and having to start over completely.

Even before reading about Jewel, I studied up on what happened to Prince, and the artist formerly known as Prince. How he changed his name to a symbol after what he called being treated like a slave and losing the rights to his own art. I'm so grateful he won back the rights to his art before he died. He was a genius and he fought hard for the dignity of artists worldwide.

Maybe it's because I'm an artist that these stories stand out to me so much, but it sure seems like things like this happen to a lot of artists. I've come to realize that people who don't create things often don't understand what it takes to create something. I've come to realize that there are creators and there are destroyers. People who destroy instead of create have no idea what it takes to create something. So they think it's easy come, easy go. But I know the truth about how an artist's creations are equivalent to a person's blood, and you can kill a person when you take too much of their blood. So many times an artist is more than happy and willing to give it, but too often, others get greedy and want to take more than an artist has to give. Or they get so accustomed to taking it that they forget they're taking it from a real living person who needs some of their own blood leftover to be able to live. And often, the ones taking the blood will tear a big hole in a person to get as much blood out as they can, leaving them to hemorrhage. They bleed out. So many artists end up losing their mind in the end. I suspect they lost all their blood first. It's devastating to me when I hear these stories.

Because every one of us is an artist in some way. We were all born to create something that didn't exist until we created it. Every one of us.

But some people destroy instead of create. They make that choice to destroy. I will never understand it. There are creators and there are destroyers. I know that we need things to end as much as we need them to begin, and sometimes things need to end **IN ORDER** for something else to begin. But I will never understand it when a person goes out of their way to try to destroy another person or their life's work.

Creating is sacred work that should be treated with sacredness. And all of us have the ability to create something that did not exist before we created it. It is so incredibly sacred.

But we can't keep creating if we give away our life force. We only have so much blood to give. At some point, we have to remove the bloodlines and we have to close down the blood bank and we have to decide what's for keeping and what's for giving away. When I went looking for myself, I found myself in a proverbial gutter. I'd been left for dead on the side of the road, still bleeding. I'd gotten desperate and hitchhiked one too many times, getting in the wrong car at the wrong time. I bled for that ride, but I got thrown out when I ran out of blood. Open wounds and all.

At least that's what it felt like to me.

So I'd become an artist who wasn't making art, but hiding. I became a writer who wasn't writing, but hiding. I became a leader who wasn't leading, but hiding. I hid while I grew new blood. And even when I started to get my strength back, all I wanted to do was hide.

And like I said in the last chapter, when Marq got hired full time by Wild West Mustang Ranch . . I thought maybe I could hide forever.

But then something happened that I hope to never forget.

Some beloved humans came looking for me and for my art. They'd actually been looking for me for a very long time, I just didn't know it. I was doing a very good job of hiding, but they kept looking for me. Some of them I knew and some of them I didn't know. They weren't looking for my blood . . . they were looking for my art. And seeing my own art the way they saw it was The Road Where I Got Found. I got found because of what I had already created.

It was like the door to the castle's dungeon got stormed down, and one by one, I heard from people who had been looking for me for months. They came to set me free. They were looking for what I'd already created. They were looking for who I am and who I have always been.

It was extraordinary and impossible to ignore the emails from so many people who had found value in what I'd created but couldn't find it anymore, and social media private messages from people saying "where are you?" "where did your work go?" like the story of Rebecca I told in my introduction. Now I want to tell you about another message I got that changed everything . . .

This one was from a spectacular woman I had never met. She had never met me. She had never even done any of my courses or read any of my books or purchased any of my art. Her name is Joy. JOY!!!! It's a long story that I could write a whole book about in itself, but Joy had a dream one night that she was supposed to buy a piece of property to hold retreats. And in the dream she was told "find Melody Ross and she will teach you how . . ."

Joy knew almost nothing of my work, but she remembered that her sister came to one of my retreats more than a decade ago. So she went on a quest to find the property and to find me. It took her several months to track me down and when I found her message in my "other" folder on Facebook, she sounded pretty desperate to talk to me. So we scheduled a call and she went on to tell me about her dream. She'd just bought the property, in a place called Hope, Idaho! HOPE!!!! And she was begging me to teach her everything I knew.

So I did everything I could to talk her out of me being her teacher. I told her I was a mess. I told her I lived in an RV and had nowhere to teach her but an old barn and a tipi. I told her I lived almost 4 hours from any airport, high in the mountains away from the civilized world. I told her I didn't even live at my own place, but I was living with my friends. I told her again that I was a mess. She said, I will drive there! I will sleep in a tipi! You can teach me in the barn! PLEASE DO THIS! PLEASE! She was impossible to say no to.

So I said yes, hands shaking, and I got going again.

And when I put the word out to a few of the people I knew . . . suddenly I had 7 women coming from all over the country to learn what I could teach them. In a barn, in a tipi, out in the middle of nowhere, at Wild West Mustang Ranch. Where I was hiding out and growing my blood back.

They didn't care that I was a mess….they all just wanted to learn how to be an art healer.

I couldn't hide anymore. After I said yes, the floodgates opened and I heard from one woman after another . . . teach me, teach me, teach me. Please teach me. I've been looking for you and I finally found you. I'm not going to let you say no. I'm not going to let you die in that gutter, they seemed to say.

So then I had to go in search of what had been lost, because not only was I very lost, but my work had been ransacked and lost too. I had to go find it all and put it back together.

So, Found Soul,

What parts of YOU could be hiding?

AND

Where will you look first?

Sometimes we are the only ones who know where our lost pieces are. And sometimes God is the only one who knows. We've got to start the search somewhere, and what we find is almost always a beautiful surprise.

And that's what the next road is about . . . The Road Where I Was Cut Into Pieces . . .

I love you.
See you there.
xo
melody ross

42

The Road Where
I Was Cut
Into Pieces

I often find things that have been left out in the weather to rot and decompose – things that were clearly beautiful and valuable at one time, but because they weren't protected and valued by their owner, they're now considered garbage. They were never meant to be out in the weather, unsheltered, so they're ruined now.

I've also watched my favorite tree fall down in a windstorm, with no way to save it, having to cut it into firewood to later be turned to fire, then to smoke and ash. Then back into the earth to grow another tree.

I've seen countless painstakingly-made quilts on plastic tables with paper tags at yard sales — selling for so much less than their worth. Lots of them say "cutter quilts" which means the quilt might not be much in its whole form, but it's great for cutting into pieces to use for something else.

I don't know which of these things I've felt like most, but parts of me have felt like every one of them.

I told you at the beginning of this book how we left Idaho to chase the sun, to try to find the right environment for my husband to heal from the lasting effects of his brain injury. I also mentioned how it turned out that I was the sicker one, the one who needed even more healing than he did.

309

Melody Ross

We ended up exactly where we were meant to be, and it has all seemed to be by design.

I had been cut into pieces and I was brought back to the very place where I would start to find them. I don't know if I fell to pieces because I didn't take care of my valuable life and left myself unsheltered in the weather. I don't know if it was a windstorm that knocked me down or if I was just so worn out that I had become potential scraps. I don't know entirely. I just know that I got blown to smithereens and so did my life's work.

At this exact moment in time, I live a few miles from one of the most majestic sights on Earth; Snow Canyon in St. George, Utah. I can actually see the enormous red cliffs of the canyon outside my window as I write this.

If you were to come see this geological wonder, just before you hit the mouth of the canyon, you'd drive past a place called Red Mountain Spa and Resort. Every time I drive by that place to get to the canyon, it's a beautiful reminder of how sometimes miracles are a long-game. Because the first time Marq and I went to see the canyon, when we moved here a few years ago, forgotten memories flooded my brain.

I had been there before and totally forgotten that it was here where we now live.

About a year after Marq's brain injury, which would have been in 2005, I was completely burnt out and exhausted. It had been a year of trying to figure out what was happening to him, and we'd finally gotten him into the Elk's Rehab Hospital, where he had a whole team of neurospecialists to help him. At that time, our children were roughly 14, 12, 9, 5 and 4. I had been taking care of them, taking care of Marq and taking care of our company. I was doing a miserable job at all of it, I am certain. But I was doing my best. I was completely exhausted though, mostly emotionally, and a friend suggested I go to the desert, to her favorite medical spa where she'd found lots of healing. It was Red Mountain Spa & Resort.

I flew alone and then had to take a shuttle to the resort. Back then, there wasn't much else out here. I hadn't ever gone on a trip like this before, and certainly not by myself. But I was desperate. I needed something to help me get my bearings. The meals were all organic and very clean. Everyone was there to heal from something. I went to my first yoga class, ever. I slept in. I went for walks. And I met with a few healers — something totally new for me.

One of the healers gave me an experience that has become a part of me I hope to never forget or take for granted. She was a medical intuitive and when I walked into her little office, she had stones and gems set out in a beautiful arrangement. My upbringing taught me to stay away from all things hippie, so I was reluctant, but something felt very good and very right. (Incidentally, almost 2 decades later, I am now that hippie myself. Surrounded by beautiful crystals and stones.)

Well, this woman and I hardly said a word to each other after I walked in, just a short hello. Then she asked me to sit down while pointing to the beautiful arrangement of stones.

She asked me to choose whatever stone called out to me or whatever stone I felt most drawn to. I chose a crystal-clear piece of quartz in the shape of a tower. It was pointed at the end and stood up straight. I held it in my hand.

She said it was the exact right stone for me, then looked in my eyes and said she had a story to tell me. It was the story of The Goddess Isis of Egypt.

You can go and read the story yourself if you're interested, but the synopsis is that Isis was married to Osiris. They loved each other deeply. They were good and fair and kind leaders in Egypt. For lots of reasons, Osiris was hated by his jealous brother, Seth, who betrayed him and left him for dead in a coffin. Isis went to find him and ultimately did find his coffin, growing in a tree where the river had deposited it. She brought him back to life because she was a goddess, after all. When Seth found out, he came to kill Osiris for good.

And then he cut him up into pieces and buried them all over Egypt.

Isis then went on a quest to find the pieces of Osiris and put them back together. It took a very long time and she never quit, and found enough pieces of him and she was able to bring him to life for long enough to conceive a son.

Melody Ross

Their love was legendary.
Her devotion to him was legendary.
She did what it took to find him and put him back together.

So this woman at Red Mountain Spa sat and told me this story, with the hippie crystal in my hand, and I sat and sobbed . . . because this was so much my story. I had been searching the world over to find the pieces of my husband so that we could get him put back together.

This woman didn't know me and she knew none of my story. But through some miracle, I chose the stone that brought the story of Isis. This story has sustained me through so much sorrow and difficulty over the years.

It has remained an anchor and a parable and a miracle to me. I want to be like Isis.

Let's call what she did ISISIZING. I know it's hard to say, but what she had to do deserves its own word, and besides, I need a word to describe what had to happen for both Marq and me.

I had to do my part in Isisizing him. He has had to do his part in deciding whether he wants to stay alive and stay together. So much of staying alive is our own choice, and I have watched him bravely decide over and over and over again, surrendering to whatever strange and brutal timeline has been meant for it all. Sometimes I have to go find parts of him that get lost, but mostly he does it for himself these days . . . he's been a tremendous example to me of how to be patient during your own Isisizing. And how very very very long it can take.

There are all sorts of experiences in life that take us from feeling whole to feeling full of holes. The experiences that cut me into pieces felt like a vengeful, hateful machete, hacking me into such small pieces that a bystander might just think they were looking at a pile of hamburger.

But I have still tried to find every piece. And I have come to know that there are pieces I will never be able to find. The earth already drank them up and turned them back into soil. I keep searching, however. Every allegorical dumpster I can find.

I hope you will understand that there are reasons I can't talk about public-

312

ly for why I ended up scouring every dumpster for miles around, looking for the pieces of my life story that I had so tirelessly created with my own hands over nearly 5 decades. It doesn't really matter how or why anyway. It's just been the greatest heartbreak of my life to see my lifework treated like foul garbage — thrown in metaphorical dirty dumpsters, set on fire, or just tossed out the window in the middle of nowhere. My creations are so much a part of me. My art, my writing, the lessons I was given to teach. After my husband and my children, they are my lifeblood. They are my appendages. They are vital organs that have kept me alive, that I want to keep alive in return. I don't know if it's healthy or right for this to be so, but it is what it is. I would never have thought it could be possible for a person to be looking at the pieces of themselves strewn out in front of their own eyes, all bloody and ragged, and that they could still be alive to witness it without bleeding to death. It's hard to fathom that some of my pieces will be lost forever, but that's where I've found myself over the last few years. I will never understand the events that transpired — a dull but powerful chainsaw hacking me into jagged and bloody pieces. Mercilessly. Ruthlessly. Callously. It was cruel. It continues to feel cruel. Although I have grown from this experience, I don't know that I will ever find the strength to embrace it as something wonderful.

But I have learned so very very much on this Road Where I Was Cut Into Pieces.

This machete felt like it had been chasing me for a long time. So I'd gather up my paintings, my journals, my sketchbooks, my hard drives . . . I'd pack them up carefully, AND RUN. I'd protect them and keep them safe. But the machete kept chasing until I was too tired to outrun it. It finally caught up with me. It had its way with me. I got too tired to protect my valuables and left them out in the weather where the weather had its way with them. And a few times, I have to say honestly, I was the one holding the machete and doing the hacking.

It's really starting to matter less and less to me who did the machete hacking, who was holding the chainsaw, who took the trash out, who set it all on fire. Sometimes you have a split second to decide whether you'll chase the perpetrator or save the one bleeding to death in the street. Because you simply can't do both.

I have just wanted to stop bleeding. I want to be whole again.

So in the last year especially, I've had to face my own Isis story. I've had to do the tedious task of Isisizing. Mine is different from Marq's, particularly in the way I've had to go in search of my own pieces, while feeling the phantom pain of having them gone. So many of my friends have shown up and wanted to help, but I was the only one who could do it. I didn't know where all my pieces were, but I mostly knew what they were. I've had so much help, but ultimately I've had to lead the charge on this journey. While bleeding, oozing and feeling like it just might kill me lots of days. I remembered to include God in my journey much of the time, and it was always harder when I didn't.

If you've ever put together a really big and complicated puzzle with thousands of tiny pieces, you know the temptation that comes and goes to just quit the whole damned thing. It feels so tedious, monumental and hopeless when you can't find the next piece among the piles and piles of pieces it's hiding in.

I have certainly wanted to quit. Mostly at night when I'm so exhausted and lonely. When the anger and the grief take over. Starting each morning, I search and search and search for ways to put things back together — and by sundown I'm just so tired. It feels so useless and even irresponsible some nights, as I think about how I could just take one of the many jobs that have been offered to me and finally let go of the possibility that I can ever reclaim and restore enough pieces to keep my dream alive, to give it a chance to grow into whatever it's supposed to grow into next. But I start over every morning with fresh enthusiasm and hope I won't bleed out before this essential surgery is safely completed. Some days my heart is so broken that I can literally feel my life force oozing out of it. Or maybe that's just what it feels like to have my heart beating again. Sometimes healing hurts worse than the injury ever did.

I have gotten to the point in this raggedy puzzle where it has started to form a picture, but there are still so many holes I know I will never find the old pieces to fill — perhaps that is meant to be. Whether or not something is EVER "meant to be," I know that I can make something of the raw materials I have in front of me. It's what I do. It's what I've always done. As I've worked to find myself through my art, my writing and my teachings, I have expanded on them, changed them and edited them. Even the pieces I've found are already starting to create an entirely different picture. I work hard to embrace this beautiful miracle, this essential truth of life's changes; and I also deeply grieve the loss of what once was.

I didn't know if I could recover. Some days I still have my doubts. I have wondered over and over again how a person can keep going when so much of them has been hacked away. But I am getting it. I am learning a lesson that I have taught to my students over and over again. That we are not what we do, we are not what we produce. What we are cannot ever be thrown away, discarded or destroyed. We just think it can, so we behave as if it were true.

When we mistake our life experiences for actual LIFE, we can be so easily tricked into thinking our life is over when our experiences are over.

I gotta say that once the bleeding was stabilized, I did start looking for who was holding the machete. It is the anger part of the grief process. I felt it was my obligation to find the perpetrator and hold them accountable, so that the machete could never come after me again.

But then I realized it was never about the machete. It was always about the power I gave to the machete . . . the story I told myself about it. I didn't feel safe in the world after that, so I had to learn that the only safety that is ever real and lasting is the truth of who I am and what I am made of . . . something that can never be destroyed.

So I had to decide to rise up. And rise up again. And again. And again.

I had to realize that we are all made of something eternal that could never really be cut into pieces…..but that we get to have myriad experiences to simply see things as options we can take or leave. No matter what happens to our experiences, we will always remain intact. That's true for you and it's true for me. My you-ness was never outside of me. It was never something that a machete could even touch or understand. It was just waiting patiently all along for me to understand and see and experience and KNOW it's permanence. The absolute, scientific positivity of how it can NEVER be destroyed.

The machete was a trick, held by a trickster. It was smoke and mirrors. It was a shell game.

When you think what you DO and what you PRODUCE is WHO YOU

ARE - you can truly believe that you are broken beyond repair when those things get destroyed in whatever way a destroyer thinks to destroy them.

My work is made of pieces. I am made of pieces. My life is made of pieces. So I collect pieces, and I put them together in ways that tell stories that are meant to teach lessons and lead people back to their own Soul Road.

My pieces were scattered all over the place. Literally and figuratively. And for me to get back to work, I had to go and find enough of the pieces of me that I could at least start to move forward again — to get back on MY Soul Road.

And I did. And I have.
I found myself. God showed me exactly where I was hidden.

But I had to go and take action. I had to meet myself and God at the trailhead.

I am gathering more beautiful pieces every day. That's the part I'd forgotten about, that there would always be more pieces to gather no matter how many I'd lost. So I keep gathering. Some of the pieces used to be me, some of them were pieces of someone else's story, discarded for some reason or another at some time in history. I am gathering gathering gathering beautiful pieces again. And those pieces are starting to form a glorious picture that is yet to be revealed. There are still lots of empty spaces, and for that I am grateful. Because every day a beautiful new pile of pieces comes into view.

And I get to choose which one to put into my puzzle, I also get to not choose any more pieces at all if that's how I'm feeling. I just know I get to choose, and that is a gift.

I am sewing a life quilt, making a soul mosaic, building a soulful collage. Just like I always have, just like I always do. I am making beauty out of whatever is in my life at the moment. Just like I always have, just like I always do. I know these things I create will not be around forever, but I will be.

I am grateful today that I have an eraser, some scissors, a seam ripper and a garbage can. I'm the one discarding what I don't want anymore. I am protecting what I don't want to be discarded or hacked at ever again. No matter what ends up remaining of what I build with my hands, I know now for sure that I can never be destroyed.

And neither can you.

Even though I know these things to be true, I still have to forgive the truth of what it has meant to lose what I got to hold in my hands for a while. I have to forgive what happened when I lost what I wanted to last forever . . . and that's what the next road is all about . . .

So Perfectly Wonderful Soul,

What have you believed is destroyed about you, and how could you perhaps be wrong about that?

AND

What pieces are you ready to discard to make room for new pieces?

I love you and I hope you'll find yourself valuable enough to search for. And I also hope you'll realize that you get to decide where the next piece goes.

Thank you for being with me. Next I'm going to take you on a road that very few of us would ever choose for ourselves. But it's a road that leads to wholeness and peace . . . the Road of Bitter Fault Lines.

I will see you there.
xo
melody freebird

43

The Road
Of Bitter
Fault Lines

The word /fault/ has different meanings. One involves pointing a finger of blame — finding the faults in a human, the other involves tectonic plates and shifts in the earth that can result in deep chasms, canyons and crevasses that often extend miles deep into the earth.

Both kinds of faults create the earthquakes that create the canyons. One between humans, one on the very ground we stand on. Both can create a need to build a bridge to get to the other side. Both sometimes stay bridgeless forever.

I don't know why forgiveness feels so daunting at times. It seems like if we were wise, we'd choose it instantly. My little girl self might be instantly and infinitely forgiving, but I have found that my adult self just isn't. Or maybe it's the other way around. Throughout the therapy I've been doing, my child self and adult self have done some kind of a merger, and I don't know who's who most days. I just know that I've found a part of me that has long been silenced, a part of me that has been very very very angry. This has been a surprising and disappointing discovery, but it is what it is. I am still bleeding.

I still remember the day my anger broke open a few years ago from a very deep place, and vile swear words came out of my mouth as I was talking to my husband about the way I was feeling. I didn't really use swear words much before that moment but they boiled over the edge of me like a pot of unwatched pasta. I said words I've not said since I was a teenager trying out cussing. Vile and angry words. I even shouted some of them out. It shocked and scared me so much that my eyes immediately burst open big and bulging, and I put my own hand over my own mouth, staring at Marq like a kid in trouble.

He actually smiled really big, started clapping and said . . . "it's about time babe, keep going . . ."

It has kept going, oozing out like molasses. But the flow is hot and cold. It doesn't flow until the heat of my anger starts it up again. So I allow it. I'm hoping it will be done draining out soon, but I just don't know. I suspect it's a lifetime of anger that I didn't know how to express. It might be a while.

Until I was almost 50, I truly believed I was born without whatever thing it is that lets us feel anger. I have just never really been able to do it. Turns out, it's been in me all along. I was just a pressure-cooker.

At my age, I don't have as much oxytocin and estrogen as I did in my young woman years, so I simply don't give as much a rat's patootie as I used to about a lot of things I used to suffer over. I don't have the gun to my head I used to have that told me I had to always be nice, accommodating and pleasant, even during atrocities. Smile and wave, sweet girl, smile and wave. Keep smiling, keep waving, keep sweet. No anger allowed for nice girls.

There are actual chemicals in a young woman's body that make her softer and more nurturing, more accommodating and patient. I suspect it was by design to get her through the mothering years. I'm grateful for how easy it was for me to be nurturing, patient and kind. And I also think those chemicals, mixed with cultural conditioning, can really mess up the internal alarms we were given to go along with it. We stop hearing our own "NO!" We stop hearing ourselves at all, actually. Smile and wave, smile and wave. No anger allowed.

Now that my age has taken those chemicals away, I have to forge my own character and defy my own biology to be soft and kind, because I know it is my true nature to be soft and kind. It's just not as easy as it used to be.

320

50 Roads To The Middle Of My Life

But because I'm dedicated to never betraying myself again, my stubborn new older self has been very reluctant to be the soft and forgiving person I used to be. My anger moved in, demanding to be heard. It screams out reminders about how I have fallen into too many crevasses and spent far too many years trying to climb out of them. It screams reminders about the blood and guts that were strewn everywhere when my life was hacked away with that machete, no matter what the machete meant. It is no longer an option to put my head in the sand about the things that push a person right over the edge of a deep canyon. I was reckless at the edges, and I have pulled my children and my husband right down there with me too many times. My anger is trying to protect me from doing that ever again.

I get that.
But I hate that I am not instantly forgiving anymore.
I really do.

I used to think it was so easy, but it was never easy, I was just ignoring it.

I find forgiveness to be so complicated. So complicated. What I am finding is that it can be an onion made of layers of very thin glass. The layers you work to peel off will often break into razor-sharp pieces — leaving you bleeding. But still, you keep peeling back sharp layers, in semi-sadistic fashion to get to a place of peace. You want to get to the center of it at any cost.

So you peel and bleed, bleed and peel, looking for the center.

Until you finally find it.

I have found every time that I am the one at the center of it. It was never anyone else. It was always me. And the core of it all was the need to forgive myself. I ALWAYS NEEDED TO FORGIVE MYSELF MOST OF ALL.

That core is made of gold. Pure gold. So it's worth the bleeding.

Over and over I have thought it was about others, but ultimately the healing only came when I saw my part, letting any other human or situation completely off the hook, no matter how heinous — and taking on the hard work of forgiving myself.

It sucks and it's difficult. At least it has been for me.

But a road built on a fault line is a dangerous thing. The fault can break open at any time and you can plunge to your death. You can also just end up a bitter woman, which is a particularly long and painful fall before you're actually relieved of it by death. So you either stay on your side of the broken-open canyon created from the effect of shaking up a fault, or you find a way to build a bridge across it. I still don't know what I should do about so many of the canyons I'm currently exploring. Stay over here or build a bridge? I'm still looking at my own part in my own earthquakes. Maybe I will be forever.

Because it's dangerous to try to get to the other side of something that deep when you don't know for sure the safest way to do it. I think there might even be times when there just isn't a safe way, at least not in your own lifetime. So you might just have to walk away from the canyon completely and find a different road. You forgive the canyon, you just don't get to cross it.

Either way, the grieving is going to come. And that's the trick to not becoming a bitter woman . . . letting yourself grieve what was once whole but now is fractured or gone completely. Sometimes the earthquakes just absolutely destroy a thing, not even leaving a big crack to look down into. Sometimes you're back to that pile of rubble I talked about driving down at the beginning of this book.

You have to grieve the rubble, too.

I want to forgive all of it. I really do. I am trying so hard. I want to forgive others and I want to forgive myself. I want to forgive life. I want to forgive God. I want to forgive broken dreams and broken promises and the brokenness of humanity . . . especially my own. But I'm finding that first I have to look at things carefully and see my own reckless and careless behavior, lest I miss the lesson and not take responsibility for things I could have prevented. I never want to go down this road again, so I'm stopping for a while to inspect how I got here. No matter how many other people or situations I feel betrayed and hurt by.

I got myself here.

What I know is that I have exposed people I love to very dangerous situations and horrific long-term consequences because of my stubborn refusal to see the dangers in dangerous people and situations. Making me a dangerous person. I've ignored a million red flags. I have ended up bleeding in the barrow-pit, barely surviving the fallout because of my stubborn refusal to see the predator in front of me who would ultimately discard me and leave me for dead. Or I've refused to acknowledge my own weaknesses and the way I put my head in the sand when leadership was needed. Or the way I begin things but have a hard time finishing them. I have so many faults, so many weaknesses. And my bleeding has bled over — making my loved ones bleed at times. I have exposed people I love to horrific things because I did not do the hard things that needed to be done, and I did not require others to do the hard things they'd committed to do. I hoped for an easier way, that by some magical means, things would turn out fine without any accountability.

I've said it before and I will say it again, I have been so incredibly reckless. And it has created so much pain and complication for my family. My kids and my husband and so many of the people I love most were damaged because of my magical thinking. Because of my naive and stubborn trust. I trusted, so they trusted. I was deeply wounded by people I trusted most. My family, in turn, was deeply wounded. That's the hard part of being an accidental leader, and that's what's kept me from wanting to ever lead anyone anywhere again.

Today I was painting on top of an old painting — adding to it, actually. I woke up at 4am and walked into my studio to greet a whole stack of old paintings I'd pulled out to finish. Or paint over. Or weep over.

My anger comes in hot when I think about the way I've done all I could do and it still wasn't enough for things to turn out the way I wanted them to turn out. It comes from situations with people I simply can't understand that only look like cruelty and negligence to me. I weep bitter tears as I'm looking back and trying to make sense of how the hell things happened the way they did.

There are so many things that might not ever make sense to me.

So I glue another beautiful old scrap to the top of an old painting, making it new. A painting that's been in so many different places with me, in so many different boxes and on so many different tables and in front of the camera and underneath other paintings. Stuck on the shelf in a storage unit, shrink wrapped in a stack in the horse trailer. Different states, different towns. In the barn. In a stack of boxes with my other paintings. Waiting. Waiting. Waiting to be finished.

So I decide once and for all I'm going to let her be finished. And I paint a swipe of pearly paint as I remember some of the people who were in my life the first time I painted this painting and I bitterly think...

"How could they have done this to me and left me for dead?"

and I cry, and glue another piece to my painting and think . . .

"How could I have done this to me?"

And I weep even more. But it's not bitter anymore, it's sorrowful.
"How could I allow this to be done to me?"

I wipe another tear. . .

"How can I stop allowing this to be done to me?"

"How can I stop doing this to me?"

and finally it comes to me....

"I wonder if I have ever done this to someone else?"
"How can I stop doing this to them?"
"This hurts."

My heart breaks until there's an opening. And the questions continue as I paste down more pieces on top of the bottom layer that used to be my life, making it new. Making it new. Making it new. The questions continue and the weeping continues too.

This particular painting is a butterfly whose body is the neck of a paper guitar. I have little jars of sparkling glass shards that I often embed into my paintings. On this butterfly, I use tweezers to put the tiniest pieces of metallic gold crushed glass as an aura all around her. I cry and cry as they sparkle in the soft shine coming from the twinkle lights hanging over my head. I spend hours with tweezers giving her the adornment she'd always deserved.

The sun finally came over the mountain and Marq came into my studio to tell me good morning. I was still crying, holding tweezers. He looked at me, concerned.

All I said to him was . . .

". . . this painting has been through so much . . ."

And I cried harder.
He kissed me on the forehead and walked into the kitchen.

I kept grieving with my tweezers.

Whose fault is it when something beautiful gets hurt or disappears or even dies? Whether it's a murder, a sickness, an accident, absolutely careless-ness, a theft or just old age? Whose fault is it?

What if you can never know? Does it still matter?

There are things I am grieving that I simply cannot fathom, I can't make sense of them. Things that are so incredibly cruel and incomprehens-able.And the conclusion I've come to is that I can only heal the things I have stewardship over. I can only heal what I know intimately enough to perform surgery on. So I set off to see my part in all of this is. And I am carefully extracting the parts that are not mine and discardig them. I've been sorting too long through the shrapnel, getting cut by the pieces of my own life. I don't need to let myself get cut by the sharp parts of others, too.

I am working hard to own my part in my own demise. I'm building a bridge across my own faults to find my truest self on the other side. This is big work, even bigger than trying to find your way across the chasms of betrayal and loss and human cruelty. I have given up on trying to under-stand why people do horrific things to each other. I have my own faults to traverse.

And so I make more art, and write more songs, and focus on the sweetness to counteract the bitterness. I weld pieces together with the gold I find at the center. Making something new. Making myself new.

I am my art now.

So, Forgiving Soul,

Where do you find it hard to forgive another?

AND

Where do you find it hard to forgive yourself?

I hope you'll remember that forgiving does not mean you believe that an atrocity was okay. It just means you're setting yourself free. Sometimes setting yourself free means setting everyone else free, too.

I love you dear one. I will see you on The Road Where We Climbed Into the Clouds.

I love you.
xo
melody freebird

44

The Road Where We Climbed Into The Clouds

I watch people a lot. At stoplights, when I'm shopping . . . anywhere, really. I watch them because I think about what their lives might be like, what they might be going through while they're looking so completely normal. Or so completely abnormal.

I remember in the early years of Marq's brain injury, I would be driving to my office or the gym after dropping my older kids off at school, after kissing my little ones and handing them to their caregiver — knowing that I'd just left my husband alone in our bed at home, not knowing whether he'd make it through the day or not. But I looked so perfectly put together and like my life might just be perfect. I remember those days, at the stoplight, looking over at people laughing and singing along to their car stereo . . . and I'd often think, "how could they be laughing and singing when life is so absolutely horrific?" Or on days when my hope was bright, I'd be singing along to the radio and look over at others and think, "I wonder what they are going through?"

Marq and I both wear hats almost every day. He often wears a fitted wool vest over his crisp button-up shirts, and we both usually have boots on. We are considered "dressed-up" a lot of the time when we are out running errands. He's always very put-together and he holds himself the way an military general would. He often gets asked what branch of the military he's in, just by the way he walks, talks, and holds himself and his life together in such an orderly fashion. His clothes are always crisp and polished, and he walks and talks with measured precision. I just dress like an artist, all layered up in fabrics and textures and colors — much like my collages.

I tell you these things because I'm always astounded at the things people say to us when we are out and about. We get comments all the time, mostly from older people, about how nice we look and how lovely our outfits are. The thing is, we both have 2 kinds of clothes . . . the ones that are covered in paint and grease and holes from the work we both do, and the few nicer, dressier clothes we have. We have nice clothes for mountaineering and hiking, and we have a few nice outfits for when we "go to town." So when we go out, we sort of stand out.

I'm astounded at the comments because of what's going on in our personal life so often when we are out running errands, things no one could ever know, often very difficult things. The last few years, especially, of trying to navigate a very fast-paced world as two middle-aged outliers who are starting over in their life. People often talk to us like we are the luckiest, most interesting people ever. While we are actually the most exhausted, perplexed and beat-down people some days. We just look interesting and colorful and happy.

On the day where we set off on The Road Where We Climbed Into the Clouds, we were wearing our adventuring clothes. Clothes we wear a lot. From the outside, we might look like a couple on vacation, getting ready to take our once-a-year hike, but in all actuality, we are just dressed in the clothes that will keep us safe, covered and ready for whatever weather shows up.

We had stopped at a gas station, like we often do, to grab some snacks on our way to the mountain trail. As it often happens, several people commented to us how "cute we look together" and "how much fun we must be having." I smiled and said thank you and so did Marq. We laughed together when we got back in the truck because our life was in such disarray. We were heading up to the mountain to literally plead with God because we had no idea how we were going to move forward. We were scared, sad and worn out.

But from the outside, we looked like a photo shoot for Instagram.

50 Roads To The Middle Of My Life

This particular day was sometime last Spring, after I fell down the cliff I talked about many roads back. Marq and I had gotten into a serious discussion about prayer, about what is possible, about miracles, and about how there's no way we were ever going to make it through what we were facing without some Divine intervention.

I know I talked a bit about my truth crisis and my changing relationship with my Truthteller, but something that has never changed is my knowledge that if I ask for help, my Truthteller always delivers. It's almost never in the way I thought it was going to be, but it always happens.

We needed help. We were like two kids lost in the dark woods. So we made a plan to go to the top of the highest mountain we could find. It's a mountain we can see from where we live, called Signal Peak, at the top of the Pine Valley Mountains. It towers more than 10,000 feet into the sky.

We drove a long dirt road to get there, it took nearly an hour just to get to the trailhead, and even though it was Springtime, there was quite a bit of snow to hike through at the place where we could hike to the top. We were prepared. We had boots and gloves and coats and backpacks. I had my journal, with a prepared speech to orate into the sky. I had a lot to say and a lot of faith in what would happen if I said it.

Marq had a speech prepared too, but it was memorized I guess, and probably not nearly as long as mine was. So we walked through the snow, through the trees, up and up and up, an absolutely stunning view of the Mojave Desert to keep us in awe. Then we got to the top.

We found a big flat boulder that the sun had warmed enough to melt the snow off of and sat down, starting together, pleading with God and any other Divine beings who were available. We took turns talking, pleading our case. Telling God how tired we were, what a long and difficult journey we'd been on for more than a decade. We said we were weary and out of ideas. Our hearts were broken and our spirits felt broken too. We felt like we were out of options. We needed help and direction. We needed to know that there were things in life that could never be taken away from us, things we could count on forever.

And then we each walked away to a private place and asked for a personal burden to be removed from our life. I asked for my addiction to food to be removed, and the 50 pounds I'd gained to go along with it. I asked that the fears that caused me to blanket my body with extra padding would be removed. I told God I was done with it. I wanted to live a different way altogether. Marq asked for his relentless bouts of depression to be removed. I don't know what Marq said to God, but I know he was earnest. We both pleaded into the sky, we begged, we asked, we cried. We believed.

A feeling of peace and otherworldliness shrouded us both. We met back at the big boulder and looked out over the valley below, more mountains everywhere of every color. Black lava, white sandstone, red sandstone. Juniper trees, mesquite trees, pine trees. Lakes, rivers and bluffs. It was absolutely spectacular. It's hard to feel hopeless when you're up that high and everything is so much bigger than you are.

We sat silently after our individual pleas to Heaven. We didn't even talk about what transpired when we went away to our respective private spots to have our private conversations. We didn't' need to talk, we'd both just been through very similar experiences and so we both knew that we each were processing in our minds and hearts privately as we sat on that boulder.

We'd never done something like this, at least not together. We'd never done something intentionally separate, right in front of each other. 30 years of doing and being EVERYTHING together. And we walked away from each other right in front of each other.

It was up on top of that mountain where I realized it was okay for him and I to have separate prayers, separate talks with God, separate dreams and separate fears. It was okay for us to have separate lives, next to each other. There was something very transformative happening up there in the clouds, it was as if we were being ushered into a brand new part of life that was coming up, right around the bend. A time when we'd get to stand next to each other, but completely on our own Soul Roads. It wasn't like anything would change from the outside, but that everything was going to change on the inside. When I watched Marq go somewhere else for his private prayers, I started to see him not as my husband, but as a soul who was on his own journey. I had always thought of us as a single unit. A couple. An entity. And for lots of reasons, that had always worked really well. But it was also a burden to our individual growth. I still don't know if this is just something that happens at our age, or if it is something that happened to us. I just know that up on top of that mountain, where we went to ask God how we could work through our trials and problems together, God showed us that we needed to learn how to work through things on our own, and then come back together to talk about what we'd learned.

It's taken me a while to understand the gift we were given that day. While it was happening, I was very curious and engaged, wondering what it meant or if it meant anything at all. But as the months pass, I know for certain that it was an ending and a beginning.

As I write this, it sort of sounds like Marq and I went through some kind of emotional separation or some other kind of marital separation. It has actually been quite the opposite. It's when we started to be okay with not being codependent. Of course, we are still a work in progress, but something changed in both of us at that moment, And it continues to evolve in the direction of he and I being sovereign beings, next to each other. Rather than two people who have no identity apart from each other. It culminated that morning in the RV when he begged me to stop doing things FOR HIM and to PLEASE start doing things FOR MYSELF.

We went to the top of that mountain to ask for things that no person could take away from us, things that we could count on to last.

We climbed down the mountain in silence, we drove home in silence. We both had a faraway look in our eyes as we let ourselves be absorbed into the scenery on the drive back to civilization. I was somewhere with my thoughts and so was he. We were right next to each other, but also zillions of miles into somewhere else, each in our own psyche. And it was totally okay.

After that, Marq started to feel better. I started to drop pounds. Over the Spring and Summer, I lost almost all of the 50 pounds I'd wanted to lose. He felt great. I felt great. We started making plans. It was a beautiful summer. I still battled my fears, but I didn't try to cover them with Cheetos and chocolate and ice cream. I spent a lot of time outside and a lot of time with animals. I helped Kami raise 10 caterpillars, complete with the honor of watching them each turn into butterflies. I held my first Soul Road Certification Training. I even started writing this book.

Marq didn't get depressed. He started feeling like himself again. I didn't turn to food to medicate my fearful feelings. I started fitting into smaller and smaller clothes. I started feeling like me again. He started feeling like himself again. It was glorious. We were cured.

Then September came and we got Covid and he broke his shoulder. And we were back to another place where we didn't know what to do. I think if this little bump in the road would have consisted of just a few days of obstacles, we would have totally stayed on our happy, hopeful trajectory.

But it's December now and it's been a rough few months with all the pain in his shoulder, the loss of mobility and strength, the inability to do the work he loves to do. He fell into a deep depression again. And I started self-medicating with Cheetos, M&Ms and warm bread slathered with butter. Lots of my pants are tight right now. My thighs are rubbing together again. I know this cycle well. But I feel really different this time. Everything feels really different this time.

I don't feel betrayed by God or hopeless that our trip to the top of the mountain was just an illusion that didn't really work. I know that what happened on top of that mountain was real. I know there are parts of it that I have yet to understand but the parts I do understand are that we had to DECIDE what we really wanted, and then we had to go home and do our parts to get there. And that NOTHING ALIVE is going to stop doing what it does, just because we want it to. Our bodies need to be supported in what we want for them. Our minds need to be supported in what we want for them. We have become very undisciplined over these last few months when it comes to doing the things that were helping us get where we wanted to be last Spring. There are reasons why it's been hard to keep giving our bodies and minds what they need to be able to thrive, but the fact is, we stopped. We started focusing on just surviving every day.
I know when we were at the top of that mountain, begging the sky to relieve us of some of our burdens, we could see SO MUCH from up there. Just like in the story of The Longest Dinosaur. I know that God was helping us, but God wasn't solving our problems for us. God was just giving us a proper perspective.

I have often taught a lesson about perspective, especially in respect to our problems, by showing others what it's like when you take a little copper penny and put it right up to your eye until it's almost touching. I tell my students…think of this penny as your problem. When you focus on it as the one and only thing that's going on in your life, you cannot see anything past it. When it's almost touching your eyeball, it literally looks like all there is. But when you take it and pull it down and put it on a table in front of you, or even across the room . . . you can see that it's just part of the rest of life. It's the same size or smaller than everything else. I put the penny with pictures of the people I love. BIG PICTURES. The penny is sitting right there next to them, but the pictures become so much more important.

I feel like THAT is what God showed us on the top of that mountain. And what we did after that is start to see everything else. We started to focus on everything else. And the problems we were dealing with started to become just another part of life, not A BIG GIANT MONSTER that obscured our ability to see everything else right in front of us.

At the top of that mountain, we asked for things that no one can take away. We were shown that there are already millions of things right in front of our face. We just weren't seeing them. God didn't take away our problems, but showed us how to put them in their proper perspective.

There just really is not a magic one-time elixir we can drink that keeps life from happening. I mean there is, but it's called death. If we are going to decide to be alive, we are going to have cycles and new problems to solve. We will all have old problems that resurface for another round of figuring out. That's where we are now. I have not stepped on the scale, and I won't, but I suspect I've put on nearly 20 lbs of protective padding because I put that copper penny right up next to my eyeball and the only way I could survive that is to eat garbage. Or at least that's what my old patterns told me.

We are also realizing that we've tried EVERY SINGLE THING to make Marq's depression cycles stop. We have done EVERYTHING we can find to make it go away once and for all. He hasn't had an episode this bad since we left Idaho. It's been 2 years. But in the grand scheme of things . . . it's just a part of our life. So we take the penny down and put it by the giant red mountains in front of us and we know it's going to pass. It's just a part of our life, surrounded by SO MUCH BEAUTY and SO MUCH OF OTHER LIFE.

Melody Ross

The Road Where We Climbed Into The Clouds taught us so many lessons. That we are okay when we are separate, especially when we are separate right next to each other. We are okay when our problems haven't been solved yet. And we are okay even when we are not okay but LOOK OKAY to everyone who sees us in our hats and boots and colorful layers.

We blend into the landscape. We are part of all of it.

And all of it is beautiful in its own way.

So, Sovereign Soul,

Where in your life do you wish to find the balance between being together and being separate, for the good of you both?

AND

Where have you gotten answers that worked in your life, but then stopped doing what worked? Will you try again?

I love you. I love being next to you on my own road.

I want to tell you now about an act that has changed everything, The Road Where I Took My Gaslight Back.

See you there.
xo
melody ross

45

The Road Where I Took My Gaslight Back

After that trip to the top of the mountain, I started trying really hard to see how I'd been making things bigger and even more difficult than they needed to be, and how the wrong perspective was really holding me back. I started seeing all sorts of things I was doing, and realized a bucketload of my own destructive behaviors.

At some point we all have to take responsibility for our patterns if we ever want to be free. We have to stop blaming others for our own messes. It is the road to freedom. Even if heinous things have happened, we are never powerless.

It's been a difficult concept for me to accept. I have to take responsibility for my patterns. I cannot blame others for my particular messes.

I want to be free.

I am on the road to freedom. But goodness gracious have I had to learn how to stop gaslighting myself, how to stop gaslighting others and definitely how to stop allowing others to gaslight me.

I believe that God gave all of us a power source inside. One that has always been meant to be used to power our own personal life. I believe it's plugged into the Source of the best kind of power, a power that never runs out. I used to be so afraid of power of all kinds, so I didn't want to even explore the possibility that I have power inside of me. I know now that it's always been my birthright, and it's yours too.

I've been experimenting with my own personal power after learning about and experiencing the effects of "gaslighting," a phrase used in psychology that I'll talk about later in this chapter. Essentially, gaslighting is a manipulation tactic used to erode the personal power of another person, making them easy to control or destroy. It's a tactic designed to get a person to believe something that's not true. This tactic involves actions that make a person question their own reality, that discount another's experience and that flat-out deceive a person so relentlessly that they start to believe that a lie is the truth. Most often, a person gaslights another to control a self-serving narrative, to make things SEEM the way they want them to be SEEN. The best way to control a person or a narrative is to make someone believe they are not capable or worthy of trusting their own inner knowing, their own inner light or their own inner power. Gaslighting is incredibly effective if your aim is to control or destroy a person — to manipulate a person.

Manipulation is utilized by someone who simply wants to get another person to do something that is for the manipulator's OWN best good, but not good for the person they are manipulating.

Others can gaslight you. You can gaslight others. You can even gaslight yourself, and that is the worst kind of all. I know this from experience.

Gaslighting is done most heinously when things happen that are hurtful or wrong or confusing, and the people involved KNOW exactly what happened, but one or more want things to SEEM like they happened very differently, or not at all.

It's used in phrases like . . .
"That never happened"
"I never said that"
"I did not do that"
"You're making things up"
"I don't know what you're talking about"
"I would never do that"

50 Roads To The Middle Of My Life

"You're crazy"
"You need help"
"That was not my intention, stop being so sensitive"
"It wasn't that bad"
"I was just trying to do what's best for you"
"You're taking this too personally"
"You're remembering it wrong"
"You just need to trust me, you can't trust yourself right now"
"I can't believe you're still thinking about that"
"I'm shocked that you feel this way"
"Just forget about it!"
"I've done so much for you - I earned the right to do that"

It happens to YOU when YOU KNOW what happened BECAUSE YOU WERE THERE. Somehow this devious tactic makes you question your very reality; and it definitely makes you question yourself and your own abilities. Others can do this to you, and you can do this to yourself. Either way, you start to question your reality and your inner light. Eventually, you forget your power and your light and start relying on any power you can find, as long as it's outside of yourself. You are convinced you are crazy and faulty. You continue to go in search of external power sources, because you are convinced you don't have your own — or that everyone else's is better than your own.

When you do it to yourself, it's like walking around with deep, open and infected wounds and constantly telling yourself . . . "that didn't happen, it wasn't that bad, I'm just remembering it wrong." Meanwhile, your body is bleeding and dying; begging you to take notice and do something about it.

Gaslighting yourself and allowing others to gaslight you KILLS your inner power. And then you just live as if you're dead.

I've spent years behaving as if I were powerless. It's true and I don't love that it's true. I've walked through the dark parts of life, looking for light, while holding the key to my own bright light all along. I just forgot I had it - both the key AND the light.

So I looked outside myself for the power needed to propel me and keep me breathing and thinking and surviving. I looked outside of myself for the light that would show me the next step on my own journey.

Looking outside of yourself for what will sustain your life is forever a dangerous endeavor. IT WILL ALWAYS BE DANGEROUS to hunt for things outside of yourself that were always meant to be found INSIDE of yourself. Because it usually means you'll find those things from another human who is also meant to stay self-contained, meaning they're also meant to wield only their own personal power over their own personal life.

A person needs power to live. When you forget you have it, you instinctively start looking anywhere and everywhere for it, simply out of survival.

The thing is, you'll always find it out there somewhere,. But it just might destroy you. And it will certainly try to destroy the power you've always had inside — you'll start living and behaving as if you have no power at all.

No one loves to live their life as though they're powerless. It's exhausting and terrifying. It's not a fun, productive or efficient way to live. It's terrible, actually.

However, living your life as a powerful person, relying on your own inner power is so much harder than it sounds. It doesn't just happen, it is a decision that must be made in just about every waking minute of life. It's a decision you can't even make until you are aware you have power inside. Even then, you often don't know how to live as a powerful person.

So lots of us spend years or lifetimes behaving as if we are powerless. It's just an old pattern, it's what we know how to do.

I used to indulge in so many fallacies regarding personal power. I have found that the word "power" sort of got hijacked somewhere along the way, and the fallacies bled into its true meaning. We started thinking that power meant dominance. And we started seeing so many abuses of power that lots of us started to detest the very word. But it was always the domination we detested, not the power. We got confused and decided to hide our own power, ashamed of it; not wanting to play any part in the abuse of power and domination. After a while, we actually started to forget we ever had any power at all — and that our power was GOOD, not bad. If we remembered we were powerful once, we were sure it was now gone forever. So we felt attracted to power outside of us because we need power to survive.

50 Roads To The Middle Of My Life

Then lots of us started getting dominated by the power of others; the kind of power that is fueled by people who forgot they have their own power — and used instead by people who are addicted to power. They need more. And more. And more. And more. But not their own, they need to take the power of OTHERS to feel powerful.

You see, power over others almost always turns toxic. The only antidote for the poison of dominance is personal power. Something has to propel us forward. Something has to give us the juice to keep learning, growing and becoming. Power is absolutely necessary and very useful. As long as it doesn't go toxic.

As long as it's PERSONAL power used in its proper capacity; which is PERSONALLY.

When we don't understand the good parts of power, we think we can run from it. Because we need it for survival, we end up being dominated by power that is outside of ourselves. We think we can run from power, but the more we run from our own power, the more we are running toward being powered by others.

We still need to be powered forward and upward and inward, even if we think we can run from power. When we don't use our own power, we become a magnet to those who love to use their power OVER us.

So we actually start thinking that being powered-over is the only way we can get powered. We get addicted to being dominated. We do have to get powered somehow, after all. Until we learn that we have everything built into OUR VERY OWN SELVES to power us, we will almost always be submitting to a life of being powered by the dominance of others.

Good things will always be abused. That doesn't mean they are not good. I'm doing my best to learn that my power is good. I'm accepting that just because power gets used in devious ways, it doesn't mean power is bad. Power is necessary. We just have to choose the source of it.

The best source of power FOR EVERY ONE OF US is our own power — born into each of us. Every. Single. One. Of. Us. Our own given personal power is the most powerful power that will ever exist specifically for us.

Like I said, I truly believe our Creator designed it this way. But like we do, we got it all tangled up to mean something else. I am on a mission to untangle it, smooth it out and SHINE SHINE SHINE.

We are meant to be powerful and to live powerfully. Once we remember how powerful we are, we have to protect our personal power while we learn the wisdom to best utilize it — so we don't become another abuser of power in the world.

It's like we're all learning to use supernatural instruments that were always meant for our good, but all sorts of reckless shenanigans happened with these powerful instruments, and that made lots of us afraid of ever using them.

For some, the temptation to abuse these instruments is just too strong to resist. As long as this is true, we have to protect ourselves and our power from those who are addicted to taking the power of others.

I know from experience that there are very good people who know the purpose of true personal power. There's nothing that can compare to being in their presence. They shine so bright that it's impossible not to feel their warmth. They control their own inner-light, like a gaslight illuminating the rooms of a grand ancient house. They know when to turn it up, and they're the only one who controls the brightness. They have no need to control anyone else, because their personal power gives them all the power they'll ever need.

THAT is true power.

When we haven't figured this out yet, we give our personal power away to people, organizations and situations. The only thing that will ever stop this horrid dance is if every human remembers, utilizes, protects and grows their own personal power.

And then supports, encourages and celebrates the personal power of others.

It's always going to get stolen otherwise. It's just too valuable. When a power-hunter sees that it's not getting used, they'll feel very justified in stealing it with the great strategy that humans use to steal someone's inner-light.

340

And then to "gaslight" a person into ever knowing or remembering they've had their own light inside all along.

The term "gaslighting" comes from an old Hollywood film called Gaslight, made in 1944, where a husband tricks his wife into thinking she has a mental illness by randomly turning up or dimming down the gas-fueled lights of their home — then going on to tell her that she's hallucinating.

He turns them up, she notices, then he tells her they're not any brighter. He turns them down and tells her they are not dimmer. She is CERTAIN that they are. She fights it at first, because she trusts herself and her instincts. She trusts what she knows. But at some point, through his relentless manipulation, she stops trusting herself and starts thinking she's crazy. And she gives her power away to him. It's just what he wanted. She stops trusting her own inner light. She essentially dies inside.

It's sick.

He literally used the external light to deceive her and made her think she could not trust herself. She forgot she had inner light to show her the way.

I hear the term "gaslighting" all the time now. It's wonderful to know that our human family is starting to shine their own lights on this very effective and very devious strategy. And it IS a very devious strategy; to break someone down over months and years, convincing them that they can't trust their own light until they forget they ever had a light at all.

Heinous, cruel and way too effective.

What I learned on this road is that the only thing able to put a stop to this abuse is to SHINE YOUR LIGHT SO BRIGHT that it will burn the hand of anyone who comes to try to dim it or turn it up the way that abusive husband did to his wife. No more hands reaching inside of you, dimming your own gaslight or turning up your own gaslight. We HAVE TO take our own inner gaslights back. NO ONE should ever have access to the turnkey that's meant for our own use.

The key to YOUR LIGHT is a key that only the owner should ever hold. That's you.
For my light, that's me.

This is a key that must be protected at all costs.

I'm finding that the best protection is to SHINE AS BRIGHT AS I CAN SHINE. So I'm practicing shining my light so hot and so bright that it burns and blinds anything or anyone who may want to come at me with ill intent.

There are lots of reasons a person or a situation would love to control your light.

I'm not having it. I'm protecting my light.

But what's starting to override my relentless desire to protect myself is simply how good it feels to be illuminated by my own light. I don't ask someone to show me my next step, I just shine my own light on it and I can see it clearly. This is such a beautiful way to live. It's a new way, and it feels so right.

When a gaslighting situation shows up, I try to look at it now as if it's literally nothing. If someone is trying to get me to doubt my own knowing, my own light, my own truth . . . I just turn it up without saying a word - SO THAT I CAN SEE WHAT I NEED TO SEE - by the light of my own power. It's not about anyone else. It's my own light in my own house. A light that was given to me by my Creator. A light that was given TO ALL OF US. When I keep things illuminated with my own light, there is never a need to go in search of power that is outside of myself.

This way, the effects of potential gaslighting are not even possible. If I'm guarding the key to my gaslight and creating a hot and bright light around it - no one can sneak in and turn it up and down with the intention of making me question my own sanity and dignity.

This is holy work, taking your own gaslight back. It takes so much practice. It takes so much focus. It takes so much discipline. But the alternative is an exhausting habit of living as if you're afraid of your own shadow while simultaneously terrified of your own light. It can make a person feel utterly insane, and then behave as if they actually are insane.

I don't want to get fooled anymore into thinking it's dangerous to shine my light as bright as it will go. Or that I might hurt others if I shine brighter than I "should."

I don't want to be afraid anymore of the villains I've been hiding from my whole life, having them give me the message that the only way my life will be spared is if I hide or stay dim.

I'm just now learning that villains actually hate the kind of light I'm talking about, and they actually don't have tools to fight it OR to steal it. They get exposed and illuminated so the brighter we shine, the more they want to run. But first they'll try to get your light to stop, and they'll work hardest at making you stop it yourself.

The best tool a villain has to destroy your bright light is to convince you that you don't even have a light . . . or to make you forget you ever did. Or that you're a bad person if you show your light. You're selfish, you're vain, you're too much. You're too full of yourself. You're obnoxious. You're prideful.

Don't be your own villain. Don't gaslight yourself. Don't let anyone else do it to you, either.

Let me tell you something I know now in ways no one can ever take from me — that NOT shining my light is the most dangerous act of all. You're actually most vulnerable and in the most danger when you're not using your power. Shining your light is the most powerful and responsible and healthiest thing you can ever do, for yourself and for everyone in our human family. We need to shine as bright as we can, for ourselves AND for each other.

I thought for a long time that if I ever wanted to shine, I was going to have to go in search of shiny things and shiny places and shiny situations. And live through their light, vicariously. It never occurred to me that the most powerful thing I could ever do, to find my own safety inside, is to shine the brightest and truest light I could ever illuminate my life with. From right inside of me. To shine even brighter, to sparkle even more.

Dimming my light never kept me safe, in all honesty. I've tried all of the ways to hide and disappear. I've tried dimming myself down. I've had to learn that frightfully walking in the dark and searching for a light outside of me has damaged my life experience more than anything else.

Ignoring the light inside of us is truly the most dangerous thing we can ever do. My safety was always to be found in the light born into me. It's born into all of us. So you're safe too.

From now on, I will shine.
And shine brighter.
And brighter and brighter and brighter.

And even brighter than that.

I hope you will too.

So, Illuminated Soul,

Where have you been gaslighted, by yourself or others?

AND

What will it take for you to shine your light as bright as possible?

I love you and I ask you to shine even brighter. We need your light. You need your light.

I will see you next on The Road Where I Stood In The Wind.

xo
melody freebird

46

The Road Where
I Stood
In The Wind

Something that's wonderful about the analogy of an old gaslight or lamp is that it's protected from the wind by the glass that surrounds it. But the wind can knock you over too — not just blow your light out.

I've had to learn how to stand upright when the wind is blowing.

When you've grown familiar with the winds of life constantly blowing, you create clever tricks to not get blown over. I had another battle to fight inside. Somewhere along the way, I either chained myself down or allowed others to do it for me so I wouldn't get blown away. It didn't even occur to me that I could become strong enough to stand in the wind without chains to hold me down. And I had chains a'plenty; pretty little gold chains keeping me upright.

Then the chains got tangled together.

And I needed to untangle and unravel them.

I can look back now and easily see that my much needed unraveling actually started when my dad died, 7 years ago. It amplified when I left Idaho. It was a supremely perfect storm. I didn't realize how much my dad was the anchor that made me want to stay grounded. I hadn't realized how closely I watched him from the time I was tiny; to know what I should do next and who I should be next. He was my North Star in so many ways, my one true thing — until Marq came along. And like Marq, he was an advocate in my life, wanting me to be my own person. Both of them were delighted constantly when I was strange and unusual, a free bird. Just like Marq, my dad saw something in me that I had such a hard time seeing in myself. He didn't want me to squander it away. It was the gift of being a free spirit. He made a great effort to express this to me from his hospital bed in the days before he died.

When he died, the reality of the chains holding me down became more clear.

A million tiny gold chains.

What I know now is that sometimes you have to unravel to get untangled. And you have to get untangled before you can fly free. I've been untangling and unknotting and smoothing myself out these last few years. It's been brutal and messy and tedious and heartbreaking and often very hopeless. I've had to tear quite a few chains apart to get them out of the knot they were in. It's been scary. It's been lonely. But I feel this strange feeling I've only recently been able to identify . . . it's the feeling of being untied after being tied down for a very long time. It's as if I've been tediously working those tiny tangled chains made of gold for years and years and years. And one day not long ago, just the right combination of rubbing them between my fingers, softly jiggling and gently pulling finally made the last knot come loose.

And I am free.

So I sit with this feeling, not quite knowing what to do with it — yet. It's still new enough that I don't trust it completely. But I actually do trust MYSELF these days, and that's a really good feeling. I finally know that I am worthy of my own trust.

As the years pass since my father died, I understand more and more why he felt it was so important to tell me to never let anyone or anything take away my free spirit. He told me that he had a free spirit too, and there were so many things he longed to do that he never did. He told me to go and do all of the things . . . to be exactly who I am and never let anything make me into someone or something else.

I have taken his edict very seriously.

Without even knowing what I was doing, after he died, I set off to untangle the chains that kept me from being free.

What I've found in the mess of these tangles is pretty magnificent. And messy. And flawed. And devastating. And wonderful. And strong. Part of never allowing anyone to change my free spirit is the decision to never allow anyone that kind of influence over my life in ANY way again. I mean the kind of influence we give to people that actually DOES make us change into someone we are not — in an effort to be more acceptable to THEM. I do not want to EVER give someone that kind of influence again. No one. Not even the ones I love most. This means I am the one who will have the most influence over my life, moving forward.

That is an enormous responsibility. With so many consequences of all sorts.

I suppose it was always meant to be this way. Some of us just have to learn it the hard way.

There are a lot of terrifying tasks that come with taking yourself seriously. It means I have to decide what kind of person I want to be TO myself. Will I continue to constantly scrutinize my own nuances, gifts and weaknesses to the point of being my own worst bully? Will I hide my own magic and my own gifts and my own magnificence so they don't ever have to be met with rejection? Or will I learn to be my most trusted friend — the kind of friend who finds beauty and potential in both my awesomeness and in my messes? What kind of friend will I be to myself?

I'm messy by nature because of my wild mind and my incessant need to experiment with every possible combination of whatever raw material is available. I'm a mad scientist of sorts, a soul scientist. It's messy work. I make SO MANY MESSES on the way to my most magnificent magnificence. And I truly don't know if there's any way around it. I've tried. In the end, I know that if I am to be most true to myself, there will always be messes to clean up. I am often the messiest mess of all.

BUT I've also been this awkward and amazing warrior all along. And I'm kind. And I have always meant well. Always always always. I know this about myself. I look back at younger versions of me and that epic wild-flower girl leaves me in awe. So much grit. So much determination. Such good intentions. So much love. She tried so hard all the time. She made so many messes but she also did so many good things. She was someone I'd admire at my age. I'd root for her and help her in any way I could because I'd see that she was doing EVERYTHING SHE KNEW TO DO with what she had. I'd want to earn her friendship.

I didn't treat her that way when I was her though, and that is a shame.

One thing I've decided to discard is my old need to be self-deprecating to pay in advance for anything wonderful about me that might show up later. Lest I should get too full of myself. I had this pervasive habit where I'd work hard to identify and call- out my flaws to myself and everyone else, to the point of MAKING that one of my greatest flaws. Relentless self-deprecation. I'd try to be small and dumb and not too much. I made myself into a joke and allowed others to do the same; a survival mechanism I just don't want or need anymore. I want to own what's unique and wonderful about me the same way I want to own what's not so fantastic about me. I want to embrace all of it. I want to be that kind of a friend to myself . . . one who takes the mess with the magic. And doesn't even WANT one without the other.

I want to invite it all with the most warm and enthusiastic welcome, the way a beloved lifelong friend greets you at the door when you're reuniting after years without seeing each other. I want to greet myself every day with the same kind of excited sparkle in my eyes that happens when I see one of my grandchildren.

And I want to do it IMMEDIATELY because I'm just so tired of these years in the same laboratory, looking at myself. I'm done thinking I'm going to find the thing that's going to cure me or ruin me. I could spend the rest of my life here and miss out on everything that feels like being a free spirit is supposed to feel.

I. AM. SO. TIRED. OF. LOOKING. AT. MYSELF.
I want to see everything else now.

50 Roads To The Middle Of My Life

It's taken years to untangle these chains. It was necessary and holy work. But now that I think I might just be totally untangled — I want to move on.

I am a free bird who wants to fly.

I really am so tired of looking so closely at myself. I just want to BE myself. Without trying so hard — without trying at all.

In the few years after my dad died, I would drive 45 minutes to the cemetery to sit by his grave. I felt so lost without him in so many ways. There was a particular day I sat at his grave and asked him to show me in some way that he was there.

A beautiful heart cloud showed up high in the sky. And it just kept forming to be a more and more perfect heart.

And then the wind started to blow and I could actually faintly hear his voice. I will never forget it. He said "Melly, you're going to have to learn to stand in the wind."

"Things are going to get harder.
You can do it. You are equipped."

Over these last years I've come to understand what that means. It's not the chains that would hold me in place when the wind would blow, it was my own strength, and the strength of my Truthteller; holding me upright.

Chains holding us down are not the best way to keep us from blowing over. Our own given and earned strength is the best way. And the trust that we have help from the other side when the wind blows harder than we have strength to bear.

So I've said it to myself countless times over these last years of unraveling and untangling . . .

"Stand in the wind, Melody, stand in the wind."

"Things are going to get harder.
You can do it. You are equipped."

And life tested me, as it tests all of us.

Life asked me . . .

Can you stand in the wind if this happens?
Can you stand in the wind if this happens now too?
And how about if this happens?
Okay, now what about this?

So many painful things have happened. Illnesses, accidents, betrayals, mistakes, crushed dreams, disappointments. Terrifying dilemmas. Losses of all kinds. Mighty winds.

And each time I've pled with God…please not this.
Please not this.
Dammit. Please not this.

Please.
Please, I beg you.
Please. Not this too!

We stood in the wind through so much of it together as a family, but then my children all grew up and don't need me in the same ways anymore. They don't want me to behave as if they need me. They don't want me to behave as if I need them. Just like Marq told me when his shoulder broke, he does not need me or want me to do his life for him. Not even his pain. He does not want me to do MY life for him. They all want to be free and they want me to be free. They learned what I tried to teach them. But I was teaching them those things so that I could live it vicariously through them. They don't want me to be vicarious anymore. They're reminding me that we've each got to stay on our own Soul Roads. And it's not a job we can do vicariously. It's one we each have to do on our own. We each get to be free, next to each other.

But it hurts when the ones you live for don't need you in the same ways anymore. It's something you have to grieve before you can feel the exquisite freedom it provides.

So much of life has felt this way. The unraveling and untangling has been a mighty wind — daring me to stay standing without being chained down.

Can you stop working long enough to feel what you actually feel?
Can you step away from the battle long enough to know what peace feels like?
Can you let yourself?
Can you do it?
Can you do what you have to do to save your own life, even if it means disappointing, confusing and even repulsing some of the people you love most?
Can you walk away from beautiful things that aren't meant for you anymore?
Can you walk away from destructive things that never were?
Can you be who you are even when it's scary?
Can you stop being who you are not; even if that's what some others may like about you best?

Can you stand in the wind?

I can. And I have. Some days the dust blows in my eyes and I can't tell if that's what's drenching me in tears or if it's just the grief. There are so many kinds of tears. The tears that come from the wind blowing in your face and the ones that come when you're so grateful the wind has stopped for a while.

I am unchained. I am standing.

I am unlabeled.

I am learning how to do this.

And now I will focus on finding joy whether the wind is blowing or not.

We are all meant for joy. I just know it. I'm ready to claim what is meant for me and to create even more of it. I probably don't have as many years left to live as the ones I have already lived. Unless you've made it past the halfway mark, I don't think you can understand what this knowledge brings. It's an urgency to choose your focus — to choose joy.

Joy in the wind.

Joy in the peace.
Joy in all of it.

Because I am finally free.

So, Enduring Soul,

In what parts of your life do you chain yourself down in an effort to not get blown over?

AND

Are you willing to stand in the wind?

I love you. I know you can do this.

Now I will take you to The Road Where I Decided to Decide.

See you there.
xo
melody freebird

47

The Road
Where I Decided
To Decide

I find myself obsessively checking my email, my text messages and all parts of the internet for something. I have been waiting for a message, a sign. I caught myself doing it just yesterday, amidst all sorts of beautiful texts, messages and emails from people I love — there was still THE MESSAGE I was waiting to receive.

The one that would change everything.

I check. I check again. I check again. I check again. And again. I put my phone down, frustrated. Scared. I start going into a familiar fear spiral. I ask myself . . . What if the message never comes? I look at myself in the mirror, an aging woman. It is terrifying on so many levels. I check my phone again. And again. I keep checking.

Then yesterday, I finally stopped in the kitchen, after checking every available place where messages can be sent through my phone. I stopped and really questioned myself — what are you looking for? What are you waiting for? What do you think is coming?

And my first answer to myself was that I am waiting for someone or something to somehow give me THE THING that's going to take my struggles away. Something that's going to make this all make sense. Something that's going to bring me back to feeling carefree and alive and joyful all the time. I am waiting for THE MESSAGE or THE SIGN that everything is going to be okay.

I guess I am waiting for a go-ahead. Or a get out of jail free card. Or a sweepstakes notification. Or even Ashton Kutcher to show up and say," HAHAHAHAHA!!! You've been punked!!!" And then I will get to go back to my regularly scheduled life, chuckling at how funny this all was, and that it was all just a prank all along.

I'm waiting for something or someone to save me again.

It's just a little part of me that does this. An unconscious part of me. Because I know what I know and I know it from experience — that no one is coming to save me, but especially that I don't need to be saved. These are just old habits. A little part of me that keeps looking out the window waiting for Santa Claus and the Easter Bunny and the Tooth Fairy and Tinkerbell to take me back to Never Never Land.

I think about the song I wrote and sang waaaaay back so many roads ago called TAKE ME AWAY. It's my default. SOMEONE PLEASE COME AND TAKE ME AWAY FROM THIS MESS I AM IN! Sometimes I just want Harry Potter's train to show up and get me, expecting me, and take me to where I belong. To say, "You never belonged here, we are going to take you where your magic is, where your potential is, where you will be seen and loved and appreciated and free of struggle for the rest of your life."

Oh gosh, it's so humiliating to admit how often this little part of me has her suitcase packed, waiting by the door for the driver to show up to get me and take me where I am supposed to be. It's just this little part of me that keeps holding on to the hope that my life has not been lived in vain, that my struggles mean something, that my magic is special somehow.

But the majority of me knows what is true, that there is magic all around me and inside of me. That I have to choose it. No one is going to choose it for me, and even if they did, I would still be borrowing knowledge from them. It would never be mine. And until it's mine, I will always be waiting by the door for the message or the driver to take me away.

50 Roads To The Middle Of My Life

We all have to get our knowledge on our own, or it will always be borrowed.

This is holy inside work. To realize that I am the driver I have been waiting for. That I hold the pen that will write the message to tell myself what I have been waiting to hear.

My greatest yearning right now is to overcome this part of me that obsessively checks for something outside of me to tell me what is worthy inside of me. So I can stop waiting for the go-ahead and remember that I have to decide to create it for myself. It's such a monumentally heartbreaking waste of time to wait for something to come and perfectly finish me, like I'm one of those hundreds of paintings in my studio that just needs the final touches to be acceptable enough to be called "finished."

I was watching a movie a few days ago called The Lost Daughter. I was tired and so I just pushed PLAY on the first thing that looked remotely interesting. It was another mirror. It was the story of a woman, nearly 50, who was reckoning with where life had taken her. What she had chosen and where she ended up because of it. What was chosen for her. What had happened that was out of her control. What had happened because of what she decided when things were in her control. She was aging. No one was coming to save her. She was finally at the age where no one was choosing her. The age where she had to choose herself.

She went on a vacation all alone, and her past flashed before her in little clips that made her realize her age; made her realize her regrets — made her realize her power. It all made her realize she was going to have to continue to choose . . . that was the answer all along.

She was not going to get chosen anymore, and that left her free to choose her own life. She watched people who were younger than she was . . . 10 years younger, 20 years younger, 30 years younger . . . and she remembered all the iterations of herself, housed in her beautiful battle-worn body. All that she'd already done and been, all that she is now, and all that she had to choose, moving forward.

Because it seems when you get to a certain age, you stop getting chosen in the ways young people do. This is both devastating and incredibly liberating. BUT YOU HAVE TO CHOOSE HOW YOU PERCEIVE IT.

Her character helped me remember that this is the most important choice of all, how we will perceive the things that happen and don't happen. I watched her on the screen, brilliantly portraying the plight of the aging woman. The thing that struck me with the biggest gust of recognition was the way she watched the beautiful younger women on the beach. And in her mind, she'd flash back to when she was young and fresh and beautiful and firm and full of possibility. And constantly hunted-after and chosen. She seemed to go from cheering the young women on, to feeling profoundly envious of them, back to cheering them on and taking her turn at being the older woman who gets to decide whether she'll be a bitter martyr or a living vessel of wisdom and freedom.

There is a way that aging women look at younger women. And you don't recognize it until you are the aging woman yourself. Whenever I see it, I want to grab the aging woman and hug her tight — look her in the eyes and tell her, I SEE YOU. YOU ARE STILL MAGNIFICENT!!! MORE MAGNIFICENT THAN EVER!

I've also wanted to grab younger women, their face in my hands, and say ENJOY THIS! IT DOESN'T LAST FOREVER! But I know a young woman wouldn't understand or care, and she shouldn't.

As of late however, I want to grab all of us at once and say . . . "All of these ages are perfect. All of them. Don't be afraid of aging, and don't think that younger is better. Don't think that older is better. All of it is perfect."

Because that's what I truly believe. But I can't say it outloud to everyone yet, because there are still too many days where I'm trying to convince myself of it.

When you are young, there are so many opportunities to get chosen. I see it in employment, relationships and casting. It's online everywhere. It is in the physical world everywhere. When you are young, you are on a tree like a beautiful apple, waiting to be picked. And you get picked a lot. You are shiny and perfect and fresh. You are in what our society calls your "prime."

When you are aging, you think you are a rotting apple on the ground, having fallen off the tree. But then something happens that makes you see the truth. YOU ARE ACTUALLY THE TREE.

I pray that every woman alive can come to this knowledge. I am coming into this knowledge.

I was about to say that HAVING THIS KNOWLEDGE WILL CHANGE EVERYTHING, but then I deleted that sentence. Because you know what? Maybe we don't need to CHANGE EVERYTHING. Maybe we just need to be a tree, and let trees do what they do. Maybe we need to understand that the only thing needing changing is how much we try to defy nature. How much we abandon and ignore the perfectly imperfect plan of becoming.

Maybe we all just need to stop trying so hard to BE SOMETHING and just allow ourselves to BE, the way nature does.

I just spent a week with my 6 and 3 year old granddaughters, and my absolutely stunning young woman daughter who is nearly 30 years old. As I played with my granddaughters, made food with them, sledded down a snowy hill with them, holding hands . . . I saw their perfect little fingers wrapped around mine. And I saw the dramatic differences in our hands.

I am aging.

I'm trying to do the math of how old my grandmother was when I was 6 years old. She was somewhere in her 50's, I think. Holy moley, my grandmother was beautiful. And as I look back, I think about the way she fretted over her own aging. She was a gifted musician and beautician, even starting her own business way back before women did that. I used to go and stay for weeks with her and my grandfather in the summer. I watched everything she did. She was so much magic to me, so magnificent. I remember being in her yard with her as she cared for her flowers. I knelt down next to her and she showed me the age spots all over her hands. Her hands were so soft and pale. Painted fingernails. They looked like a gorgeous topographical map, blue veins and freckles. They smelled like cold cream.

It's a fresh memory what she said to me . . . "my hands used to be so beautiful, and now they are so wrinkled and old."

She looked into the distance as she was saying it, her voice trailing off...

she went somewhere else. I am at the age now where I know exactly where she went . . . to the place where you are trying to remember something you once were.

As her young granddaughter, I was shocked and confused. All I could think was . . . "That is what a grandma's hands are supposed to look like!" To me, they were the most beautiful hands in the world, they were my grandma's hands.

My granddaughters look at me the way I used to look at my grandmother. She used to let me rifle through her button box, through her jewelry and through her lovely things. She let me wear her horn-rimmed rhinestone bejeweled reading glasses. She loved beautiful things and she let me touch and hold and enjoy them. She would give me scraps and a needle and thread and let me sew clothes for my dolls. She would help me. She would put on records of the music she loved most and I could see the light in her eyes that lit up the dreams that were inside of her, on a stage in her own mind. She was the most magical creature I knew.

My granddaughter calls me on Facetime several times a week. She always asks if I am busy and if we can please talk for a long time. She shows me everything. She wants to see what I am creating and what I am doing. She props the phone up and dances for me. Her eyes are so full of everything you'd ever want a 6 year old's eyes to be full of.

She wants me to be my age. She needs a grandmother.

So I decide to decide. I decide to decide that I will BE HERE NOW. I will be the age I am now. I will see the gifts of NOW. I will decide who I am at this age. I will decide what message to write for myself. I will decide what signs I will make for myself. I will decide what train I will create to take me to the magical place where I belong.

I belong wherever I decide I want to go, that is where I belong.
So I decide where I want to go.

I have tremendous examples all around me of what it means to age magically. I think of my grandmother, I think of the many close friends I have who are 15 and 20 years older than I am and how I would never want them to be younger than they are, or to look younger than they are. I think of the way they make me excited to keep going to another level in this game of life.

I remember the first time I met my friends Terry and Patrice. They were in their 50's when we met and both of them are in their 60's now. I remember after meeting them, I wasn't afraid to get older anymore . . . because they are the most beautiful, creative, unique, stylish and wonderful women you could ever imagine. They get more beautiful and vibrant every year.

It's the same with my friend, Lisa. She is more than 15 years older than I am, and we are just two funky little girls when we are together. She is another one who just seems to get more beautiful and vibrant and authentic every year.

I often come back to this short little poem by one of the women in my life who has consistently taught me about holding on, but mostly about letting go. About allowing. About choosing. About making the most of what is right in front of you and deciding not to abandon the gifts in your hand to go in search of something you may not ever find. She is a mentor, sister and soul friend to me . . . Orly Aveneri. She is the most prolific artist. She has had the most epic life. Born in Israel and now living in rural Oregon, where she makes art and curates beauty from the things right in front of her, always. And she is constantly letting things go, constantly. That is the thing I always remember about her most, how the peace and beauty she exudes largely comes from how she never holds on tight to anything. She allows everything to become what it wants to become next, and she appreciates it while it's in her hands.

These are her words I carry with me. And I look at them often:

It's okay to change.
It's okay to retreat, then join back in.
It's okay to leave and never come back.
It's okay to leave and come back differently.
It's okay to close doors and open others.
Gracefully, for yourself, and for others.
-Orly Aveneri

Orly and our other artist friend Katie were visiting a few years before we left Idaho. The week they were there, a fox or hawk or raccoon was getting into our chicken coop every night. And every morning, I'd find another dead chicken. I was devastated. Then a big tree fell down and died. Then I told Orly about all of the things in my storage unit. She kept telling about how much happier I would be if I could just let things go. Neither of us had any idea that a few years later, I'd be doing just that.

Her words have sustained me over and over.

She is aging too. I don't know how old she is and I don't care. She is ageless to me. All of my favorite people are.

So I sit here in my 2.25 strength readers, typing the last of these roads with wrinkled hands. I think about the way my husband and I have become older people who sit next to each other on the couch and watch our favorite shows together, mostly in silence, taking turns bringing each other dinner, to be eaten on our little wood trays as we laugh or cry over whatever show we are watching. We adore each other and we have earned this comfortable silence with each other over more than 31 years of life's different stages and transitions. We are madly in love but it's so much different than it used to be. I think of the way we love each other now. How we pause the show when our kids call and put on our reading glasses so we can see them on the screen. I think about the way we take our vitamins in the morning and kiss each other goodnight every night, several hours from when we will actually go to sleep in separate rooms. Because we are valuing sleep more than passionate nights these days. I think about the way we hand each other reading glasses at the store when one of us has forgotten ours, so that we can read the labels and the prices. How we laugh about the things aging people laugh about, things younger people have yet to understand, but will. How we go on dates to the grocery store and stand in the aisle, talking about how much bread used to cost. We have become the older people. We are cool and eclectic, but we are the older people.

And I decide to decide. That this is all so beautiful, all of it. Even in the beauty, I decide to release everything, every day. So that every new day can be what it's meant to be — NEW.

I decide to release everyone I love or have ever loved of any obligation to contribute to my life or my happiness in any way. I release my grudges, my old "need" for things to be made right, for apologies. I release the martyr in me. I set everyone free. It sets me free.

50 Roads To The Middle Of My Life

I decide that I will stop waiting for THE THING. I will stop waiting for the call or the text or the message or the sign. I will take what I can find and make it into something beautiful. I will release what cannot be found and what is not meant for me.

I decide to decide. For I am the one who has to decide or it will by default, be decided for me.

And that is the opposite of free.

I decide to keep living. I decide to keep experiencing. I decide to take my turn at being in my 50's instead of desperately searching for a way to be in my 30's. I decide that I will also take my turn at being in my 60's, 70's, 80's and 90's. And that I will do it just like me. Colorfully, awkwardly, amazingly, joyfully, sorrowfully, FULLY. I will fall, I will fail, I will succeed, I will make it, and I won't make it. I will decide to keep holding things, but I will mostly decide to not hold on so tight that I ever have to RELEASE anything ever again. I will let everything just go when that time comes. I will hold my hands out and let things rest there, to be seen and appreciated, and then when they're ready to take flight like a brand new butterfly, I won't put them in a cage . . . I will watch them go.

There will always be more butterflies.

No matter how things happen, I will grow. That is the one SURE THING. I will grow if I am moving. I will grow as I see other things and people moving. I will change and transform if I am moving, whether it's my body that's moving, or the river inside of me that's moving.

Stagnation is the greatest threat, not failure. This I know for sure. It's the trying to go backward to fix what never happened or to try to live in something that doesn't exist anymore. It's the death-grip on things that expired a long time ago that threatens our existence. It's the being anywhere but RIGHT HERE and RIGHT NOW that is the biggest threat. It's the waiting that will steal our life from us.

So I decide to decide. And when I decide, I immediately decide that I will keep deciding. No matter how scary it feels, no matter the consequences.

I am done waiting.

I am here, and I am who I have been waiting for.

It is time.

So, Becoming Soul,

Where are you resisting your own becoming and your own aging?

AND

How can you make the rest of your life the best of your life and stop waiting?

We are all in this together. The sooner we embrace every age, the sooner we will have the kind of wisdom available for young people they need most. And the sooner we will see that we are truly living the best years of our lives.

I love you and I will see you on The Road Where We Flew Wing to Wing

xo
melody freebird

48

The Road Where We Flew Wing To Wing

I used to send out a daily email called, A Little Bird Told Me. This message was simply a bit of truth that had been given to me from somewhere divine, and I wanted to pass it on. I did this for over a decade, every weekday. Hundreds of thousands of people got those messages in their inboxes 5 days a week. It was the greatest song of my life, and I loved singing it. I wrote my heart out as I was gifted those messages from somewhere up above. And I loved sending them, it was easy and joyful.

Until the little birdie lost her voice.

Then a few years ago, in the midst of recovering from my wings being clipped and my voicebox being sold for ransom, I gave myself a new name — Melody Freebird.

When Marq and I set out on the road, we called ourselves Freebird Nomads. We called our RV our Freedom Home.

But I always thought I was a little sparrow, or a barn swallow. Or a little chickadee. A little song bird. Marq was always the eagle.

When Marq had his brain injury, we lived on Beacon Light Road in EAGLE, Idaho. He was an EAGLE scout when he was only 13 years old.

Melody Ross

Then we moved to Star, Idaho — onto the ranch where we would hold our retreats, and the ranch was on bird sanctuary land right along the river. Birds of every sort lived there. Herons, ducks, geese, hawks, falcons, and eagles. The barn swallows would come every evening in the warmer months and give us an acrobatic show right in our own backyard. More than a few times, I'd look out the window and see a giant horned owl sitting on our lawn, he lived in one of the tallest tress on the ranch and you could hear him at night. You could hear the doves constantly cooing. The yellow finches came in the hundreds every summer when I put out the bird feeders filled with thistle seed. One would show up, and by some inaudible communication, they'd tell their finchy friends for miles around where the action was. Within a few days, we'd have swarms of yellow wings right outside our window. The quail families used to love living underneath our wild blackberry bushes or back by the pond, under the brambles of vines and tree roots. I loved watching their brood strut across the property, mama, daddy and a long line of baby quails in tow, headdresses bouncing with every step. Because our house on the ranch was clothed in big windows all the way around, we would often hear an alarmingly loud thud as birds tried to fly through them, only to be knocked out cold on impact. I'd run to the window and almost always they'd sit for a minute, shake their birdie head and then fly away. A few times the impact killed them, and that was always heartbreaking. It happened to fat robins, young hawks and quail the most. Every bird was so beautiful, so valuable. I loved living on that ranch and being up so close to them. After being there a few years, it's as if they trusted us enough to let us be part of their habitat, and I communed with them daily. I still miss them all so much.

In the couple of years that preceded our exodus from Idaho, we were seeing eagles everywhere. Mostly bald eagles. The first time I saw them up close was the beginning of a long string of seeing them over and over again, SO OFTEN! We were canoeing up in the mountains, sometime in late summer or early fall. It was warm enough that we could be in a canoe, but it wasn't warm enough that we'd want to be in the water. We ended up in a slow-moving part of the river that had a lot of curves and turns. Somehow, hundreds of salmon had found themselves trapped there. The river was literally the dark orange color of salmon. We could reach down into the water and touch them . . . hundreds of them all around us. It was surreal. I couldn't stop gasping and taking pictures.

Then Marq pointed up, and 2 ENORMOUS bald eagles were perched

364

right above us in the trees. They found their endless buffet.

We sat for at least an hour in that spot. I couldn't believe how HUGE a bald eagle is up close. So majestic. So stunning. We pulled the canoe onto a sandbar and found a big boulder to sit on because I wanted to see them swoop down into the river. I want to capture it on film. It never did happen. They just sat up on their perch together, the two of them, happy as can be. Marq said they were probably already stuffed and just waiting until they got hungry again. It was a rare moment. We were right next to them, viewing them up close the entire time.

After that, we started seeing bald eagles everywhere. One particular time, we were on the way back from Sky & Pixie's place and a really freaky thing happened. About every mile, a bald eagle would be sitting on the fence on the side of the road. We saw the first one and commented how strange it was. Then we went down the road a little further, and another . . . doing the exact same thing . . . and another . . . until we saw 8 of them, just perched on the fence next to the road. It was absolutely extraordinary.

I could tell you several more experiences like this, but the point I'm trying to get across is that it seemed like we were being put on notice to listen to the eagles, or notice the eagles . . . something. It felt like a message.

When we had our 25th Anniversary recommitment ceremony, our dear friend actually blessed us with eagle feathers from his Native American upbringing and teachings. He had found them after a cougar tried to attack the female eagle and the male eagle tried to save her. They both perished in the fight and our friend harvested their feathers to use them in the sacred ways he'd been taught. He told us that we held the spirit of the Eagle.

Over the last months especially, I have felt less and less like a little bird. And more like an old crow. But the eagle kept coming back to my mind. And just last week, another bald eagle flew right across the highway and in front of our truck, in a way that I could not miss. He or she was wanting me to take notice. God kept nudging me to listen listen listen.

We met with our friend Nicole, who was gifted with EXTREME intuitive abilities after 2 different near-death experiences. We met just after my 50th birthday, Marq and I together. She told us so many things that she perceived about us, but the thing that stuck with me most was when she told us that we are both like eagles. That he and I together had the spirit of an Eagle. WHAAAAAAAAT? But I thought I was a little chickadee type of a bird! Or an old crow, like I said. But an eagle?

So I finally did a little search on what is so sacred about the eagle and I was astounded. It still makes me weep to think about it. I will just copy and paste what I found on Google. The first question I asked was whether eagles mate for life. I'd heard that they do and that was one thing I had in common with them. Here's what I found on Google:

Are eagles monogamous?
Bald eagles are solitary, but monogamous animals. Although they spend winters and migrations alone, bald eagles maintain the same breeding pair year after year. A mated eagle pair finds a nesting site and produces offspring each year.

Why do eagles mate for life?
Bald eagles stay hitched until death do they part, often returning year after year to the same nest. While there, the pair continuously adds to the structure, so that after many seasons it assumes gargantuan proportions and stands as a symbol of their fidelity.

What do eagles fear?
Bald eagles fear humans at all times, but will tolerate much less disturbance during the nesting season, than at other times of the year. A nesting pair will seek isolation, and any human interference, if prolonged, may drive the birds away from the nest.

AND THEN . . . I searched the spiritual meaning of an eagle and found this:
(from pure-spirit.com)

. . . .
Symbolism and Power
The eagle is the chief over all the winged creatures. Eagle conveys the powers and mes-sages of the spirit; it is man's connection to the divine because it flies higher than any other bird. The eagle brings the message of renewed life because it is associated with the east winds - the direction of spring, dawn and rebirth.
If an individual has been going through a hard time, eagle not only signals a new begin-ning, but provides that person with the stamina and resilience to endure the difficulties. If eagle has appeared, it bestows freedom and courage to look ahead. The eagle is symbolic of the importance of honesty and truthful principles. Summon the eagle when you are

about to embark on a challenge, a massive life change or a creative endeavor.
Eagle people are seen as visionaries, those who are seekers and who are willing to push the limits of self-discovery and personal freedom. The eagle person is a born leader and may become impatient with those who cannot fly as high or as fast. Despite the fact that eagle with hold aloof or retreat to the skies, people will naturally gravitate to them.

The Lesson
When Eagle appears to you it means that you are being put on notice. Eagle totems appear to inspire (push) you to reach higher and become more than you think you are capable of. They tell you to be courageous and really stretch your limits and see what you can do. They bring a sense of courage and a desire to explore and grow. To dream of a flying eagle or one who is perched high signifies good fortune or victory coming your way. If it scares you or attacks you it means there are some self-imposed limitations you need to push through.

The lesson of the eagle is to take a look from where it sees. You must have the courage to relinquish stale and comfortable habits and beliefs to soar into unknown realms and new realities - continually expanding your view. Now is the time to take full responsibility for your life and be prepared for instant destiny. As your spiritual awareness increases, the positive and negative ramifications will become more immediate and have greater force.
....

I used to think the whole spirit animal and animal totem thing was weirdo woo-woo. Now I'm the biggest woo-woo weirdo there is, after spending these last few years in nature and letting God teach me about the creations here for us to learn from and enjoy. Many days over the last few years, the only meaningful communication I would have with another living creature was with an animal.

I have always been drawn to anything in the sky. Clouds, stars, sunsets, sunrises, the sun, the moon. But mostly the birds. I thought I was a little tiny birdie once, but I've come to realize that I AM an eagle of sorts. And I have tried to fight that knowledge for many years. Little birdies are cuter, and sweeter, and they get to hang out with lots of other birds. Eagles lead a more solitary life. And they are kind of intimidating. Not something you'd ever want to mess with.

But it all made sense for me when I read about how they mate for life. They are solitary but very devoted.

Marq and I took off in our RV together 2 years ago. Freebird nomads. In my mind was a picture of two cute little barn swallows. I was so grateful that we'd get to be in that tiny RV together so that I could have him all to myself after so many years of so many things keeping us apart for much of the time.

I thought . . . Are we done being apart yet so that we can be together forever and ever and ever, amen? Every minute, through every single thing? So I can hug you and squeeze you and touch you and hold you?

So I can be okay?

But we weren't little birdies. We've been eagles all along. Both of us. It's never changed. And I've always tried to make it something different instead of embracing the gifts inside of it.

"**Although they spend winters and migrations alone**, bald eagles maintain the same breeding pair year after year. . . Bald eagles stay hitched until death do they part, often returning year after year to the same nest."

Marq and I lose each other almost every winter. It is hard. Just like the devoted eagles, we seem to go our separate ways in the winter. It has felt heartbreaking. He goes somewhere in his mind and I go somewhere so I can cope with the heartbreak. But as I look over the last 31 years, we have always done big things separately and then come back together. He's taken people on pack trips that last weeks. There have been many summers when I've only seen him for a few weeks between his trips. I've traveled the world for business. He goes and does his thing, I go and do mine. Then we come back together.

So it's always been just right. We fly together when we are together. We fly solo when we are solo. The important part is that we fly, instead of staying grounded, thinking there is some perfect thing that's going to happen to make it possible for us to fly. WHAT WAS BUILT INTO ME IS WHAT MAKES IT POSSIBLE FOR ME TO FLY, NO MATTER THE CONDITIONS. WHAT WAS BUILT INTO HIM IS MAKES IT POSSIBLE FOR HIM TO FLY, NO MATTER THE CONDITIONS. And sometimes we get to fly together, and that is awesome.

But we gotta fly solo sometimes, too.

For us, it seems to be a lot of the time.

I think of the story of the ugly duckling. The little bird who was so differ-ent from the other ducks that she thought she was ugly and wrong. And then she found out she was actually a swan. She was a perfectly perfect swan, not a duckling at all. Melody Freebird thought she was a chickadee or a sparrow, or a barn swallow.

But she was an eagle all along.

It's time to fly.

So, Soaring Soul,

Where in your life have you denied your own majestic abili-ties?

AND

Who could you be if you didn't feel the need for someone else to complete you?

We get to fly wing to wing a lot in life, and it is wonderful. But when we can't, we really will be okay on our own.

I love you. You can do this too if the time ever comes that you've got to, I promise.

Thank you for being here with me. I will now take you to the glorious Road Where I Heard New Birds.

See you there.

xo
melody freebird

49

The Road
Where I Heard
New Birds

When you make a sacrifice, you never know if anything will come of it. I guess that's part of the sacrifice, the risk that you could be trading something you truly love for something you feel you need even more than the thing you love, only to find that you are left with nothing at all.

Life can feel like that sometimes, like our sacrifices yield nothing. But I don't really think that's even a possibility. There is always something being born from something dying, or while something is dying. There is just ALWAYS something being born for us if we have eyes to see it and ears to hear it. Always.

But are sacrifices the only way to find ourselves? What if life is more merciful than we thought it was? I know that life has often felt more cruel than I could imagine. But if I'm honest, the mercies of life have far outshined the cruelty.

Sometimes you find out that a sacrifice was never required of you to begin with, you just thought it was, and you find that you actually sacrificed YOURSELF on a manufactured altar, to try to pay for a debt that was also manufactured.

What can be born of that? It just seems so tragic.

Melody Ross

A lot can be born of it actually.

A couple of stories stick in my mind like a napkin for a bookmark, impossible to ignore. I don't even know if I'm remembering them right, but there are 2 stories I don't know that I could ever forget, and they are very similar.

One is about a person who saved everything they had to get somewhere on a ship. It was a very long voyage. They sacrificed everything they had to buy the ticket, and then packed some very meager provisions. Canned food, low quality food to get them through the journey. They stayed in their room so they would not have to watch the people who could afford the good food offered on the ship. They stayed in their tiny room, sea sick and full of cabin fever, eating their salty old food, alone.

When the trip was over, they found out that the delicious food the ship was offering actually came along with the fare. They could have been eating that food all along. It was meant for them.

The other story is about a guy who walked through the desert to redeem himself — to make some kind of sacrifice to pay for his existence. He nearly starved. He nearly died of thirst. He suffered tremendously as he prayed and prayed. In the end, he came back and said that what he learned was that there was never a reason he would ever have to do that. There was no redemption needed. He just thought there was. He nearly killed himself, trying to pay a debt that never existed.

But he learned.
And the person who passed-up the beautiful ocean views and fresh food learned too.

They just learned it the hard way, like we sometimes do.

My favorite movie of **ALL TIME** came out in 1996. I have watched that movie at least once a year since it was created. It's called Phenomenon and it stars John Travolta, Kira Sedgewick, Robert Duvall, Forrest Whittaker and many other stellar actors. I could probably quote 20 lines from this movie word for word, but the part in it I could never get out of my mind was when John Travolta's character, George Malley, is explaining something beautiful he'd just learned about the potential of human beings if they only realized their divine connection to everything alive, he said:

"Now we were talking about a partnership. Do you know what the largest living organism in the world is? Ok, it's a grove of aspen trees in Colorado…acres of aspens. Ok, now, they thought they were disconnected, separate, but indeed they found out that they weren't. That there was one giant organism with the same root system."

There is so much more to this scene. A backstory and a forward story. It defined so much of the movie for me. But I bring it up because one of my greatest dreams from that moment forward was to visit that aspen grove. When my dad died, my friends even put together a fund to plant more aspen trees in Colorado in his name. I had always planned on finding it and visiting it.

Well, just this year, I learned something absolutely miraculous. It was that George Malley was wrong. That aspen grove actually is NOT in Colorado. It is in Utah. And for the last 2 summers, I just happened to live right smack in the middle of it — I just didn't know it.

It's called Pando.

I'm going to say more about this place, but first I want to tell you what I was doing in the weeks before we left Idaho. I was saying goodbye to the birds. I was saying goodbye to the trees. I was saying goodbye to the river. I was saying goodbye to the mountains.

The month before we left, I told myself that no matter what time I woke up, I was going to put my shoes on and go outside and walk for at least one hour. I had a lot of saying goodbye to do. And I did it. Most often, it was around 4am. I would walk out into the darkest of dark, hours before dawn, and walk around our ranch, down the street to where my in-laws live and where we built our first house. And I'd talk to the trees, mostly. I'd thank them for all they'd meant to me. I'd cry and tell them I'm sorry I had to go, that I hoped someone else would take care of them. I'd ask them to remember me. I'd walk around the pond and see the mountains in the distance. I'd hear the river. I kept telling it all goodbye. It was a sorrowful time. I didn't want to leave that essential part of my life. I couldn't believe I actually lived on a bird sanctuary property, next to a river, surrounded by trees. I was leaving behind everything I loved. I felt that it was getting pulled from my very fingers. I knew that life could never be this beautiful anywhere else, and I knew I was going to have to sacrifice all of this to find healing for my husband. Because I loved him even more.

I would walk and walk until the sun came up. And just before the sun came up, the birds would start to sing. Someday I would love to know what their songs were saying . . . what the words are. But I suspect they sing in a beautiful parable, meant to mean something different to everyone who hears their song — meant to be the exact message the listener needs.

When the birds would start to sing on those mornings, I would really start to cry. I could not imagine my life without these birds, and I knew it would be one of the greatest sacrifices of my life. But then I'd look over at the RV where we had already been sleeping, and think about how if we didn't find something to help Marq, I would lose him too. We had to sacrifice.

Losing the birds was a big one for me. Losing the trees. Losing the mountains. Losing the river. Losing this place that welcomed me like I was truly a bird myself. Losing my home. Losing my community.

Well, imagine my surprise last summer when I found out that I'd been living right in the middle of the largest Aspen grove in the world?

Because guess what? I was in my proverbial ship room, eating old saltine crackers from my suitcase . . . not letting myself leave my room because I thought I had to pay my way.

When we left Idaho, we first moved to St. George in the winter, but as soon as it got too hot, we'd head up to the ranch with West and Kami . . . the ranch that is nestled in the land of Pando.

Kami would coax me out of my RV, where I was working tirelessly to put our life back together, and she'd take me on drives and hikes to show me her favorite places. The first time we drove up the hill and I started seeing the expanse of Pando, it took my breath away. It was Spring and so the leaves were not on the aspens yet. They were just beautiful, elegant white sentinels that towered into the air. . . millions and millions and millions of them, For miles and miles.

I still didn't know where I was.

Kami also showed me the river that ran from the very top of the mountain, at Fish Lake, all the way down the mountains, through the ranch and beyond . . . through Capitol Reef National Park, which is the opposite direction of the heart of Pando, but just as close to the ranch.

One day, when I had committed to go on a nature adventure with Kami, I walked out of the RV at dawn and heard it. BIRDS.

BIRDSONG!

SO MANY BIRDS. They were new birds, birds I didn't even know existed.

I had not heard them until that moment because I was too busy making my sacrifices.

That day, I finally saw it all. That if I could find the courage to come out of my sacrificial cave, everything I left behind was waiting for me right where I was, and more.

That summer, and the summer after, it was as if Mountain Bluebirds planted themselves everywhere we would end up. Like they were our tour guides. If you've never seen a Mountain Bluebird on the white bark of an aspen tree, please Google that image right now. It is one of the great and beautiful collaborative art masterpieces of this earth's existence.

Beautiful new birds, beautiful new trees. New to me, at least. Ancient in the grand scheme of things.

Around that time, I had a dream where I was sitting in a room with a beautiful little mountain that I had sculpted with my own hands. I never left that room because I needed to be with my mountain, and I didn't want anything to happen to it. When people would come to see me, I would show them my precious mountain. In the dream, I had to leave that room and leave my mountain, and I thought I would die, but life led me to somewhere else. Where there were ENORMOUS MOUNTAINS everywhere. Everywhere. And they'd been there for millenia. And they'd be there long after I was gone.

There was never any reason to hold tight to my little mountain made of kinetic sand, thinking it was the best I'd ever have, the only I'd ever have. There wasn't ever even a need for me to protect it, because the real mountains already existed. I didn't have to build them or pay for them, just experience them.

I don't know why, when I said goodbye to the birds and the trees and the water I'd enjoyed for more than a decade at Brave River Ranch . . . that I really thought I was saying goodbye to those kinds of beautiful things once and for all. I was willing to make that sacrifice.

It was never required of me, though.

I don't know why so many of us try to pay for our suffering once and for all, a balloon payment of sorts, when there was never a debt to begin with.

But this is one of the greatest roads I have ever found, and one that I still travel daily.

The sun rises here. The sun sets here. The birds sing here, too.

The birds sing everywhere. Maybe they aren't the same birds, but the song follows you everywhere you go, sung by a different choir, but it's the song of life all the same.

The birds sing everywhere.

So, Beloved Soul,

What gifts are right in front of you, gifts you are missing because you are trying to sacrifice your way into earning them?

AND

When will you next listen for the birds?

I love you. We are almost there.
xo
melody freebird

50

The Road Back Home

To tell you about this road, I've got to tell you about when the tipi flooded this summer.

One of the things we kept when we left our home at the ranch in Idaho was our big giant tipi. It IS ENORMOUS. You can fit 40 people inside on big comfortable chairs. We've had so much life inside that tipi. It used to sit between the chicken coop and the river at our ranch in Idaho. Marq harvested every pole with our sons and a few of his soul brothers. They scraped the bark off with special tools and hand-oiled them. The poles are 3 stories high.

This tipi is epic.

Our daughter got married inside of it. Marq had several men's retreats inside of it, and I had the women from my very last retreat at the ranch inside of it for a few very special campfires to wrap things up. Just me and Hilarie made the last magic retreat at the ranch. We hung vintage sari quilts from every pole. We surrounded the fire with daisies. It was a work of art to us.

Marq and I drove it to Utah before we ever knew we would end up living here. We entrusted it to West and Kami because we knew they would honor everything about it, and West had come to Idaho and experienced his first man camp inside of it. It was a special place to him too.

So we made a 9 hour journey, hauling poles that are longer than a semi truck, driving through the mountains to that magical place nestled inside of Pando, Wild West Mustang Ranch. And the tipi and poles sat in the barn there until this summer.

Over the summer, we worked hard to build the beautiful labyrinth together and then we made a space for the big tipi. We set it up so that I could hold my first Soul Road certification training inside of it. You know, the one where Joy from Hope, Idaho begged me and I said yes?

The tipi was the last bit of home we had to offer to anyone. Or so I thought.

West and Kami have 2 tipis of their own already. They are beautifully painted, and there are wood floors and beds and electricity in them. People come from all over the world to stay in them. Our big tipi would be the one where we would have our gatherings, and theirs would be the ones where everyone would sleep.

So 9 epic humans came from all over the country. The nearest airports were more than 3 hours away so everyone had a long road trip through the mountains to get to us. I was so relieved when the last woman arrived. It was Joy.

Joy arrived.

Carl and Hilarie drove all the way from Idaho and stopped on their way to get all the groceries. They set up their own tent out back in one of the horse fields. It meant everything to have them there. They cooked for us all week, they held space for the miracles to come.

Well, the second night of the training, we experienced the wildest and most torrential downpour. A monsoon, to be exact. It lasted for days. Thunder and lightning, too.

It flooded all 3 tipis. Noah's ark level flooding.

We gathered around the tables in the only shelter left to keep us dry, the barn. We watched unimaginable sheets of water pouring down on everything, while West used a big push broom to try to keep the water from flooding the barn. He worked this broom for hours.

Marq was several mountains away on a job, building someone else's home. He would have been alongside with a broom. But even with West's great efforts to keep most of the water out of the barn, the barn ended up flooding too.

Kami ran out, through the pouring rain, to see what was happening inside the tipis and just as we feared, the bedding was soaked in every single one. The carpet and furniture was soaked in the big tipi, and it was getting darker and colder outside.

I had a moment. Of tears. Of defeat. Of anger. Of feeling like a failure and a huge disappointment to everyone who had come such a long way to have this experience.

Of feeling like I was doomed and bringing everyone else to the point of being doomed.

But then my incredible students, my teammates, decided this was an awesome adventure — that we were making memories. That this kind of problem-solving and resilience was EXACTLY what we needed to learn together. Sherri, Summer, Sandy, Joy, Ann, Amy and Cheryl. I will never ever forget this little family we forged that week.

It kept raining. Pouring. Flooding. Hours and hours of it.

So we ran out together and gathered all the bedding and clothing. We sorted through it and hung sleeping bags and blankets all over the barn to dry. Kami started what would end up being loads and loads of blankets in her dryer in the house.

And I had to gather myself. Because I'll tell you what I had wanted to happen; I had wanted to create an absolutely magical experience for these precious women who were bringing me back to life with their pleas for me to teach them my teaching methods — so that they could go on and help others with them.

I wanted to give them an experience of HOME.

I had used much of the money they paid me to buy beautiful fur blankets, lovely pillow cases with pom pom fringe. Silky bed liners. Fur chair covers. Beautiful hand-crafted macrame wall hangings to decorate the tipi. And twinkle lights, of course. Incidentally, when those macrame wall hangings arrived in the mail in a giant box, Marq opened them and had no idea what they were. He brought them to me and said…"I don't know why you need so many mops, but your mops are here."

Perhaps it was a prophetic statement.

Because all of it got soaked. All of my beautiful things I bought to create a beautiful home environment for everyone. For me, too. And we ended up sitting around a plastic table in the barn, nearly yelling to hear each other over the sounds of the rain.

And nobody cried about it. In fact, there was a whole lot of laughter.

The training went on. We bonded. We had to stop the lessons many times because the rain was so loud on the tin roof that no one could hear me or anyone else.

So we chose those times to write our lessons in our journals.

We each held ourselves together and then came together as a team too, as a family. We solved problems. We ran out into the wind and water for each other. We cooked together, we ate together, we learned together. We became more of a family with every new experience. We experienced HOME.

It actually turned into its own unforgettable magic. Things happened that I never could have planned. Things that brought us to beautiful places together. Things that brought us back to ourselves. Things that taught us each who we are. Alone and together.

West and Carl put giant tarps inside of every tipi as an extra ceiling, keeping the rain off the beds. So everyone was able to sleep in the tipis despite the rain. But all the beauty I worked so hard to create was overshadowed by a different kind of beauty that week. The beauty of working through a hard journey together. And separately.

50 Roads To The Middle Of My Life

Every night and several times throughout that week, I would walk back to my RV in front of those women I so badly wanted to gift with a magical experience. On the first day we were all together, I would get in my trailer alone and think about how disappointing it must be to them to see their leader walk away to her little old trailer. It certainly wasn't an impressive home I was living in. I fought the humiliation I felt.

Turns out it was just the opposite. They were not disappointed at all. And they were seeing my real life. The real me.

And even if they would have been disappointed, that was never the point. It never has been the point. They didn't come to be impressed. They came to learn. They were learning.

By the second night, I'd go back to my trailer alone and I'd start to laugh when I looked out at the tipis, completely soaked with rainwater. The rain falling on the top of my trailer was as loud as the rain in the barn.

It became a rhythm, and I'd just think…..

I once had a house, and I had to leave it.
So I moved into a trailer.
I didn't have a home to bring people into.
So I brought my beloveds to my tipi,
but the tipi flooded.
So we went to the barn.
Then the barn flooded.
So we found home somewhere else.
A place that we can take anywhere.

Inside of ourselves.

Inside of ourselves.

Inside of ourselves.

WE ALL DECIDED WHAT HOME WAS THAT WEEK.

I had a big wake-up in that moment about my relentless need to make everything okay all the time for everyone. Not just okay, but SPECTACU-

LAR and BEAUTIFUL. In all honesty, I had to make everything okay so that I COULD FEEL OKAY. I had to earn my way so spectacularly that I would never get kicked out of HOME.

I thought about how life kept giving me new opportunities to learn what I'd needed to know all along. Forever and ever I have looked around me, desperately, in difficult situations to find the resources to create something beautiful to make everything okay for everyone. So that I could be okay.

If I don't have a house, I will have a trailer, if I don't have a trailer, I will have a tipi. If I don't have a tipi I will have a barn. And I will make it all okay.

But what happens when the barn floods too?

What happens is that you are still okay. Everyone is.

It was never about the place. It was always about the love. It was always about everyone taking responsibility for their own experience.

So what is HOME, anyway? I have had to ask myself that question over and over again. If you don't have your own place, are you homeless? What does it mean if you are homeless?

For me, I have always wanted home to be the place where you can be exactly who you are and not have to be anyone else. I have wanted it to be the place where you are loved, no matter what. But can you always control that? And when you are living in a place where you cannot be who you are, or you are in a place where you are not feeling loved, are you still home even if you live in the house that has your address on the front?

What is home?

I have lived in some beautiful houses. Most of them also felt like home. I've lived the picket-fence life, with the decorated front door for each new season. We have mowed the lawn and planted flowers in the summer, we have tilled the garden in the spring, we have cleaned up weeds during autumn, and used the snow shovel in the winter. We raised our children in those houses. We had parties and house guests and sales people at the door.

And we've also been without a house.

Do you have to have a house to have a home?

Not the kind of home that is most important.

As I was writing this book, I found a piece of marketing copy I wrote to explain my work to others, to tell others what I offer . . . and it occurred to me that if I would write these words TO MYSELF, I would know that when I treat myself the way I wanted others to be treated when I worked so hard to create all of the homes I have created…I would always feel like I AM HOME.

Like I am HOME WITH MYSELF.

So I offer these words to you, to turn them around on YOURSELF. I added my own name in front of every sentence that I was writing to others. I invite you to do the same.

Melody - I want you to be on YOUR OWN SOUL ROAD.

Melody - I want you to be awake to your life. I want you to feel self-respect. I want you to be able to spend your minutes and your hours doing things that really matter to the overall life you want to live and the story you want to be the main character of.

Melody - I want you to be reunited with the soul that is YOU, the one you may have forgotten.

Melody - I want you to have the courage to live your life as WHO YOU ARE, not who you think others want you to be.

Melody- I have all sorts of tools to help you do that, and to help me do that. Let's walk on our Soul Roads next to each other. <3

....

There is a popular phrase I've always loved. I believe it was first spoken by Ram Dass. It says simply, "we are all just walking each other home."

What I learned on The Road Back Home is that I better know my own

address. I better know exactly where home is, because sometimes I'm gonna be walking myself home.

I've been looking for someone to walk me home my whole life, and almost
always, I wanted them to tell me where home was before they took me
there. Again, I believed that home was somewhere outside of myself.

We can live in a house, we can live in a trailer, we can live in an apartment,
we can even live in a tipi. I've done every single one of those things. But
the one place I've always had to live, no matter what place was housing me
on the outside, is INSIDE OF MYSELF.

I've learned that when we don't accept our own inner-world as our true
home, we will always feel like drifters, vagabonds and even refugees. We
can always get evicted from places that are outside of ourselves and we
will always be left looking for another home, no matter where we are.

Our truest home has been inside of us all along.

I'm getting it. I am creating the home inside of myself that I have been
looking for and longing for my whole life.. I am memorizing my own inner
address.

When others DO walk me home, it's no longer because I don't know my
own address. It's because I want to be with them and they want to be with
me. And on the days when I have to walk myself home, I am the one who
knows the way best. I know the shortcuts, I know the scenic view, I know
the places to steer clear of if I don't want to get bitten by rabid dogs.

I walk myself home a lot these days.

And when I get there, I make myself a warm cup of tea, build a fire and
put out the fresh flowers I gathered along the way. And I sing myself a love
song. Because it's been a long and difficult journey and just like everyone
alive, I deserve a song that's written just for me. I know the words by heart.
So I grab my guitar and start the serenade.

After that, I turn on the twinkle lights, I fluff the pillows on the couch.
I grab myself a cozy, furry blanket. I light the candles. I settle in. I slow
down.

Then I smile warmly and say to myself, "I am so happy you're here."

I am home.

So, Dear You,

Do you know your address by heart?

AND

What do you do to make your home inside beautiful, wonderful and comforting for yourself, no matter who is or isn't there with you?

You are worth every good and beautiful thing. Please memorize your address. It's the best place you could ever be.

I love you forever.
melody freebird

Afterword

This is a picture of a group of hikers I ran into earlier this week, the day I finished this book. It's January of 2022 and we've all been in lockdown from the Covid Pandemic. Because I've been living a very isolated life, Pandemic or not, I hardly ever see people I haven't planned on seeing. I want to tell you about what happened when these people showed up, but first I have to tell you what I was doing before they arrived.

I'd hiked to the edge of a cliff a few miles from where I live and asked God if I could finally be free of some of the sharp shrapnel this story brought up to the surface of my life. Whatever it was, it was aching and stinging and right under my skin. Over the course of an hour or so, I sat with little-girl sobs on that cliff — anger and sorrow and the like . . . the kind of deep sobs that make your nose run and take your breath away. I screamed out words over those cliffs that I hadn't ever been able to say audibly. I told God every single thing that still hurts and I just kept saying DID YOU EVEN KNOW THAT? DID YOU EVEN KNOW THAT? WHERE WERE YOU???????? Spit and snot flew, I screamed and screamed. I wiped my eyes and my nose and screamed some more. I paced and paced those cliffs and kept screaming the same sentences over and over and over into the sky. With as much as I've shared in this memoir, I won't share what those sentences were. They came as a big surprise and came uncontrollably. But they gave me such a glimpse into the pain

I've held for so many years, and what the root of it was. I just wanted to hold my little girl self and never let her go. I thought the sobbing and the screaming wouldn't end.

But then it did.

And I felt free.

I sat there in silence for a long time with the kind of relief you feel after a sliver gets pulled out. It's the kind of relief that comes as a huge surprise after feeling so much pain just a moment before.

Keep in mind I was out in the wilderness where I hike a lot. And I never see another soul when I'm out there. So I felt safe to scream and sob . . .

But then I turned around and saw off in the distance, but not too far away, that a big group of hikers was coming. They were headed toward the cliffs from the direction I needed to go to get back home. We were going to collide on that trail whether I wanted to or not.

It's been so hard for me to talk to people or even see people.

I put my headphones back on so I wouldn't have to talk to them, but then as they got closer, I felt myself wanting to see them and feel their presence so badly. As they got closer, I realized they were all at least 10 or 20 years older than I am. They were all decked out in hiking garb, with walking sticks and backpacks and the kind of sparkle you get in your eyes when you take really good care of yourself. From far away, I couldn't have known they were older people because they were all so fit and walked with the same spring in their steps as someone in their 20's.

The trail is thin so two people can't fit on the same spot at once. I looked around and found a big rock on the side of the trail to stand on so I could let them walk by. I stood on the rock and waited for them to get closer so they could go their way and I could go mine.

The first one smiled so big at me as they approached. I immediately pulled my headphones off and smiled back. Then I shouted out . . .

"You guys, right around the bend is the most beautiful view you will ever

see in all your life!"

Someone shouted back,

"Thank you! That's where we are headed!"

And then I just couldn't help it…they were all so alive….I wanted to be alive too!! I couldn't stop smiling.

As soon as they got close enough that they could all easily hear me, I just started pretending like I was their welcome committee and I put my arms out wide into the air and yelled . . .

"HAPPY FRIDAY!!!! WELCOME TO YOUR BEAUTIFUL LIFE!!!! ENJOY IT!!! YOU ARE HERE FOR A REASON!!! THIS IS ALL HERE FOR YOU TO ENJOY!!! WELCOME WELCOME WEL-COME!!!!"

And they each walked past me, laughing or smiling as I said the words to them that I needed most, like I often do.

The guy who was last walked by me and winked and said "Thank you."

And I don't know if they could see it or not, but tears started rolling down my face. I could feel something bubble-up in me while I joyfully yelled those words out to them. It bubbled up just like the shrapnel had. But it wasn't sharp and painful. It was something different.

I'd decided earlier that week after talking to Rebecca, the epic life-coach, neuroscience angel who showed up in my life about a year ago, that I was going to have to decide to LOVE MY LIFE. No matter what.

She was one of the ones who'd been looking for me and my work, a student of mine from the beginning. And when she found me and begged me to bring my work back, I became a student of hers. And she's become one of my very best friends. An unexpected gift along the way.

She's no-nonsense and doesn't let you drown in your own quicksand. She's been teaching me the power of my own thoughts and my own perceptions about myself, about life and about others. And how I have to design all of

391

it or it will get designed for me — by default.

So I'd been getting up every morning and hitting the trail as soon as I could see the first glimpse of the sun. I'd say I LOVE MY LIFE, I LOVE MY LIFE, I LOVE MY LIFE over and over and over again until my brain started picking up on it and pointing out evidence of it everywhere I looked. That's what brains do . . . they act out what we currently believe. So you can DECIDE what you want to believe and then keep giving your brain that to-do list instead of leaving your brain to scavenge through the thoughts you've thought the most in the past. And your brain will automatically choose the thoughts it thinks you need to be able to stay alive; thoughts about threats and danger and pain and how to avoid anything uncomfortable. Until you start avoiding EVERYTHING and seeing EVERYTHING as a dangerous threat.

I decided to start designing my own thoughts. And my new thought was I LOVE MY LIFE.

And I started walking right into this new belief I was designing.

On one of the first days of my new sunrise walks, out in the middle of nowhere, I found an old camera slide. A REALLY OLD ONE. Turns out, the image is a place in Israel where a famous battle was won and a famous battle was lost. It was a cliff that looked just like the one I shouted my pain out to God on. When I did some deeper investigating about the place on this slide, I found an article that said this place, as legend tells it, will be the place where the final battle between Good and Evil will take place.

I don't know what evil is exactly, but the best definition I can find is that evil is something akin to an absolute lack of love. That's the only definition that even comes close to making sense to me. It's the same with light and dark. Light is light, and dark is just a lack of light.

I don't take the message of this found treasure for granted. I have battled dark and light. I have battled love and a lack of love. And I will have to do it over and over and over again. I've lost some of my battles and I've won some of them. But I will WIN this war.

Because I choose love.
I choose good.

I choose life.

And I love my life.
I LOVE MY LIFE!
See you on the trail, beloved. Stay on your own Soul Road, okay?

Xoxo
Melody freebird

P.S.

I'd love to hear from you! Would you write and let me know how this book resonated with your own life experience? I have a special email set up just for this. melody@melodyrossmedia.com

and . . .

Would you leave me a review on Amazon and pass this book on to anyone you believe may benefit from it? I'm shopping for a major publisher so any and all recommendations are appreciated.

I love you, beautiful soul!
xo
melody freebird

About the Author:

Melody Ross has been a worldwide known teacher, artist, author and entre-preneur since her twenties, building one of the most collected and sought after brands in the designer paper, gift, fashion, and home decor indus-tries, creating thousands of products over her 25+ year career and winning countless awards. Melody has authored and published over 20 books and written and taught more than 50 courses focusing on living a meaningful life and developing grit and resilience to overcome life's challenges. She teaches and coaches both in-person and online with students all over the world. Melody and her story have appeared on countless television pro-grams and in countless magazines and blogs.

As an entrepreneur, Melody has created 2 other international, multi-million dollar companies aside from Soul Road Media – she is the founder and creator of Chatterbox, Inc, a designer stationery company from 1997-2009 and the founder and creator of Brave Girls Club, a worldwide women's self-development company from 2009-2019. Melody and her business partner closed Melody's Soul School in 2020 during the Covid Pandemic and Melody created a new way of home-learning through self-guided workbooks and YouTube videos centered around creative soul-searching.

Melody and Marq have been married for more than 30 years, they have 5 children and 5 grandchildren and enjoy time with their family living the outdoor lifestyle of the West. In 2019, they gave away most of their belong-ings and set out on an epic adventure. Melody writes, creates and makes videos while visiting all sorts of beautiful places as she and Marq travel to see and collaborate with old and new friends from all over the world. Find her work on Amazon or at

www.melodyrossmedia.com and www.soulroadacademy.com

Made in the USA
Coppell, TX
09 June 2022